The Healthy Edit

Ch 2, 9, 3, 10, 11, 12, 6, 7

The Healthy Edit

Creative Editing Techniques for Perfecting Your Movie

John Rosenberg

Illustrated by Michael Rosenberg

ELSEVIER

Amsterdam • Boston • Heidelberg • London
New York • Oxford • Paris • San Diego
San Francisco • Singapore • Sydney • Tokyo
Focal Press is an imprint of Elsevier

Focal Press

Focal Press is an imprint of Elsevier
30 Corporate Drive, Suite 400, Burlington, MA 01803, USA
The Boulevard, Langford Lane, Kidlington, Oxford, OX5 1GB, UK

Notices
Knowledge and best practice in this field are constantly changing. As new research and experience broaden our
understanding, changes in research methods, professional practices, or medical treatment may become necessary.

Practitioners and researchers must always rely on their own experience and knowledge in evaluating and using any
information, methods, compounds, or experiments described herein. In using such information or methods they should be
mindful of their own safety and the safety of others, including parties for whom they have a professional responsibility.

To the fullest extent of the law, neither the Publisher nor the authors, contributors, or editors, assume any liability for any
injury and/or damage to persons or property as a matter of products liability, negligence or otherwise, or from any use or
operation of any methods, products, instructions, or ideas contained in the material herein.

Library of Congress Cataloging-in-Publication Data
Rosenberg, John.
 The healthy edit : creative editing techniques for perfecting your movie / John Rosenberg.
   p. cm.
 Includes index.
 ISBN 978-0-240-81446-9 (pbk.)
 1. Motion pictures—Editing. 2. Motion pictures—Production and direction. I. Title.
 TR899.R663 2010
 778.5′35—dc22   2010040568

British Library Cataloguing-in-Publication Data
A catalogue record for this book is available from the British Library.

For information on all Focal Press publications
visit our website at www.elsevierdirect.com

10 11 12 13   5 4 3 2 1
Printed in the United States of America

Working together to grow
libraries in developing countries

www.elsevier.com | www.bookaid.org | www.sabre.org

ELSEVIER   BOOK AID
            International   Sabre Foundation

To Debbie, Michael, and Sarah

Contents

Foreword   *xiii*

Acknowledgments   *xv*

Introduction   *xvii*

Chapter 1   Prescriptions for Success   **1**

Strong Medicine   1

   The Film Doctor   2

   The Editor   3

Principles of Filmic Medicine   3

   Cardiology   4

   Genetics   4

   Anatomy   4

   Psychiatry   5

   Surgery   5

   Instruments   6

   Bedside Manner   7

Chapter 2   Mastering the Art of Film Editing   **9**

Heart of the Matter   9

The Scalpel   9

   The Great Experiment of Dr. Kuleshov   10

Dynamic and Continuity Editing   11

The Rules   12

   Match Action   12

   Cut on Action   12

   Let the Camera Settle before Cutting   12

   Create Visual Bridges   12

   Don't Cross the Line   13

   Maintain Eyelines   14

   Vary the Cuts   14

   Cuts Should Be Motivated   14

   Cut Before (or After) People and/or Objects Enter the Frame 14

   Pay Attention to Physical Continuity   14

   Respect the Rule of Three   15

Contents

Chapter 3   The Film Doctor Is In   17

The Profession   17

The Approach   18

    What Is the Scene About?   19

    Filling the Gaps   19

    Who Is the Scene About?   22

    What Does the Audience Learn from this Scene?   24

    Further Diagnosis   24

    Wrestling with Material   24

When Poisons Are Medicines, Accidents Are Intentions   25

Chapter 4   The Instruments   29

Linear and Nonlinear Editing Systems   29

    In Praise of the Physical Body   29

An Editor's Tools   31

    Medieval Medicine: The Moviola   31

    European Renaissance: The Flatbed   33

    The Modern Revolution: Nonlinear   35

    Early Electronic Systems   35

    The Mouse That Roared   38

The Edit   39

    The Frame Matters   40

    One-Stop Shopping   43

    You Must Remember This   45

Chapter 5   Alternative Medicine   47

Nontraditional Treatments   47

    The Match Cut   49

    Continuity Errors   50

    The Goodies   52

    Off-Camera and Off-Track   53

Chapter 6   Genre Editing Styles I   57

Expectations Posed by Genre   57

    Conventions   57

    Crossing Genres   58

    The Ritual Object   59

    Expectations   59

The Western Rides into the Sunset   60

Science Fiction and Fantasy   61

Visual Effects   61
Computer-Generated Images   64
Compositing   64
Motion Capture   65

Chapter 7   Genre Editing Styles II   **67**
The Comedy   67
Surf the Laughter   70
Sight Gags   70
Romantic Comedy   71
Action Adventure   71
Guideposts   73
Crank   75
Emphasizing an Action   77

Chapter 8   Genre Editing Styles III   **79**
The Horror Film   79
Blood Suckers   81
The Thriller and Mystery   82
Family Films   83
The Documentary   84
Playing with Blocks   85
The Auteur Editor   88

Chapter 9   Internal Medicine   **91**
Coverage   91
The Master Shot   92
The Establishing Shot   92
The Wide Shot   92
The Medium Shot   93
The Close-Up   93
The Over-the-Shoulder Shot   94
The 2-Shot   94
The Reverse Angle   94
The Insert Shot   94
Sync   95
From Chaos to Order   96
Finding Order   97
Story Order   100
Reducing Bloat   102

Contents

The Gap   103
  Examinations   104
  The Puzzle   104
  Saved in the Editing Room   105
  Shot List   106

Chapter 10   Surgery   **109**
What Goes and What Stays   109
  Practical Considerations   110
  Trimming for Health   112
  Tarantino and Time   113
The Lift   116
  The Way of the Lift   118
  Lift and Separate . . . or Not   118

Chapter 11   Psychiatry of Character Disorders—Part I   **121**
Dialog   121
Subtext   122
  The Overlap   125
  Exposition Infection   127
  Show, Don't Tell   127
New Territory   128

Chapter 12   Psychiatry of Character Disorders—Part II   **131**
Performance   131
  Tracking the Beats   131
  Substitution   132
  The Cutaway   133
  Words Like Skin Tags   134
  Improvisation   134
  Bingeing   135
  In Good Shape   137

Chapter 13   Genetics   **139**
Story Problems Inherent in the Screenplay   139
  Romeo and Juliet   139
  Inherited Traits   140
The Montage   143
A Telling Story   145
  Information   145

Chapter 14   Cardiac Unit   **147**

Pace and Rhythm: The Editor's Unique Tools   147

   Visual Music   149

   Pick Up the Pace   151

   The Power of Pace   151

   Anticipation   152

   Overstated   153

The Heart of the Matter   154

   Rhythm Is Life   155

   The Graduate   156

   Finding the Flow   157

   The Battleship Eisenstein   158

Scene-to-Scene Transitions   159

   Overdose   161

   Blacking Out   161

   Ban Banners   161

   Narration   162

   Shot Size   162

   The Pre-lap   163

The Intercut   164

Chapter 15   Bedside Manner   **167**

Politics of the Editing Room   167

   Bedside Manner   167

   No Surprises   168

   Screening the Rough Cut   168

   The Best Policy   169

   All Ears   169

   Staying Seated   170

Dailies and Rough Cuts   171

   The Answer Is Yes   171

   The Poor Craftsman   171

   What's the Big Deal?   172

   The Strength of Weak Ties   174

   Committing to a Project   174

   Film Doctoring   175

Chapter 16   Triage   **177**

Emergency Procedure   177

   Two Weeks   177

   Symptoms   178

Contents

Audio Issues   179
Video Ills   182

Chapter 17   Post-mortem   **185**
From Final Cut to Exhibition   185
    Made in Heaven   186
    Affairs of the Heart   187
Reediting   187
    The Free-for-All   188
The End Is Near   189
    The Specialists   190
After the Hard Labor: Delivery   193
The End Backward   195

Glossary   197
Index   209

Foreword

My first "cut" as a fledgling editor was just that: I was given a roll of film and a pair of scissors and told to cut and paste the pieces of a travelog together. Of course, the edges never matched. Luckily, I soon graduated to a splicer, but even then editing was a world away from today's situation. I was working on an upright Moviola with 16 mm film, which had a tendency to shred, and a monitor image the size of a postcard.

I found editing a universe I loved to inhabit, but I wanted to learn the craft in depth. This was in the days before film schools were as omnipresent as Starbucks stores (which didn't exist then). UCLA, USC, and NYU required four years for a bachelor's degree or two for a master's, and you had to spend your time studying the full span of film crafts. I could find no programs in the United States where I could study only editing.

What I wanted, what I needed then, was a complex editing course in a bottle. If only I'd had *The Healthy Edit*.

I worked hard and progressed as best I could, editing documentaries, industrials, and commercials, and, finally, a low-budget feature.

Then I had the good fortune to work as an apprentice on the classic movie *One Flew Over the Cuckoo's Nest* (with Richard Chew editing). Later, in another chance to watch real pros at work, I was lucky enough to be an assistant on *Apocalypse Now.*

In those days an assistant often spent time in the editing room with the editor (and sometimes the director as well), finding trims or putting up rolls on the KEM. In today's digital editing room, the editor rarely needs that kind of at-the-ready help, and the assistants are usually in another room doing digital housekeeping and maybe temp effects, so now it's harder for them to see the editor's working process or the director/editor dynamic.

Which is another instance where *The Healthy Edit* fills a need by offering the kind of voice and experience that editors used to provide in the editing room.

When I became a feature editor, I was lucky enough to work with certain directors on several films in a row: Robert M. Young, Sam Raimi, and Wayne Kramer. I also had several single-film experiences with other interesting directors. All with different styles, in film and personality.

Fortunately, every project I worked on interested me. I feel proud of all of them. Besides *Beverly Hills Cop*, *The Mask*, and *Spider-Man*, certain ones come to mind in particular: *Triumph of the Spirit* for its unflinching look at the Nazi death camps; *American Me* for a shocking view of Mexican Mafia gang life in prison; *A Simple Plan*, a chilling story wonderfully told by the actors and the director; and *Running Scared*, a pedal-to-the-metal adventure.

Foreword

As varied and helpful to me as those experiences were, John Rosenberg offers something more. He culls from not only his own experience but that of numerous other editors, to provide a greater range of background than any one editor could pass on.

Most of my work consisted of editing features from start to finish, but I also did a doctoring pass on *Monster*, with Charlize Theron's Oscar-winning performance. The original film had been well edited, but I believe I was able to change enough things to take it to another level.

The ability to bolster a film's health has imbued the film editor with special status throughout the history of the medium. There are tales of veteran editors whom studios retained on payroll, waiting in the wings to resuscitate troubled productions. My good friend John Rosenberg is one of them. He has been the health insurance policy on contract to independent film studios and summoned in to minister to major studio productions.

Yet this essential topic has remained untapped until now. John brings a unique perspective to the art of filmmaking in general and to editing specifically. An excellent communicator, he's been a popular lecturer for many film programs. Students and professionals are fortunate to have this comprehensive volume full of valuable insights, reflections from other top professionals, and informative examples.

Editing often requires long hours and long work weeks, and it often places the editor in the crucible of strong wills and personalities. Things can go awry, minds fatigue, and tempers fray. It's a fast-moving film world these days. All the old challenges of editing analog-style on film are still there, and they have been overlain with a raft of new complexities to perplex and confound the unprepared.

Read and absorb the Rx's in this book, and both your films and your state of mind will be healthier for it.

Arthur Coburn
Los Angeles, California

Acknowledgments

Just as an edit is more than the sum of its parts, an editing book includes the generous contributions of many. Above all I'd like to thank Debbie Glovin, who suggested the idea, cheered me on, and is the best book editor and researcher an author could work with. I owe my heartfelt gratitude to my endlessly helpful, flexible, and dedicated editor at Focal Press, Dennis McGonagle, his attentive assistant Kara Race-Moore and my delightful and supportive project manager, Anne B. McGee. And special thanks to George Lucas, who generously gave me permission to use his remarks reflecting the core concept of this book. Also, my deep gratitude to my program director Pascale Halm, founding director Ronnie Rubin and Dean Cathy Sandeen at UCLA Extension, department chair David Schreiber and President Laura Soloff at The Art Institute of California, Norman Hollyn, head of the editing track at the USC School of Cinematic Arts, along with graduate production coordinator Pablo Frasconi, department chair Michael Taylor and Dean Elizabeth M. Daley. I owe a great deal to my students, who have brought as much to my life as I hope I have brought to theirs. To the talented filmmakers who generously give their time and insights by guest lecturing to my students throughout the years, I wish to thank Mark Adler, Alan Baumgarten, Conrad Buff, Richard Chew, Arthur Coburn, Philippe Denham, Michael Economou, William Goldenberg, Andrew Golov, Michael Gottlieb, Bruce Green, Michael Knue, David Macquilling, Jed Nolan, John Norvet, Richard Pearson, John Poll, Jonathan Sanger, Garry Schyman, Ken Shapiro, Martin Spottl, Norman Wallerstein, and John Wiseman. Some of their words also appear in this book. If I left anyone out, my apologies, and you'll be in the next edition. My sincere gratitude to those who helped me create or obtain images and permissions for the book, including artist Michael Rosenberg, Joe Bogdanovic of West L.A. Post, Scott Laster of Christy's Editorial, Joel Marshall of Atomic Film Company, Ron Mandlebaum of Photofest, Merrideth Miller of the *The New Yorker*, Laura Muhlhammer of Lucas Films, Ltd., Hugh Neeley of the Mary Pickford Foundation, Jim Turner of Moviola and Michael Steven Gregory who generously contributed footage for the companion website as well as encouragement for the book. To Tom Walls and Robert Brown, who mentored me in the early years, I offer my deep thanks. Appreciation also belongs to the late Arthur Schmidt and Ralph Winters who shared their creative insights with me. My profound gratitude extends to the feature film directors with whom I had the privilege of working: Doug Barr, Ron Ford, John Hancock, Neal Israel, Mark Kolbe, Mike Mendez, Philippe Mora, Jed Nolan, Bob Rafelson, Stewart Raffill, Alan Rudolph, Andrew van Slee, Kurt Voss, Dan Wechsler, and Yuri Zeltser. Special thanks to Lisa Axelrad, Nina Fallon of Double Negative, Irv and Jeanne Glovin, founders of the Oskar Schindler Humanities Foundation, Kim Marienthal, Nancy Ong, Emilyn Page, Inge Price, Steve Smith, Steve Weinberg, and Internet maven Sarah R. Rosenberg. And finally to my brother James, the doctor; to my late brother and penultimate entertainment attorney Daniel; to my mother Maryanne; and to my father Frank, whose great command of storytelling and love for filmmaking inspired me even as he advised me time and again to go into a saner line of work.

Introduction

The Art

Editing is not a simple art form. It can take years to master and great technical skill to perform. It changes due to technological developments and cultural upheavals. Where a writer can survive on a pen and paper or a painter with a brush and canvas, an editor requires the support of expensive, highly complex equipment, as well as the efforts of often hundreds of people. These crews work together to deliver to the editor the raw materials—the dailies—with which to perform his art. He depends on them, and they depend on him.

Postproduction and editing encompass everything it takes to bring a film to completion. This includes storytelling, dialog, pacing, color, sound, visual effects, music, titles, and more. It is an art form that consists of part aesthetics and part high-technology. Today the discipline of film editing has gone from a quiet, nearly invisible profession to a driving force. In that regard, this book not only speaks to the advances in modern film editing but also to the filmmaking process in general.

The technology can be daunting with respect to the intricacies of running the editing machine and understanding the film and video medium in general. Unlike paint and pencil, the medium with which the film artist sketches is, in itself, highly sophisticated. It consists of colored gel layers imbedded with silver salts on celluloid strips or, in the case of video, binary codes imbedded on magnetic and plastic surfaces. The same person who will arouse an audience with a well-orchestrated kiss, scare them with a loud sound and jump cut, or send them into fits of laughter with a well-placed punch line must also understand timecode, frame rate, 3/2 pulldown, codecs, greenscreen, 3D, aspect ratio, DI, IN, 7.1, anamorphic, and a plethora of other technical concepts.

Nonlinear editing, in the guise of such systems as Avid, Final Cut Pro, Premier Pro, and Vegas Pro, has revolutionized the art form. This is possible by the affordability and accessibility of the equipment, coupled with the opportunity to create and archive multiple versions, to experiment without the consequences of physically altering the film, and by instantly rendering optical and visual effects. Even if the film is accentuated with jump cuts, undercranking, slow motion, and other potentially distracting images or sounds, the effect for the audience must be seamless. It must create a consistent universe, "a vivid and continuous dream," as the novelist John Gardner called the storytelling process.

While not as obvious as a cinematographer's or director's work, the editor's impact is so pervasive as to make or break a film. Among the early Russian filmmakers, the great film theorist and director Sergei Eisenstein believed that editing held the highest position in the art of cinema. Since his time, Hollywood producers, acknowledging editing's influence, have generally reserved the right of the final cut for themselves, not the director. Over the last 50 years, the *auteur* theory as espoused by the French New Wave has held that the director is the true author of a film. Ironically, the New Wave's greatest contributions, such as the use of jump cuts, derived from innovations of the editing bench. Today, postproduction exerts an influence that exceeds any of the past.

George Lucas has declared that postproduction is the most important aspect of the filmmaking process and that it should be afforded as much time as possible. Granted, his films are postproduction miracles, but he was not speaking merely of manufacturing images through motion capture and computer modeling. He was referring to the assembly process in general. This is the stage where a film truly realizes its identity and where some of the greatest discoveries are made. It is also the place where some of the most grievous mistakes occur. It can take a film to the edge of death. And, when that happens, it is time to call the film doctor.

Today's Editor

Despite the unprecedented access to editing equipment, today's aspiring editors often lack the crucial experience and mentoring that have informed and launched previous generations of editors. From a small handful in the 1970s, film schools now abound. By last count there were well over 1000 film programs worldwide, signifying the prominence that film has taken as an art form and an interest within the culture. Film school editing professors vary from those who work actively in the film industry as editors to those who began as assistants but switched to academia before acquiring the position of editor, to those who studied the process but have never worked in a professional film environment. This book fills the ever widening gap that has opened with the introduction and proliferation of new digital editing systems and the commensurate decline in mentorship due to digital technology's lessening need for assistants. In the foreseeable future, all postproduction jobs may eventually meld into one as editors become their own assistants, apprentices, sound designers, mixers, color graders, finishers, and even distributors. They will also have to serve as their own mentors through the time-consuming process of trial and error, with perhaps a little help from a guide such as this.

 Doctor's Note

Like an MD, the film doctor has privileged information about his patient. He has seen the dailies, the flubs, the crossed lines, the broken frames, the dolly bumps and the botched performances. To a certain extent, he keeps it to himself. In this book, where I have permission or the patient is known or the case obvious, or where filmmakers have spoken publicly about the process, as in my classes or film forums, I'll refer to the films by name. In other instances, the identities are obscured, as is often the case in medical journals.

Figure 0.1 *The film doctor's caduceus.*

Throughout this book the reader will encounter medical terms analogous to the editing and film doctoring process. These will help him or her to remember the basic concepts and put those into an overall context. With this in mind, he or she may venture forth confidently into the uncharted territory that every film presents to the editor, whether novice or veteran.

Doctor's Note

The Roman god Mercury, known as Hermes in Greek mythology, was the winged messenger who carried a staff encircled by two serpents that Apollo had presented to him. He was said to move between the highest and lowest, from gods to humans, from alpha to omega. In the filmmaking process, the editor is that mercurial messenger. At times he becomes the audience, naïvely viewing the film from the point of view of the uninitiated. Other times the editor gains omniscient powers, seeing the film through the director's eyes and carrying that vision to the world. Ultimately, as an editor, he is attached to no one—not the script, the set, the dailies, the actors, anyone. Yet he services them all. His ultimate goal is to discover the best way to tell the film's story.

Like the chemical element that bears his name, Mercury flowed unencumbered, working his way around any obstacle, determined to deliver his message. Those wings of Mercury and that staff are reiterated to this day in the image of the medical caduceus, a symbol adopted here with two coiling strips of film.

But wait a moment. Mercury's caduceus, which is generally associated with medicine, is the wrong caduceus. Appropriately, the medical caduceus actually belongs to Asclepius, the god of healing. His rod bears no wings and only one serpent coiled around it. The rod of Mercury, bearing his wings and two serpents, was mistakenly adopted by the Army Medical Corps, who were probably thinking of Asclepius's design. As happens, this image took hold and has propagated to this day. Since Mercury was a trickster, thief, (see Stealing a Shot, Chapter 3), athlete, and messenger, his symbol is probably most appropriate for a book on filmmaking.

R_X

To define, amplify, or guide, the following sidebars are distributed throughout the chapters.

- Doctor's Note: Amplifies or adds additional information.
- Doctor's Orders: Offers an important suggestion.
- Case Study: Supplies firsthand experiences reflecting chapter topics.
- Warning: Flags an urgent issue.
- Tech Note: Elaborates on technical issues as they relate to chapter topics, generally involving nonlinear editing systems such as Avid or Final Cut Pro.
- R$_X$: Suggests an exercise or reviews a concept.

Chapter 1

Prescriptions for Success

If, as the media philosopher Marshall McLuhan once observed, Gutenberg made everyone a reader and Xerox made everyone a publisher, does Final Cut Pro make everyone an editor? Today powerful, inexpensive software such as Apple's Final Cut Pro and Avid's Media Composer rule the independent filmmaking world. Anyone with a couple hundred dollars, a computer, and an idea can become an editor. Or can they?

If you put 100 monkeys in a room with an Avid, it is unlikely they would eventually edit the great American movie. Though anyone can do it, not everyone can do it well; following the rules and knowing how to operate the software are not enough. Despite the accessibility of equipment and user manuals that describe such basic editing concepts as matching action, preserving continuity, and maintaining eyelines, many films today fail. But often the intervention of a film doctor can make the difference between a healthy movie and one that flatlines.

Strong Medicine

The difference between a cut that is not working and one that works is often striking. While time and polish may burnish a film's rough edges or improve a performance, an edit in the hands of an editor with a strong point of view and the means to fulfill it can give the appearance of a completely different film. This is particularly true in the documentary genre where the editor often shapes the movie from haphazard or unscripted footage. In the case of a fictional narrative, the recut film appears as if new footage has magically materialized in the hands of the film doctor, that a life has flourished inside the narrative, and that energy has flowed into the characters. Just as a healer's good hands, insight, and compassion can alter the patient's prognosis, so too the touch of an accomplished editor can change the course of a film.

This assurance extends to the audience, the most important recipient of the new vigor. The viewer relaxes and gives himself over to the images before him. Seeing a good film is like falling in love. One's resistances

The Healthy Edit. DOI: 10.1016/B978-0-240-81446-9.00001-9

break down, an innocence and vulnerability blossom, and, in this attitude of surrender, the ego's constant chatter and self-protectiveness ease to allow something new.

For the most part, films are entertainment, something that takes us away from ourselves. But the really good ones compel us to examine our lives, our goals, and our values. The filmmaker who can look into herself and rally a unique approach, rather than the obvious or banal solutions that come from dealing with the surface, stands a chance of affecting the consciousness of the time.

Viewed as a puzzle or labyrinth, the filmmaking process can best be solved by the strategies employed in attacking any maze: retrace your steps. During the editing process, all the foibles, failings, and virtues of the script and production become clear. If one views the filmmaking process as a three-step translation from the writer's idea to a script, from the script to dailies, and from dailies to final edit, it becomes clear where elements break down. Something is often lost in translation. To be a good film doctor, one must not only address the patient's ailments but, even better, suggest modes of prevention.

There are strategies for success but no guarantees. Unlike the real world of medicine, filmmaking is not a science, yet like medicine it requires intelligence, preparation, and sometimes great leaps of faith. And time is always of the essence. When viewing the dailies, mistakes in production become clear. When viewing the first cut, mistakes in the script become clear. When viewing the final cut, mistakes in the editing become clear. It is easy to be an armchair quarterback in the comfort of the editing room, and one thinks of the assistant who mumbles "The script sucks, the director's an idiot, the movie's a disaster, I could've done it better," to paraphrase a cartoon found in some editing rooms and projection booths. But probably at the time of production, considering the budget and time constraints, the footage may be the best it could have been. Ultimately, everything ends up on the editing bench, and it is the editor's job to make everyone else look good, even at the expense of the perfect cut. Some shots may not match, some continuity may waver, some choices may appear odd, but if everyone looks good and the film works, the editor *has* created the perfect cut.

The Film Doctor

What is a film doctor? Simply put, the film doctor is the person who promotes the health of the film. At times he saves its life. Film doctoring involves many considerations. It can be as subtle as intercutting parallel stories rather than letting one play out fully before introducing the other. It can require taking the movie's ending and splicing it to the beginning. Or it can involve completely redesigning the ending. All this demands a solid understanding of story, genre, and pacing. The riveting, suspensefully edited climax of the hit thriller *Fatal Attraction* replaced a previously diminuendo conclusion, tediously played out on the close-up of an audio tape that fortunately ended up on the cutting room floor.

Film doctoring can be as simple and unexpected as the projectionist neglecting to thread up the first reel of *Lost Horizon* during a preview screening. When the film played better before the unsuspecting audience, the studio realized that the first 10 minutes were superfluous and cut them out.

Or film doctoring can involve an editor replacing the soundtrack with a new song: "Do Not Forsake Me, Oh My Darling," played throughout a dynamically edited and failing western that became the classic *High Noon*.

The metaphor of film doctor serves as an abbreviated way to examine situations that can occur in any editing room on every film, from an indie movie produced for a few hundred dollars to a studio blockbuster weighing in at well over $300 million. Except for the level of politics, the sophistication of the technology, and the number of accountants, the two are surprisingly similar. Like twins who were separated at birth, the differences reside in the environmental influences and opportunities—nature and nurture—afforded to each.

> ## THE CUT
>
> Electronic nonlinear editing has introduced many new terms to the editing vernacular. Some older terms remain, occasionally altered in meaning. What is referred to as a sequence used to be a *cut. Cut* also means the physical or, in current use, virtual separation of one section of media from another. Geographically, the place where one shot is joined to another is at the *cut*.

The Editor

If the director and writer are the film's parents, the editor is the pediatrician. In many cases the editor has been doing his job a lot longer than either of the others. Like a doctor, he has gained vast knowledge, diagnosed many ailments, and learned how to remain objective while still caring deeply for his charges. And he probably spends long hours doing it. Through all this, he must maintain a childlike sensitivity and naïveté.

Case Study

In my conversations with the late Arthur Schmidt (whose editing credits include *Forrest Gump, The Birdcage, Back to the Future,* and *Pirates of the Caribbean: The Curse of the Black Pearl*), I was surprised to hear him refer to himself as "naïve." How unusual to hear a man of such knowledge and sophistication—a connoisseur of opera, music, and fine food—refer to himself as naïve. Yet that naïveté is the crux of film editing. It gives the editor the chance to discover treasures, to ask questions, and to conjure answers that will erase confusion for the audience. The editor approaches the film with the naïveté that mirrors the audience's shared innocence that envelops them as the lights dim. Through answering the questions for himself, the editor supplies the answers for his audience, allowing them the great joy of a communal, uninterrupted dream. That is why many editors spend as little time on the set as possible. They want to avoid preconceptions. As Richard Pearson (*The Bourne Supremacy, Quantum of Solace, Iron Man 2*) told me, "I don't usually like to hang out on the set. I don't want to know how long it took to set up that Steadicam shot. Then I'd feel obligated to use it."

Principles of Filmic Medicine

To a film doctor, the basic medical disciplines apply: cardiology, genetics, anatomy, psychiatry, and, ultimately, surgery. Along with it all, proficient use of the instruments and a good bedside manner make everything run smoother. If we want our film to have a life of its own, we must attend to all of these. In the following chapters we will explore each discipline of the editor's craft.

Cardiology

As the heart gives the body its pulse, then the pace and rhythm achieved by good editing give a film its heart. This is accomplished through the editor's three main choices: the selection of shots, the length of shots, and the placement of shots. The selection of shots influences the scene's performance, focus and point of view. The length and position of shots influences the subtext, the pacing and the rhythm of a scene and consequently the overall film. A shot can appear on the screen for several frames or, in the case of the opening sequence of *The Bonfire of the Vanities,* for the length of half a roll of film.

In the case of Alfred Hitchcock's classic *Rope,* or the more recent *Russian Ark,* one shot runs the duration of the entire film. *Rope* incorporates hidden cuts to allow transitions from one film roll to another, while *Russian Ark* uses the entire length of a specially modified high-definition video cassette. But those are exceptions. Usually it is necessary to cut and to cut often.

Doctor's Note

Rope was intended as an experiment in nonediting. In actual practice, the director and editor of *Rope* had to construct invisible cuts to knit each reel together, since 35 mm motion picture film is supplied on 1000-foot rolls that, running at 24 frames per second or 90 feet per minute, last about 11 minutes. Every 11 minutes or less, depending on thread-up waste, a changeover had to be choreographed into the onscreen action. At that point an actor would back up toward the camera, obscuring the scene so the frame went completely black. The cinematographer then changed the film roll. The new roll began with the actor stepping away from the camera. A splice joined the two black frames.

Genetics

In life there are certain conditions that are inherent in our makeup—our heredity. In medicine such conditions as diabetes, some cancers, and some heart disorders are a product of genetics. In the editing room the editor also encounters inherited conditions. These begin with the script. Issues of motivation, character arcs, story structure, genre expectation, beginnings, and endings confront the editor as she tries to create a coherent and compelling movie from a compromised script.

Anatomy

Structural anatomy is an offshoot of the inherited conditions of the script. Some of us are taller, some shorter, some wider, and some leaner. The editor's job is to build a full, living being starting from a skeleton. But first she has to get the bones right.

Case Study

In my classes at UCLA and USC, I often begin the course by handing each student a piece from a giant jigsaw puzzle. The puzzle depicts fire engine with enthusiastic firefighters and their Dalmatian. The students' job is to work collaboratively over a large table to build the puzzle within the deadline, usually one minute. Many presume this exercise's analogy to film editing before I even point it out. But all are surprised to discover that one of the pieces is missing. Unknown to them, I have hidden the missing piece behind the podium. They look to for the errant element, and when everyone shakes his and her head, they realize they are stuck without the final piece. Now their mission has changed. They have to figure out exactly what the missing piece should look like. Occasionally I even throw in some pieces from another puzzle which they must discard.

Some students realize that the puzzle's box top, with its picture of the completed puzzle, is analogous to the script and will help them decipher the challenge. Others use their imagination. Either way, after some discussion, they conclude that the missing piece would consist of a firefighter's hand on one side, part of the ladder, and some textured metal from the fire engine's flank. This kind of investigation mirrors the editor's job. Any editor can put together a movie's puzzle pieces, but only innovative and well trained editors can successfully fill the gaps that will enhance a film's story, characters and rhythm.

Psychiatry

The practice of psychiatry is concerned generally with character and mood disorders. In the editing room the film doctor must possess a profound understanding of character and the way that characters reveal themselves through dialog, subtext, response to other characters, and reactions to the tensions placed on them by the story's obstacles. When a performance is not working, when it sounds clumsy, arbitrary, forced, or unrealistic it may indicate a faulty upbringing: the script. But there are other forces as well. Performance is the additional element that is not part of the script. This, like the director's vision, overlays the script. Bad acting and poorly conceived directing can handicap a previously healthy story.

Surgery

When all else fails, there is always surgery. What goes and what stays form the crux of the editing process. A classic joke states that Michelangelo, when asked how to sculpt a horse from a marble slab, replied, "Simple—chip away everything that's not a horse."

Similarly, in filmmaking, once the editor has removed every line of dialog, every action, every scene that does not absolutely pertain to the story, he is left with the best possible movie. The trick is knowing where and when to cut. Like the *New Yorker* cartoon in which a group of surgeons huddle over an anesthetized patient and one says, "Let's just start cutting and see what we end up with," this is as ill-advised in filmmaking as it is in medicine.

Essentially, one must have an orientation to the scene, the film, and the patient. It is not enough to know how to cut images together. Just understanding the basic rules of matching action, establishing eyelines,

"Let's just start cutting and see what happens."

Figure 1.1 *Courtesy of* The New Yorker.

preserving continuity, and so on will not suffice to create a compelling motion picture. As full of constant refinements as editing is, it is not arbitrary. Neither is surgery. Like surgeons, no two editors are alike. There will be as many versions of a scene as there are editors to cut it. Ultimately, however, there are those approaches that work and those that don't.

Instruments

Along with all these disciplines come the tools—the scalpels, forceps, and hemostats—that allow the editor to perform his elusive magic. The instruments have always required a quick mind and an adept hand. These tools have expanded from the mere scalpel of the editing block to today's complex, software-driven editing systems. As will be reiterated throughout this book, the tools constantly change—more so today than ever. Ultimately it is not the tools but the editor who cuts the movie.

Bedside Manner

Lastly, through all of this, the editor, like the doctor, must discover in himself a bedside manner, a way of approaching the work and the people in it. Some call it politics, some call it diplomacy, and some call it playing the game. It amounts to a way of sustaining your creative vision, cooperative attitude and mental health throughout the marathon of filmmaking.

Exploring film doctoring is a way to illuminate the practice and art of film editing. A well prepared editor can generally avoid the need for a doctor. He's a doctor himself. As with getting plenty of fresh air, good food, and exercise, understanding the fundamentals of good editing becomes the best preventative medicine. It will make life easier and create movies that will stir the emotions of audiences for years to come. Doctor, cure thyself.

"Watch two movies and call me in the morning: *Russian Ark* and Hitchcock's *Rope.*

Chapter 2

Mastering the Art of Film Editing

Heart of the Matter

The editor has propriety over a realm that belongs to no one else in the filmmaking process. While the cinematographer has his lights and lenses, the costume designer her clothing, and the production designer his sets, only the editor bears the responsibility for the pace and rhythm of the film. And that, as much as anything, influences the outcome of the film. It is the beating heart of the medium.

That may sound like a rash assessment. It is not as intuitive, perhaps, as our perception of what is said or how it is said. Yet when it is said, and for how long, including pauses, glances, and reactions, supplies the emotional subtext to the film.

How is this achieved? Pace and rhythm are certainly more elusive elements than the concrete aspects of set construction, wardrobe design, and other material essentials. Though pace and rhythm remain less tangible than these other elements, they, like music, pull on our heartstrings to a an extraordinary degree. The mode for achieving these feelings is as simple as this: a cut. With a simple pair of scissors, a splicer, or a virtual click, the editor makes a cut. Ultimately, that is all he has to work with.

The Scalpel

What is involved in a cut? A cut is merely a section of dialog or a moment of action culled from the larger whole: the dailies. When the editor views the footage that was shot the day before, he is watching a collection of *scenes* and *takes*. The scene is the larger element from which smaller elements, the takes, are derived. The scene and takes, such as Scene 45 Take 3, comprise the coverage. How a scene is covered allows an editor to transition smoothly from wide shots to medium shots to close-ups without interrupting the narrative flow. During production, all or part of the dialog and action in a scene is repeated over and over from different camera positions. It is up to the editor to decide which camera position, or angle, best serves the meaning of the scene at that moment.

The Healthy Edit. DOI: 10.1016/B978-0-240-81446-9.00002-0

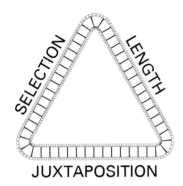

Figure 2.1 *The Editing Triangle.*

Does the editor employ a close-up for intensity or a wide shot for orientation? Does she link two characters through an over-the-shoulder shot or rely on singles? Every time an editor makes a cut, she must make three basic decisions. She must select which is the best piece of footage to use. She must determine how long it will remain on the screen. And she must decide where to place it in relation to the other pieces. Selection – Length – Juxtaposition: *the editing triangle.*

The Great Experiment of Dr. Kuleshov

What constitutes a cut has been the central concern of editors since the beginning of narrative filmmaking, in particular with the Russian filmmakers. In 1922, filmmaker and theorist Lev Kuleshov discovered the theoretical model for film editing. He was not a doctor, but he might as well have been. Kuleshov believed so firmly in the power of montage that he felt it "overrode all other aspects of filmmaking." His approach directly influenced the famous Soviet directors Sergei Eisenstein (1898–1948), Vsevolod Pudovkin (1893–1953), and Dziga Vertov (1896–1954), who in turn influenced the future of world cinema with such groundbreaking films as *Battleship Potemkin, Mother,* and *Man with a Movie Camera.*

In a brilliant experiment, Kuleshov solved the riddle of montage. It is a test that is sometimes attributed to Hitchcock, since he tried it once, even though the actual experiment occurred many years before his prominence.

To accomplish his experiment, Kuleshov collected random film clips from previously shot—and completely unrelated—footage. Then he asked the popular matinee idol of the time, Ivan Mozzhukhin, to perch in front of his camera and make no response as he gazed into the lens. Mozzhukhin had no idea how the director/editor would place the image. After the film was processed, Kuleshov spliced the shot of Mozzhukhin's face next to the other images he had previously collected. When Kuleshov placed a shot of a bowl of soup after the image of the actor's face, he achieved a different meaning than when he placed the image of a child's coffin or of a pretty girl next to the actor.

In the first case, the audience interpreted the scene as meaning that Mozzhukhin felt hungry. In the second instance, the audience experienced sadness over the grief Mozzhukhin exhibited for the dead child. In the third, the audience saw the stirrings of desire in the actor's eyes. At the time, the great Russian director Vsevolod Pudovkin commented that the audience "raved about the acting. . . . But we knew that in all three cases the face was exactly the same." The viewer had unknowingly supplied the emotional connection in his own mind.

To Kuleshov this revealed the basic premise of film editing—that connecting neutral, seemingly unrelated images can liberate a new and deeper meaning. This meaning, and its ensuing emotions, far exceeds the value of the individual shot. That is the power of film editing.

Figure 2.2 *The Kuleshov effect. (Photo credits: Public domain, author, U.S. Air Force/Staff Sgt. Daniel DeCook, and Scott Brock.)*

Figure 2.2 shows an approximation of Kuleshov's experiment. In the first shot, you see a neutral image of Mozzhukhin, then an image of a bowl of soup, then the same shot of Mozzhukhin repeated, then a coffin, then the same shot of Mozzhukhin, and then a pretty girl. These are the same subjects Kuleshov chose to intercut with shots of his actor. If you look back and forth between the images, you'll get a sense of what the Russian audience experienced when viewing the film.

Dynamic and Continuity Editing

Editing falls into two main categories: *dynamic* and *continuity*. Continuity editing is generally used in feature films and dramatic television. In general, this approach belongs to productions where scenes can be covered from multiple angles repeating the same action and dialog and creating a consistency of time and space. Dynamic editing, on the other hand, often works in documentaries and music videos. In dynamic editing, concepts of matching and continuity rarely apply. Shots are ordered by meaning but not necessarily by their relationship to one another in time or space. A documentary filmmaker photographing a leopard taking down a gazelle does not have the luxury of asking for a retake or another angle. Generally, he only gets one shot at one angle. Because of this, he will need to string together discontinuous shots to create meaning and tell his story.

Though various rules apply to all aspects of editing, continuity editing generally makes greater demands—such as the requirement to match action—than dynamic editing. In recent years, however, the lines between these two approaches have softened as documentaries and music videos borrow techniques from feature films (think of the recreations in many National Geographic documentaries) and feature films borrow techniques from documentaries, music videos, and video games—consider *The Matrix*, *Crank*, or *Zombieland*, for example.

The Rules

Here are some rules of editing.

Match Action

In matching action the editor knits one shot to the next. This maintains a sense of reality and flow. A jump in action or *jump cut* (common in dynamic editing) tends to disrupt the flow. By covering a scene from multiple angles, the director creates the opportunity to emphasize various aspects of character, action, and object throughout the scene. In order to weave these varied views into a seamless whole, the director repeats the action and dialog again and again with each take and each angle. When cutting from a wide shot of a woman raising a drink to her lips, for instance, the action begins in one shot and is completed in the next shot. This gives the illusion of continuous movement (i.e., raising a glass) even though it has been interrupted by a splice. By employing this technique, an editor can focus on a particular action one moment while widening the field to include additional information the next, all without interrupting the narrative flow.

Cut on Action

Just as a magician conceals the mechanism of a trick by distracting his audience with a sudden hand movement, an editor can improve the trick of continuous movement by cutting on action. Our eyes naturally follow movement, tracking an animal in the wild, spotting a thrown object, or locating a stealthy predator. This survival instinct remains hardwired in the human psyche. An awareness of its function helps an editor make more effective cuts. An actor's or an object's movements tend to draw our eyes—and therefore our attention. This helps to disguise a cut, making it more fluid. Static images, on the other hand, tend to make a cut more obvious. Where possible, cut on action.

Let the Camera Settle before Cutting

Another rule, however, suggests that we shouldn't cut on camera movement. Let the camera settle before making the cut. For example, begin with the camera steady, and then let it move. This gives a sense of completeness and allows the audience to anticipate the cut.

Create Visual Bridges

The discussion of action leads to another important concept: visual dominance. The term derives from the Colavita effect, which describes our underlying bias toward visual stimuli. In experiments where observers were bombarded with auditory and visual stimuli, they tended to respond primarily to the visual signals. In film, as well, audio remains subservient to the video image. Within the video image it's important to discriminate between essential and inessential information. Good directors and art directors fill the frame with compelling visuals, but only particular objects and characters are emphasized.

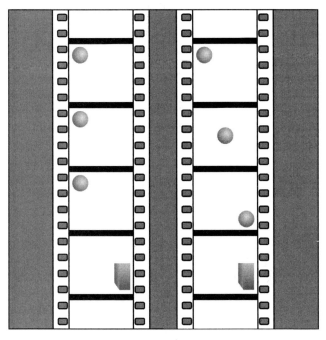

Figure 2.3 *A visual bridge.*

When you watch a film, pay attention to where objects and actors reside in the frame. The important ones should be visually dominant. They catch your attention. In doing so, they draw the eye to a particular portion of the frame. When the editor selects an action shot, he must determine where the viewer's attention will fall within that frame. To help create a seamless cut, he needs to ensure that the next shot picks up at approximately the same point in the frame where the previous shot left off. Otherwise an unintended jump occurs. The jump registers when the eye must leap from one part of the frame in the first shot to the opposite area in the next. Figure 2.3 illustrates how the problem is solved by introducing a visual bridge—an interim shot that moves the eye from one side of the frame to the other.

Doctor's Orders

Always determine where the viewer's eyes will be drawn to in the frame.

Doctor's Note

Despite sound's secondary position, it has tremendous impact on the visuals. This includes sound's ability to direct a viewer's attention. Particularly in wide shots, the placement of a sound effect connected with an object will draw attention to that object, such as the ticking of a clock or the snap of a stick underfoot.

Don't Cross the Line

Since film takes place on a two-dimensional plane, it is important to maintain screen direction. In this way the audience remains properly oriented in terms of movement and eyelines. This is accomplished by respecting the *180-degree rule*. The rule states that all action must take place within an imaginary 180-degree arc. Anything on the other side of that arc is considered "crossing the line" and will disorient the viewer. If you have coverage that takes place on both sides of the action line, it is important to place a neutral shot

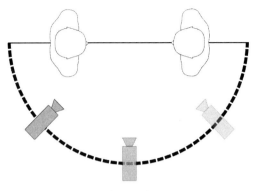

Figure 2.4 *The 180-degree rule.*

(one where scene direction isn't obvious) between a shot on one side of the line and a shot on the other side. Figure 2.4 illustrates this concept.

Maintain Eyelines

A corollary of the 180-degree rule resides in the need to maintain eyelines. Few cuts are more disorienting than those where two characters converse face to face and, rather than looking at each other, appear to stare past each other. In many cases the editor is at the whim of the director and DP who have supplied the shots. Generally, if Character A is on the left side of the frame and looking right, then Character B should be on the right side of the frame looking the left. When eyelines don't match, the editor can sometimes alleviate the problem by repositioning the frame or, in a few extreme cases, flopping the shot.

Vary the Cuts

As becomes apparent when viewing Hitchcock's *Rope*, if we stay on a shot too long, it tends to dissipate the energy of the scene. For this reason, Hitchcock continuously moved the camera in order to change angles and emphasize important details. Editing mimics these camera moves. Therefore, the editor should always consider incorporating a variety of angles when composing a scene.

Cuts Should Be Motivated

This is a corollary to the previous rule. In choosing a variety of shots with which to build a scene, an editor should avoid arbitrary selection. Each cut should be motivated by the one before it. For instance, if in the first shot the actor points at an object, then it follows that the next shot would be a view of that object. Unfortunately, this is not always as obvious as it sounds, particularly when cutting dialog. More about this in Chapter 11.

Cut Before (or After) People and/or Objects Enter the Frame

Another common editing practice requires objects and people to enter the frame from off-camera. When leaving a shot, they should completely clear the frame. This notion avoids the potentially jarring effect created by cutting to a moving object—such as people walking or cars speeding by—when they are already in the frame. It also avoids a false connection of a character leaving one scene and arriving in another.

Pay Attention to Physical Continuity

Perhaps you have seen movies where in one angle the actor holds a cup of coffee in his left hand, then on a cut to another angle the cup has mysteriously shifted to the right hand or maybe disappeared completely.

These are continuity errors. The script supervisor on the set and the editor in the editing room need to pay attention to continuity. A breakdown in continuity can damage the pretense of reality that a film seeks to create.

Respect the Rule of Three

In life a balancing factor exerts itself on many aspects of behavior. Events often occur in sets of three. In the news, when two prominent people die within days of each other, the anticipation arises that a third will soon follow. Despite its disturbing implications this notion reflects the psychological affinity for symmetry. A fulcrum with a counter balance on each side, the Rule of Three applies to many aspects of aesthetics. Take Shakespeare's famous "Friends, Romans, Countrymen..." or France's tripartite motto "Liberté, égalité, fraternité." Or, in our case, the Editing Triangle of "Selection, length and juxtaposition." Some equate it to the ease of remembering three items. In constructing a scene or a film, it becomes vital to pay attention to the primacy of three.

In a sense the editor's work amounts to proving a point and the editor should provide his proofs in parcels of three, whether they occur within a joke–with its set-up, elaboration and pay-off–or a threat that, repeated twice, is finally carried out on the third occurrence. This symmetry also helps construct sequences of shots, for instance an explosion can be dissected into three shots to give it greater impact. Likewise, in composition, if the subject sits in a third of the frame rather than the center it generally produces a more compelling image. For symmetry, memory and proof, remember the rule of three.

Such are the basic rules of film editing. Simple enough to outline, not always easy to follow. And, as we'll see in subsequent chapters, sometimes it is best to completely disregard them.

Review the basic principles of editing:

- Match action
- Cut on action
- Let the camera settle before cutting
- Create visual bridges
- Don't cross the line
- Maintain eyelines
- Vary the cuts
- Cuts should be motivated
- Cut before people and/or objects enter the frame
- Cut after people and/or objects leave the frame
- Pay attention to continuity
- Respect the Rule of Three

Chapter 3

The Film Doctor Is In

The Profession

Where do editors come from? Why do people become editors? It has been said that the editor is someone who, if he were more ambitious, enthralled by working with actors, or loved to move the camera around, would be a director. In this sense the editor was a frustrated director. Many editors have, in fact, become directors, most notably David Lean (*Lawrence of Arabia, The Bridge on the River Kwai*, and *Doctor Zhivago*) and Robert Wise (*The Sound of Music, West Side Story*). But people who become editors do so because they love the challenge of story structure, the subtleties of character and the sublime experience of rhythm.

In my university classes I used to begin by asking everyone who wanted to be a director to raise his or her hand. Scores of hands would shoot into the air. Then I would ask who wanted to be an editor. Maybe one or two hands would float up from the crowd. Today it is different. In the same course taught ten years later, the majority want to be editors, not directors. Why the change? Perhaps because the once nearly anonymous job of editing has moved to the forefront. Perhaps because more and more people have access to equipment by means of Avid, Final Cut Pro, Premier Pro, Vegas Pro, and others. This coupled with other software, such as Photoshop, After Effects, Motion, Soundtrack Pro, Pro Tools, DVD Studio Pro, and Maya has alerted the computer generation to the influence of postproduction.

An editor responsible for many hit films confided that he never wanted to be a director. He took a Zen-like approach to the editorial process and professed that, unlike the director and producer whose minds were occupied with the film day and night, from the development of the script to the key art on the one-sheets, he left everything behind in the editing room at the end of the day. He began fresh each morning and enjoyed the direct participation with the new material before him. During those hours in the editing room, the dailies became his whole world, and by uncovering the treasures within the takes, he would compose a film.

The Healthy Edit. DOI: 10.1016/B978-0-240-81446-9.00003-2

Doctor's Note

When Arthur Schmidt won the Academy Award for *Forrest Gump*, the ad the next day in the *L.A. Times* listed the film's other winners but not the film editor. When I pointed this out to him, he just shrugged, taking it all in stride. Editing has been called an invisible art. Sometimes its practitioners are invisible as well. Perhaps for this reason the film editors' honorary society, American Cinema Editors (ACE), presents its annual forum of Academy Award nominated editors entitled "Invisible Art/Visible Artists."

Almost all films today, from *Kick-Ass* to *Inception*, are postproduction miracles to one extent or another. Even movies that on the surface appear to have no need for special effects, benefit from high-tech postproduction, including the Facebook drama *The Social Network*. The latest version of *Pride and Prejudice* starring Keira Knightley reportedly required a special effects team to replace the dull, overcast English skies with attractive clouds. *Miss Potter*, the film of nineteenth-century writer and artist Beatrice Potter with her fanciful drawings of bunnies, ducks, and gardens, mixes motion tracking and animation in order to tell the tale. Today, the opportunity to shape a film through the extensive tools afforded editors attracts many to the profession. It remains essential, however, to remember the basis for all of this marvelous technology—the need to tell a good story.

Experienced editors at the top of their game do more than put images together in enticing ways based on a plethora of techniques handed down from one master to another. They analyze the narrative and all that is involved in telling a good story. In constructing a scene, an editor needs a solid approach to the material. And, if called upon to nurse an ailing film, he or she needs to know how to diagnose problems.

The Approach

Beginning editors often concern themselves with the principles of editing or mastering the use of software. They want to know how to make a match cut or where to locate the title tool on Final Cut Pro or when the latest version of Avid is coming out. But the essential question they must ask is "How do I approach a scene?" What thought and feeling processes are needed to discover the right way to cut a scene? This is more important than technical expertise. Here are some of the basic questions an editor should ask for each and every scene before starting to cut:

- What is the scene about?
- Who is the scene about?
- How will the scene begin? How will it end?
- What are the beats that need to be met or addressed within the scene?
- What do the characters want in this scene? Why do they want it?
- How does this scene affect the overall film?
- Is there anything missing?

One is reminded of the Zen artist who endeavors to paint a picture of a single tree. Wishing to capture its essence, the man sits for hours gazing at his subject. The hours become days. And the days become weeks.

People wander by, wondering when he will paint the picture, but he doesn't move. Then one day, in a flurry of sudden activity, he dips his brush in ink and rapidly dashes it across the paper. In a matter of seconds, he has created the most stunning painting anyone has ever seen of that tree.

Such is the way of the editor. In working with narrative motion pictures, he should watch all the dailies before making his cut. These days, with the tight schedules, he may be the only one to see all the performances, as was the case of Chris Innis and Bob Murawski, the editors of Hurt Locker, speaking in Allan Holzman's film of *Invisible Art/Visible Artists*. Even the director, who used to screen every take, may not have that opportunity.

As the editor views the dailies, he should let the sounds and images flow through him. He should note the special moments that jump out at him. He should remain alert to the take that wants to begin the scene. And then, and only then, when he has truly seen the potential of the footage in front of him, should he begin to cut. The time he has consumed in watching the dailies will be repaid in the alacrity and smoothness with which the cut will come together. And, though his movements may look rushed, his decisions come from a place of unhurried perception.

What Is the Scene About?

Scenes are minimovies. Like the overall film, each scene is about something. In a sense, each scene is a self-contained movie. In *Up in the Air*, Ryan Bingham (George Clooney) jets around the country firing employees for companies who won't do it themselves. The deepest desire of this charming and unattached corporate hit man is to achieve the rare distinction of logging 10 million Frequent Flyer miles. Yet the scene when he finally achieves his lofty goal is not about victory. Visited by the plane's captain (Sam Elliott), who presents him with the coveted Executive Platinum award, Ryan's long-awaited celebration becomes a realization of his rootless life, the fact that he has no home and no relationships. That's what the scene is about.

Knowing what a scene is about guides the editor's decision-making process. In determining what a scene is about, the editor must ask a series of questions. These include:

* What does the audience learn from this scene that makes this scene necessary?
* How does what they learn influence the eventual outcome of the story?
* Does this scene reveal something new about the character or her needs?
* What's the underlying, or subtextual, meaning of the scene?
* What feeling should this scene elicit from the viewer?
* Does the scene, as shot, have enough coverage to fulfill its objective?

If you can answer these questions, you're on your way to assembling a successful scene.

Filling the Gaps

Remember the missing piece of the jigsaw puzzle in the first chapter? That piece is discovered when the editor tells himself the story. Discovering the whole story is like seeing the whole landscape from a mountaintop. Immediately, one can point out the town, the river, the forest. Knowing the whole story allows the editor to compare the footage she has with the footage she needs. Sometimes they match up. Sometimes they don't. If she doesn't have the footage she needs, she must find it.

The story the editor tells herself is not necessarily the story as written. It is the transcendent tale that forms the basis of the scene. Perhaps it is an archetypal plot that operates behind the contemporary story as scripted. Ultimately, there exist only so many plots in the world. Depending on whom you ask or which book you read, the count seems to vary between 4 and 36 master plots. These are the stories and the myths that power your editing as well.

Case Study

Early in my career I was hired to coedit, with Dennis O'Connor, *Prancer*, a Christmas film about a girl, Jessica (Rebecca Harrell), who finds a wounded reindeer in the woods. Believing it belongs to Santa Claus, she coaxes it home and hides it in the toolshed on their farm. As she nurses it back to health, she's careful to keep it hidden from her strict and tormented father (Sam Elliott). Eventually, the reindeer escapes from the barn and is discovered by the father, who sells the animal to the butcher for display at a Christmas tree lot. Only after the little girl makes a heroic attempt to rescue the reindeer, braving a snowstorm and nearly catching pneumonia, does her father come around. He realizes how his grief over his deceased wife and his failing farm has overshadowed his love and attention for his only daughter. In an attempt to reconcile with Jessica, he buys back the reindeer from the butcher. At this point the stories of the girl and her father cross. The once hard-hearted father is willing to allow the fantasy that the reindeer really is one of Santa's, while the disappointed daughter rejects that possibility. She declares, "I never want to see that reindeer again." After a tender scene, beautifully cut by Dennis, where father and daughter reconcile, I was given the farewell scene to edit, beginning at the point where the father carries his daughter through the downstairs crowd of concerned neighbors and into the snow where Prancer awaits in the back of their pickup truck. At this point, Jessie has agreed to accompany Prancer out to Antler Ridge and release him into the wild, in time for Christmas.

The climactic scene involves the girl's farewell to her beloved reindeer, while the father looks on from a distance. Everything has built toward this moment. Yet when it came time put it together, a gap appeared in the jigsaw puzzle. There wasn't enough footage to allow the scene to play as it should. After sitting through 90 minutes of a story where nothing is more important to this girl than the life of this animal, the audience deserved a satisfying farewell. Yet without the footage to support it, the potentially vital scene was destined to play anemically. It was clear that other footage was needed.

Why did it become obvious? Because in viewing the dailies I found a story within this story, a story that directed the editing choices. Yet I couldn't find the necessary elements to complete the story. Without a concept, without an approach, without a story driving each scene the editor constructs, he is like the surgeon in the *New Yorker* cartoon in Figure 1.1. The story guides you. It provides the fire that burns away everything false; it tells you what to look for. In this case the scene wasn't just about a girl opening the tailgate on her father's flatbed Ford and releasing a dumb animal back into the wilderness where it was born. It could be cut that way, but it would have been wrong. The scene was about much more than that. It was a

---

love story. Two lovers are saying their final farewells. They will never see each other again. The life of each has been enriched by the other, but now it's time to go. Circumstance and nature will not allow their union to continue. And each has a job to do: the reindeer to return to his kind or, if he's truly Santa's, to help deliver presents the world over, and Jessie needs to go to school, play with her friends, and grow up. Despite their love for each other, the two must do the right thing and part, forever.

Where have we seen that story before? How about that postwar film starring Humphrey Bogart and Ingrid Bergman? A little girl is not Ingrid Bergman and a reindeer is not Bogie, but in a sense they are playing the same roles. Remember the end of *Casablanca* where Rick, played by Bogart, has secured the rights of passage for Victor Laszlo (Paul Henreid) and Ilsa (Ingrid Bergman)? Ilsa thinks Rick is going with her to continue their affair, but he has other plans, honorable plans. He's not just solving the untenable love triangle, but he's allowing Ilsa to continue to pursue her cause. In order to do this he's decided to stay behind. Once he announces these plans, the story's trajectory shifts and becomes a final farewell. But Ilsa doesn't just hop on the plane and fly away. She and Rick exchange words with each other, profess their love, their sense of duty, and recall that they'll always have memories of those days in Paris. Likewise, in *Prancer*, Jessie's last words to the reindeer promise, "I'll always remember you." In *Casablanca*, having left his beloved, Rick remains behind with Captain Renault (Claude Rains), whom he tells, "Louie, I think this is the beginning of a beautiful friendship." Likewise, we have the sense that Jessie and her father are seeing the dawn of a new relationship.

With this in mind I constructed the scene. All the elements were there, but not in the profusion necessary to fill it out. Jessie's dialog was well covered and the director, John Hancock, had elicited a wonderful, heartfelt performance. But in order to construct the scene as mentioned, more footage was needed of the reindeer. After all, if it were a love scene, it needed to be able to give equal weight to both sides of the equation: the girl and the animal she loved. So the assistants were sent on a mission—to locate all the footage they could find of Prancer. It didn't matter where it occurred in the film or for what scenes it was actually intended. Just so it fit the needs of this scene. The only requirements were that it was shot at dusk or night—around

(Continued)

Figure 3.1 *In* Prancer, *a discontinuity that is obvious in this series of still frames is practically invisible in the flow of the story.* Prancer, *1989. Copyright © Nelson Films, Inc. (Photo credit: Orion Pictures/Photofest.)*

Case Study (Continued)

the same time as the existing footage, that it was from a low angle—to represent Jessie's point-of-view, and that the reindeer's harness, complete with bells, was strapped to its neck—as was the case in this scene.

Ultimately, the assistants returned with stolen footage that fulfilled two of the three categories. They found excellent low-angle single shots of the reindeer, and these were at night. The fact that there was no other footage with bells had to be ignored for the moment. Armed with this material, I was able to build a scene between the two lovers, cutting from Jessie's dialog to the reindeer's reactions. As Jessie speaks, Prancer's response is intercut with hers. At the scene's conclusion, as Jessie throws open the tailgate releasing the beast into the wild, Prancer rises up, leaps over the camera, and disappears into the woods.

To make this work, I had to break rules remorselessly. Fortunately, editors aren't arrested for such transgressions. And few are ever fired for such boldness. The ones who suffer are those editors who hold too firmly to convention and distrust the audience's ability to become immersed in a good story with compelling characters. Unlike filmmakers, most audiences know nothing of film theory. All they know is what works and what doesn't. When it became a choice of using a shot of Prancer without bells or leaving out the shot, I chose to remain with the shot (see Fig. 3.1). The reasoning was this: if the audience isn't involved in the scene, it doesn't really matter whether the reindeer is dressed in a jingling harness or if it's naked. If the audience becomes involved in the scene, they probably won't even notice.

Eventually, in the final mix, the sound crew and director chose to place a slight, subliminal jingle on the soundtrack whenever Prancer moved, thereby reinforcing the bell's presence. Also, audiences don't tend to remember variations in discontinuous shots. If Character A performs an action in the first shot, and then we cut to Character B, when we come back to Character A, he may have shifted position, but if it wasn't drastic, the discontinuity won't register with the audience. Conversely, if Character A's action in a close-up is different in the shot that follows directly—in a wide angle, for instance—the change will be more pronounced and obvious. In the case of Prancer's bells, until it was pointed out, nobody noticed. In this case, breaking the rules of continuity created a better movie. It allowed the scene to develop fully as writer and director intended it. The satisfying ending may have even helped the movie become one of the top-grossing films during its release, returning, like Santa, each Christmas to TV, stores, and the Internet.

STEALING A SHOT

When editors speak of stealing a shot, they're referring to the use of material in a way that is different than was intended by the director.

Who Is the Scene About?

Many characters appear in the course of a movie. Some scenes are populated with dozens of characters, while other scenes may center on two people talking. In a simple dialog scene, for example, it is easy to cut back and forth between actors speaking. But to truly make it into a scene, the editor needs to know *who* the scene is really about. Discovering this will determine who will be given emphasis and whose role will be diminished. This in turn informs such choices as shot selection, shot length, and overlaps.

Doctor's Note

Bringing personality to animals can be tricky. As is often acknowledged, "The eyes are the windows to the soul." This notion, combined with the Kuleshov phenomenon of eliciting an emotional response from a neutral facade, helps explain how editors anthropomorphize animals, imbuing them with human-like characteristics and feelings. In the animal's neutral expression the viewer reads human responses. A close-up of an animal's eye, while completely neutral in nature, can serve to develop character and emotion when intercut with humans or objects that interact with it. Look at films such as *Babe, Black Beauty*, or *Prancer* to see how a shot of the eyes brings the creature's character to life.

In *Mannequin: On the Move*, the closing scene involved a ballroom filled with people. The coverage displayed many of the participants, and it was easy to give a sense of the chaos by cutting to all the different people. But the scene was about Jason (William Ragsdale), who has disguised himself in order to sneak into the grand presentation, that will include Jessie (Kristy Swanson), his cherished mannequin-turned-human. Even though the scene was peppered with other colorful but unknown characters, it was important to continually return to Jason, to show his progress through the crowd.

Figure 3.2 Mannequin: On the Move, *1991. Copyright © Universal Studios Photographer: Francois Duhamel. Still courtesy of Universal Studios/Photofest.*

What Does the Audience Learn from this Scene?

How does this scene influence the eventual outcome of the story? Does the scene reveal something new about the character or introduce a new character? Many of the questions asked by editors when they begin the long marathon of cutting a feature film emerge for the film doctor at the other end of the process. Once a film has been assembled or, in some cases, reached initial completion, the questions return again and again until resolved.

Case Study

As an assistant, I sat with a film doctor, listening to him converse with the producer who had hired him. "Why does (the main character) do that?" "What happened to the watch he was holding?" "Does this all take place in one day?" and so on. The producer became increasing agitated and flustered at his inability to answer most of the questions pertaining to his film. But these questions needed to be answered. The more loose ends, the more likely the final result will come unraveled. I suspect this editor's verbal approach was also a political move, pushing the producer off-guard, diminishing his authority, and reminding him why he needed this editor. Other editors take a more genial approach, asking themselves the questions internally and then going off to enact their solutions in the editing room.

Further Diagnosis

As with the human body, there are many things that can go wrong with a film. Fortunately, with humans, our immune systems usually protect us from viral or bacterial intruders. And homeostasis—an amazing phenomenon that is rarely apparent to us until it is disrupted—rules the day. When something is off-balance, however, such as in a fever, sudden pain, dizziness, it becomes immediately obvious . . . and overwhelming. As editors we need to develop the same level of acuity. If a scene runs too long, a performance lacks honesty, or a transition proves jarring, we need to recognize it as if it were an unexpected and grueling stomach ache. Conversely, like the return to normalcy after a protracted illness, we revel in a successfully executed scene.

Wrestling with Material

Part of being a good editor is learning to trust your feelings. One day, putting together a dialog scene consisting of many characters, the editor might find himself stymied by the approach he has taken. The scene just isn't coming together. It should have—after all, it was a simple dialog scene. Following several hours of wrestling with the scene, the editor comes to the obvious conclusion: he has lost his touch. Most artists confront this disquieting insecurity from time to time, the feeling that they are fakes, cheats, charlatans; how dare they even accept a salary? Obviously they are in the wrong profession, and it has taken this long for them to realize it.

Cut! Full stop. What about all the other scenes in the film that are working well? Who edited those? The same editor who's struggling with the current scene. Maybe there is something wrong with the scene.

Maybe it is not working because the editor is not feeling it. Or rather, the editor is not feeling it because some element is not working. Step back and examine the patient again. What went wrong here? Perhaps it's a lack of coverage; perhaps the dramatic situation feels contrived; perhaps the performance looks forced and the editor is not willing to admit it; perhaps there are too many people in this simple scene, and they're all talking, and what they're saying, for the most part, is unimportant. The editor is bored. And the audience is going to be bored. Trust your feelings. The scene isn't working because the scene is a lousy scene. But you can fix it or, at least, make sure it doesn't harm the rest of the film.

Not all scenes, even those by brilliant, accomplished writers and directors, can work as shot. If you know how to cut, if you've taken the time to review the dailies and discover an approach to the material, and it's still not captivating you, there's probably something wrong with the scene. At that point, it becomes necessary to reevaluate. In some cases, the cut should be trashed, and the process should start over from the beginning.

These days it's easier to scrap a scene and begin anew. All the dailies are waiting in virtual bins, as intact as when the editor first began. In earlier times, scrapping a scene took nerve. Only one version of the dailies existed, and it resided on a physical medium—film—so every cut was a commitment, a potentially destructive move severing the child from its mother. Reconstituting a scene required breaking apart every shot, finding the roll it belonged to, and splicing it back into the original dailies. Considering this today, one should not hear complaints when an editor is confronted by the task of starting over. Not only have the digital dailies remained undisturbed and ready to serve up their images again at any time, but also the editor can hedge her bets by making a copy of the previous sequence. This helps if, for some unknown reason, it turns out that the first version was the better one. Or to prove to the director why it wasn't.

When Poisons Are Medicines, Accidents Are Intentions

One of the film doctor's secret medicines resides in the accident. Just as the poisons foxglove, belladonna, and datura have been used in a multitude of valuable cures, so too the accident that is generally considered unusable footage can, in small doses, help or even save a scene. One such example is addressed in detail in Chapter 13 as a case study of the film *Horseplayer*. But there are many occasions where an unintended event, by nature of its realness, finds its way into the final film. That is the virtue of accidents—they reveal reality. In most cases a filmmaker would not wish for an actor to stumble, a prop to fall, or a camera to continue running past "cut." Yet when these events occur, they offer new possibilities to the editor.

Actress Kym Karath told me that at five years old, when she played little Gretl in *The Sound of Music,* she couldn't swim. In the scene where the Von Trapp children and their governess (Julie Andrews) row up to their home dressed in clothes fashioned from curtains, director Robert Wise preferred not to use a stunt double, so Karath agreed to play the scene herself. The plan was for the boat to capsize and, as Karath and Andrews fell off one side, the elder actress would catch the younger. The first take went as planned, but on the second take Karath fell forward while Andrews fell backward. Karath hit the lake and sank to the shallow bottom, swallowing a good amount of water. The quick action of the assistant director saved her. But rather than use another take when this one failed to proceed as planned, the director—a former film editor

(*Citizen Kane, The Magnificent Ambersons*)—chose to include it as part of the scene. In the final version, the accident occurs, and before Karath is rescued by the AD, there's a cut, and she is carried from the water by Louisa (Heather Menzies). Ultimately, the accident's inclusion evoked a truer, less staged, and more dramatic moment.

Doctor's Note

In *The Sound of Music*, after the second take when actress Kym Karath was carried from the water by Heather Menzies, her onscreen sister, Kym threw up the water she'd swallowed. This was an accident that did not make it into the film.

Case Study

As the editor assigned to cut the chase sequence in the family action film *Mac and Me*, I found myself immersed in footage of swerving cars, sprinting FBI agents, and a determined boy cradling an alien as he navigated his wheelchair downhill through heavy traffic. It was excellent action footage shot by a veteran director, Stewart Raffill. But during the shooting of this scene, an accident had occurred. The stunt double who was piloting the wheelchair miscalculated. A pickup truck plowed into him as it passed, sending him to the hospital. Fortunately he was okay. As happens when editing on 35 mm film, the spoiled take wasn't printed. Instead the script supervisor marked it as N.G.: no good.

Later, in the editing room, it occurred to me that this accident might be of value, since it was full of real jeopardy. I asked the assistants to order a print of it from the film lab. At first, I received some disapproving looks, as if I had a morbid interest in accidents. I was reminded that the scene was not about the boy getting hit by a car, but about him successfully maneuvering his way through traffic to avoid the FBI's clutches. Having read the script, I was aware of this. But I felt that the footage of the collision could somehow be used to improve the scene's intent.

The take arrived and I watched it. As it played out, the camera followed behind the wheelchair-bound boy. In an instant, a truck appeared and smacked into him, sending him flying. Perfect. I realized that I could use the take up until the actual impact. One frame before the collision, I cut away to the reverse angle of the boy passing the truck and heading toward the camera. When the two pieces were cut together, they played as an extremely close call. When the director saw it, he was thrilled. After the sound effects and Alan Silvestri's music were added, the scene became even more exciting. Whenever I watch it with an audience, they elicit the kind of visceral reaction I'd hoped for. As the truck speeds past, they gasp, sensing how close it was, relieved that it misses the boy, and completely unaware of what actually happened.

R̽

To fill the gaps that occur in a scene, consider the following:

- What element is lacking in this scene?
- Is there any footage I can steal to help tell the story better?
- What's the essential story that should drive this scene?
- Whose scene is it really?
- Are there other human moments that should be included?
- What makes this scene vital to the rest of the film?

Chapter 4

The Instruments

Linear and Nonlinear Editing Systems

The digital revolution has triumphed. It has succeeded in supplanting the old order. We stand bathed in the digital dawn. An unimpeded rush of breakthroughs in processing speed, computer memory, and software development flood the market. Devices such as hex core processors, ATX motherboards, RAM chips, and graphics cards have infiltrated the nomenclature of today's filmmaker.

Just as part of the history of medicine is reflected in the development of technology, such is the case with motion picture editing that has advanced from simple, physical devices to a complex virtual realm.

Case Study

The tables have turned. When teaching a beginning production course, I pass around clips of 35 mm release print in order to acquaint students, who have grown up with picture phones, digital still cameras, and amateur HD video, with a medium that, at this moment, still holds a grip, though perhaps tenuous, over the world of theatrical motion picture production. Despite recent improvements in video, film still offers the best latitude, greatest depth, and widest venues. These students' questions are not the questions that were asked a decade earlier. They want to know if the celluloid stuff runs at 29.97 frames per second, if the information on it can be written over, and how many megapixels it uses. These questions highlight the collision of two different paradigms that are still active at this time.

In Praise of the Physical Body

Film, that celluloid strip of images with perforations punched along its edges, has been postponing its final bow for longer than predicted. Something about its clarity, richness, and depth keeps it in the limelight or, rather, the Xenon light of the theater projector. Despite its expense and veteran status, film still finds favor

The Healthy Edit. DOI: 10.1016/B978-0-240-81446-9.00004-4

among higher-budget productions, such as those produced by the studios, and among some network television shows. Part of its attraction derives from its makeup. The fact that it is a physical medium made of light-sensitive silver salts suspended in gelatin layers contributes to its vast color range and depth. As the exposed film stock bathes in the chemical solutions that will reveal the latent image, it acquires microscopic plateaus and valleys. The images etch the surface in relief that, when projected, transfer to the motion picture screen. The people and settings appear to come alive. Even more than the artificial design of 3D projection, all motion

> ### PROGRESSIVE
>
> *Progressive scan* is an advance from the original *interlaced* video format that requires the image to be constructed from two frames, each displaying half of the image—one with the odd-numbered lines and the other with the even-numbered lines. Progressive video displays each frame in its entirety.

picture film displays actual depth. Film has depth where video, including high-definition video, is shallow. For many years this point, both practical and metaphoric, was not lost on filmmakers as video comprised the world of network television, a medium that with a few brilliant exceptions existed basically to sell soap, beer, and cigarettes. But TV has become bolder, smarter and, in some cases, less commercialized. And the paltry scanned image that made us voyeurs peering through the narrow Venetian blinds of 525 *interlaced* lines has advanced to high definition's 1080 lines of *progressive* images.

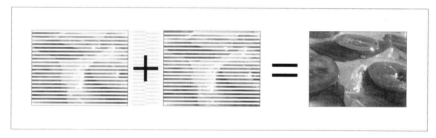

Figure 4.1 *The interlaced video frame, as used in standard- and high-definition formats.*

> ### Tech Note
>
> Current video has become the new tower of Babel. It comes in so many different formats and configurations that it is sometimes daunting to decide which applies to a particular project or what is the best capture mode for editing machines. The basic differences arise between standard definition, as determined by NTSC standards in this country, and other formats, such as PAL or SECAM abroad, and high definition. Within the standard definition realm the question for many years has been between analog and digital. High definition, which by nature is digital, divides into various resolutions ranging from 720 to 1080 lines, various frame rates from 24 to 60, and a choice between interlaced and progressive scan.

As the human world continues its departure from the physical, editing joins in the march. Veteran editors speak of the attractive feel, look, and even the smell of 35 mm celluloid film. The magic of its image, liberated through photochemical baths, entrances their imagination. Some miss the connectedness that comes with physically touching the material, feeling the weight and texture of a film roll, coordinating its movement through the editing machine, severing it, and reconnecting it on the splicing block. Others declare good riddance to the unwieldiness of it all. Historically, this is not a new occurrence. The movement away from the physical began at the dawn of civilization when hunter/gatherers, finding it more efficient to plant seeds than to forage for food, settled down on their land, built farming communities, and made way for priests and artists to hold up a mirror to their lives. From that moment on through to the Industrial Revolution and into the Information Age, humanity has shed more and more of its physical requirements. Yet, ironically, we remain highly physical beings, and those who negate this part of themselves often suffer for it.

Even if an editor will never work with celluloid, it helps to have some familiarity with the medium, if only to understand from where the current paradigm derived. To hold up a piece of film to the light is to understand what a frame really looks like. Understanding a frame helps the editor to envision the length of a beat (about eight frames) or to conceive of a second of screen time (a foot and a half). Physically making a splice on a metal splicing block reinforces the consequences of each decision. But most of all, physically handling the film brings the person into a relationship with the medium in which he works, and that is indescribable. It is a relationship that resides in the realm of the senses and not the intellect.

We have moved from the skills of physically manipulating materials to the mental manipulation of commands. Is this inhuman? Hardly. If humanity is the sole purveyor of technology among the animal kingdom and all new technology will ultimately be used—from the printing press to the atom bomb—it's best not to become too attached to any particular instrument or machine. Even Avid and Final Cut Pro will be supplanted by another storytelling instrument better suited to its time.

An Editor's Tools

As an art form heavily reliant on technology, editing has experienced several epochs in the advancement of its tools. While benefiting from the greater ease and options brought on by innovation, editors must always remember that the real work derives from within.

Medieval Medicine: The Moviola

The scissors, magnifying glass, and banana oil film cement with its ubiquitous aroma that entranced the senses of filmmakers from the earliest eras gave way to a wider array of instruments, including splicing blocks, trim tabs, grease pencils, and the world's first editing machine. Its inventor, a Dutch-born electrical engineer Iwan Serrurier, dubbed his home movie player the *Moviola*, a take-off on the home music player of the time, the Victrola. It used sewing

---

PERSISTENCE OF VISION

A phenomenon where the mind briefly recalls the previous film or video frame, blending the images in order to create the illusion of movement. This theory has been questioned in recent years.

Figure 4.2 *The original Moviola. (Photo by Jim Turner of Moviola.)*

machine type motors, belts, and pedals. One pedal supplied variable speed, while the other, operating a more powerful motor, controlled the constant speed motor. A Geneva drive, an element that was first used by Swiss watchmakers, converted the motor's continuous rotating motion into intermittent motion by use of a gear shaped like a Maltese Cross. Intermittent motion combined with persistence of vision created motion pictures.

It wasn't until an editor at Douglas Fairbanks Studios realized that the machine could be used for viewing dailies that the Moviola gained prominence in the motion picture industry. From then on it became the standard machine in editing rooms for over 60 years. In a sense, it was the first nonlinear, random access system, since the takes could be broken down into individual rolls and lined up in any order. Since the picture and soundtrack were wound up together on each roll and secured with a labeled *trim tab*, the editor could grab any take she wished to view, run it through the Moviola, mark it, cut it, and go on to the next. A spindle on the machine's side allowed for quick rewinding of the film strips into a roll.

With its sewing machine–like parts and mechanical chatter, the Moviola incorporated the accouterments of the seamstress's profession. Some early editors even spoke of the three-foot length of film, often determined to be the correct length for an establishing shot, as a *schneid*. This term, originally shortened from *Schneider*, a Yiddish and German word for tailor—literally a "cutter"—represented a length of fabric stretching from the tip of the master's nose to the end of his outstretched arm. This reinforced the physical stitching together aspect of the editor's art.

Because of its simple design, the Moviola could usually be repaired by any editor or his assistant. If the screen went dead, it usually meant that a bulb had blown out. If the film didn't advance, a belt may have broken and could easily be refitted. If the sound stopped working, a fuse in the amplifier could be replaced. This reinforced a connection between the machine's operator and the machine. Today, according to author and lecturer Pete Markiewicz, most young people "use technology constantly, but have little idea how it works." Even fewer could take a computer apart and put it back together. Markiewicz likens this naïve trust in technology to "earlier generations who welcomed processed food and food additives" but had no idea how these commodities were produced. In terms of computers, the basic concept of binary codes evolving to machine language evolving to higher-level languages as they relate to electronic switches that were originally vacuum tubes but now reside within extremely dense microprocessors is not hard to grasp, but many prefer to accept some sort of arcane magic operating at the most basic levels of computer design.

Doctor's Note

Mark Serrurier, the son of the Moviola's inventor and head of Moviola, displayed the same kindness as doctors who treat patients regardless of their ability to pay. If an impassioned but impoverished young editor needed a Moviola to begin his craft, Mr. Serrurier told him, "Pay me when you can," and gave him the machine. Today, of course, most editing equipment is sold by large corporations whose only human contact may be a customer service rep on the other end of the phone.

European Renaissance: The Flatbed

After decades of the Moviola's rein, a new kind of machine appeared on the Hollywood scene in the 1970s. These were flatbed editing machines, designed in Europe and used as far back as the 1930s. The two main flatbed manufacturers were Steenbeck, which garnered most of its attention from East Coast editors, and KEM (Keller-Elektronik-Mechanik), which came to dominate West Coast editing rooms. Both were manufactured in Germany. Moviola produced its own version of a flatbed that became popular with editors who worked with 16 mm film.

Employing sets of sprocketed rollers and rotating platters to transport the film through picture and sound heads, the flatbed machine allowed for easy screening of full rolls of film—up to 2000 feet in length—on large monitors. Unlike the Moviola that used the Geneva movement to supply the intermittent motion, the flatbeds used a rotating prism. Consequently the image, though larger, was not as sharp as the Moviola's. In order to engage and disengage the multiple film plates, as well as to determine the direction of spin, the flatbed required more buttons than the Moviola. Its three main buttons, the forerunners of the J-K-L computer keys, operated forward, stop, and rewind.

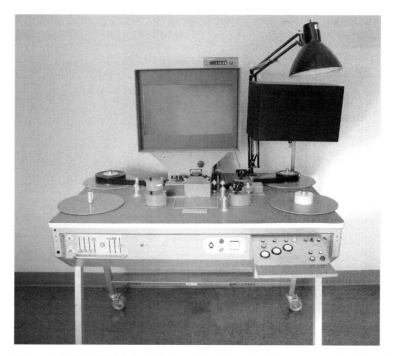

Figure 4.3 *The KEM flatbed editing machine. (Reproduced by permission of Joel Marshall, Atomic Film Company.)*

The most popular flatbed, the KEM Universal, used eight plates to hold picture and sound film, and supported interchangeable picture and sound modules. In this way multiple tracks or multiple camera angles could be evaluated simultaneously. Dailies, as well as the *cut workprint* and *worktrack*, were assembled onto 1000-foot *KEM rolls*, one for picture and one for sound. These were labeled using black and red ink, respectively. A 35 mm workprint had to last the editor for the duration of the process. Consequently, it was essential to treat it with care, guard it against too many nicks and scratches, and avoid cinching it, which would scatter microscopic nicks throughout the roll. The KEM's larger screens and improved audio system allowed for presentation of the cut workprint to larger groups. The flatbed's multiple camera and multiple sound-track features were the precursor to the vast array of tracks that electronic nonlinear systems now offer.

After the 1970s it was not uncommon to see both the KEMs and Moviolas coexisting in the same editing room. Editors accustomed to the speed of selection through random access of Moviola rolls preferred to produce their first cut on the more archaic machine and then finesse it on the KEM. Even though a Moviola equipped with special arms could run 1000-foot reels of film, the KEM made recutting simpler because of the fast rewind speeds, the less cumbersome loading, and the large viewing screens.

 Case Study

For a while, the Eagle Eye Film Company, one of the main vendors and renters of KEMs, placed engraved plaques on their rental machines bearing the names of previous features cut on those machines. In many cases multiple KEMs found their way onto films employing multiple editors and assistants, and consuming vast amounts of film. According to Jim Tucci, Eagle Eye's CTO, the editing room of *2010*, the sequel to *2001: A Space Odyssey*, required 10 KEMs in use at one time. The tiny brass plaques on these KEMs were a tribute to the artistry of the handmade creations that were crafted at these machines. The practice ended around the time of *Heaven's Gate*, a huge film that was an even bigger flop. Superstitiously, many editors refused to cut on those KEMs.

The Modern Revolution: Nonlinear

After decades of dependable use, the Moviola and KEM saw themselves unseated by the rise of the electronic revolution. As computers became more accessible and memory storage larger, software developers conjured up the idea of editing movies in a virtual environment. Video editing by use of timecoded playback and recording on video tape had been around for a long time, so the concept of capturing the images and storing them as digital media and then editing them in a virtual format was truly novel. Early systems such as *Montage*, a system preferred by Francis Ford Coppola, *Editflex*, and *CMX* were popular but still fairly cumbersome to use. They lacked the user-friendly graphical interface that would appear in later years. Editflex and CMX, for instance, used banks of laserdiscs to store media and required the editor to type in the beginning and ending timecode as well as a duration for each and every cut. In modern systems the click of a virtual button automatically generates timecode that corresponds with the beginning and end frames of the selected clip.

Nonlinear editing or *NLE* systems—those allowing random access to dailies as well as the ability to insert a shot at any place in the sequence without having to rebuild the sequence from that point onward—were initially *offline* systems. This allowed for speed of assembly at lower resolution. The lower cost of these systems, compared to the high cost of online editing, also meant that editors could expend more time in developing the cut. After a final cut was achieved, it was reassembled at full resolution on an *online* system using an *EDL* or *edit decision list*. In the case of film, the editing machine stored the film's *keycodes*. Like video timecode, the film keycode designated every film frame, allowing a *negative cut list* to be generated as a guide for the negative cutter who would conform the original negative based on the editor's final cut.

With the potential to capture high-definition video at full resolution or to reassemble a downconverted, lower resolution cut in full resolution on the same system, the distinction between offline and online editing is disappearing.

EDL: EDIT DECISION LIST

An edit decision list, commonly known as the EDL, is a log generated during the offline editing session, reflecting the in and out points and duration of each cut as well as indicating the original source material. The EDL is used to recompile the editor's cut with original footage in an online session.

Early Electronic Systems

In some early systems the computer linked to videotape players while other systems linked to information on large laserdiscs. George Lucas's system, the *EditDroid*, was another system to use laserdiscs. While still requiring that the dailies be burned to two redundant laserdiscs, EditDroid offered a graphical interface with a timeline, source, and record monitors, much like current nonlinear editing systems. Although it received fairly limited use, it was the true pioneer of the timeline-based systems in use today. One of EditDroid's disadvantages lay in its use of laserdiscs that had to be burned professionally, usually at a remote laboratory.

Avid's solution of allowing the editor to digitize media onto hard drives in the computer was a big breakthrough and led ultimately to its predominance in the field. Because of the cost and bulkiness of early media storage, the maximum drive size was nine gigabytes, costing roughly $1000 per gigabyte, an astonishing figure by today's standards. Because of the low processing speeds coupled with minimal memory, analog dailies were *digitized* at low resolution. In this regard, the image was far inferior to the picture viewed on a Moviola or KEM. But the increased speed of editing as well as the capability to render effects, such as titles, fades, and matte keys, that previously were sent out to the film lab made the new systems desirable.

Figure 4.4 *The Avid Media Composer. (Photo courtesy of Christy's Editorial.)*

With advances in technology, NLE systems moved from digitizing standard definition analog video to *capturing* high-definition digital video.

Some editors, unable to make the transition from physical to virtual, left the profession, in spite of the fact that the Motion Picture Editor's Guild made a point of educating their members about the new NLE systems. Yet editors accustomed to film editing discovered something else. They discovered that the time they used to spend mulling over a cut, those valuable moments that occurred while the film was rewinding on the KEM or while an assistant was hunting down a clip to extend a trim had disappeared. They missed the chance discoveries made while the cut sequence or dailies rewound on the flatbed. The arrival of NLE systems allowed the editor to scroll quickly through masses of film and edited footage by dragging the picture head through the scroll bar. This greatly accelerated the decision-making process without the accompanying time allowance to consider each cut. Avid, and systems like it, bring instant gratification, speed, and the opportunity to make multiple versions.

Doctor's Note

Keep in mind that most editing systems were not originally designed by editors. One of the exceptions was the editor-designed system *Lightworks*. It is now obsolete, except in a couple of editing rooms that have kept it alive, including that of Martin Scorsese's editor, Thelma Schoonmaker. This PC-based system even had a slightly video game–like interface, where you entered a graphic depiction of an editing room door. Once in there you removed your project from shelves before loading it up, and so on. If you wanted to delete something, you called upon a shark (a reference to some less appetizing aspects of the film business?), which came and devoured the offending item.

Just as the Moviola had lingered well after the introduction of the KEM or Steenbeck to editing rooms, the KEM and Steenbeck remained for years after the introduction of the Avid, allowing assistants *matchback* of the editor's virtual cut to the actual 35 mm workprint for projection in test screenings.

MATCHBACK

Matchback is the term for film dailies that are transferred to video and then conformed back to film after they are edited. By tracking time code and key numbers, the nonlinear editing system can create an edit decision list for matching the video edits back to the original film negative.

Doctor's Note

In some cases, the common film nomenclature has become corrupted, so a term that had a particular meaning in the film world has come to mean something different in the digital nonlinear world. *Clip* is one example. In film, the word *clip* referred to several frames of a scene. It was a portion of film that had been cut away from the whole. In Final Cut Pro, *clip* can refer to the entire take, represented by an icon of a 35 mm film strip. In film, a *bin* was an open metal box on wheels with a rack above it. The rack had pins that held the stray clips, or trims, of film that accumulated as the editor culled material from each take. In the Avid and Final Cut Pro world, a *bin* is a window or folder, respectively, that contains raw media. It might contain some clips, in the traditional sense, but it generally contains whole elements, such as the dailies. In most

(*Continued*)

Doctor's Note (Continued)

professional editing rooms the NLE bins are labeled by scene number, so each bin contains all the raw footage for that particular scene. Other bins contain music, sound effects, titles, or whole sequences. In Avid parlance, the single icons representing each take are known as *frames*, even though frames traditionally apply to the series of images that comprise a take. From tabs at the top of the Avid bin you can select *text view* or *frame view*.

The Mouse That Roared

Apple, the company that originally supported Avid technology, eventually got the idea to produce its own editing system. With similar functions as the Avid, Apple's system was software-based, meaning it could run on various Apple products. And it was far less costly than the Avid, where a full system could range at times from $60,000 to $150,000, including decks and monitors. For under $1000 an aspiring editor could cut his movie on Final Cut Pro. It was an extraordinary move and influenced a new generation of editors some of whom, to this day, refuse to transition to the older system, despite Avid's many other advantages. In an effort to regain its once overwhelming market share, Avid launched its own competitively priced system, the Avid Express, a simplified version of its studio models. Recently, to raise the ante, it offered Media Composer, an excellent and sophisticated software that has lived in professional editing rooms for years, at a low price.

Doctor's Note

Contrary to popular belief, the editor's ubiquitous white glove entered the editing room as a covering to protect the editor's hand from sharp edges of film not initially as a way to keep the film from getting scratched or fingerprinted, since the workprint would eventually be conformed to the original negative and new prints made.

With the rise of nonlinear, digital editing, Latin terms supplanted the more basic film terms of *picture* and *sound*. These were *video* and *audio*, respectively. What was once a *workprint* became a *sequence*, and the *soundtrack* became the *audio track*.

Doctor's Orders

Always back up your project. Having a system crash and losing media or project information is the surest way to remember the importance of saving the project after every session and, preferably, to multiple places such as the desktop and a separate flashdrive. This is one issue that film editors never had to deal with, barring a natural catastrophe. Film has an enduring quality that digital and magnetic media do not.

The Edit

During the majority of filmmaking's history, a cut consisted of a few simple steps. After marking the selected piece of film with a grease pencil, the head of the shot was placed on a splicer and severed from the rest of the body. Then the feet were cut off, and the resultant clip was joined to a series of other clips, assembled into a parade of images, the workprint, which eventually comprised the entire two-hour motion picture. Perhaps it is no coincidence that the guillotine splicer sparked allusions to the French Revolution and its liberty, equality, and fraternity. Today a new revolution has spawned a variety of choices when making the same simple move. Depending on which system the editor is working on, he or she has various options for affecting the cut.

Tech Note

To make a simple edit in Avid, the selected take is loaded into the Source monitor either by dragging or double-clicking the frame representing that take in the bin. Once in the monitor, the editor selects the beginning and end of the shot by pressing I (for in) on the keyboard and O for out, or by selecting the *mark in* or *mark out* icon from the button bar below the monitor. After making this decision, the editor has a choice of two buttons, either a yellow insert, also known as *splice-in edit*, or a red *overwrite* button. Clicking on one of these automatically loads the selected material into the Record monitor where it will be reflected in the timeline as a new sequence, or at the edit point of an existing sequence, designated by the *playhead*. Alternatively, one can employ the keyboard command V or B, respectively, for insert or overwrite.

In Final Cut Pro the take, as it resides in the Browser window, is loaded into the Viewer by way of double-clicking or dragging. Once it is marked, by using the I/O keyboard keys or by clicking on the mark in or mark out icon below the monitor, a whole other set of options present themselves for adding the selection into the Timeline. One way involves clicking on the image in the Viewer and dragging it across the way to the Canvas Edit Overlay, and over a mosaic of commands consisting of a yellow Insert box, a red Overwrite box, a blue Replace box, a green Fill to Fill box, and a purple Superimpose box. To the right of the yellow and red boxes are adjunct boxes of similar color that allow the shot to be loaded with a transition effect. Upon releasing the mouse button over the desired command, the image loads into the place designated by the playhead on the Timeline. As with the Avid, the editor can select a yellow insert button or a red overwrite button at the bottom left on the monitor window. Or he can use the keyboard shortcut F9 for an insert edit and F10 for an overwrite edit.

Another approach uses drag-and-drop editing. In this case, the editor has designated the cut by marking in and out or by supplying markers. The take in the Viewer window bypasses the Canvas and is dragged directly downward into the Timeline. This procedure also avoids positioning the playhead but instead allows the editor to visually pinpoint the edit and aim the clip toward the target. With the use of FCP's Snapping option, which instantaneously corrects for approximate positioning of a clip by snapping it into place directly beside another, the thumbnail clip is dragged from the Viewer onto the desired place in the Timeline and locks into place directly next to another clip upon releasing the mouse. An arrow pointer feature on the Timeline

(Continued)

Tech Note (Continued)

allows the editor to immediately decide whether to position this clip as an insert edit or as an overwrite edit. Upon approaching the Timeline, the thumbnail clip encounters a thin, gray line on each audio or video track. When the cursor's pointer encounters this line, it changes into a forward arrow above the gray line or a downward arrow below the gray line. The forward arrow inserts the shot, while the downward arrow overwrites an exiting shot with the new one. At the same time a solid (overwrite) or outlined (insert) box appears representing the clip's length.

Figure 4.5 *The anamorphic process. The upper part of the illustration shows the image as the camera's viewfinder sees it. The middle portion displays the squeezed image as it resides on 35 mm film. The bottom portion reveals how the subject will look on a theater's screen. Notice how the initial wide, rectangular image has been squeezed by the camera's taking lens into a square film frame and then expanded back to a widescreen image.*

All this is a far cry from the simple act of cutting the head and tail off of a spool of film and pasting the selected clip beside another. Ultimately, a cut is just a cut. You mark an in point and an out point, and somehow—even after much acrobatics—add it to the sequence of other cuts in the timeline or on a film strip.

But it's important to remember that it is the editor and not the equipment that makes the cut. Until recently all thermometers were glass probes with a bulb of mercury on one end. As the mercury rose through the thermometer's graduated shaft, it indicated the temperature. Today most thermometers contain heat-sensitive circuitry and digital readouts. They have little resemblance to the original instrument. But both ultimately do the same thing: they reveal a patient's temperature. Editing, despite the vast assortment of new possibilities, ultimately remains about one thing: the juxtaposition of images based on the footage provided. This is known as the cut. All editing machines, no matter how simple or sophisticated, perform this essential function. In that regard it does not matter if the device is an ancient pair of scissors, a simple computer program like iMovie, or the most sophisticated and advanced Avid system.

The Frame Matters

The first 35 mm movies used the entire film frame, which appeared nearly square. This was later adapted to TV, which fit inside a box with a 4:3 aspect ratio to accommodate the limited transmission scan lines. After decades, the square

ANAMORPHIC

Anamorphic describes the widescreen process that involves squeezing the image through the taking lens of the camera, then unsqueezing it at the projection stage. This allows a greater amount of information to be optically compressed into the film frame and then displayed across a wider screen area. The process was originally developed in France by Dr. Henri Chrétien, and then purchased and renamed Cinemascope by 20th Century Fox. Following its introduction, many other widescreen processes appeared, including Technirama, Vistascope, Superscope, VistaVision (where the film moved through the camera sideways), and Techniscope (using half-sized frames that were stretched into full frames in the lab).

Tech Note

A current approach to some films that have no expectation of ending up on the big screen but will spend their lives on Blu-Ray discs is to shoot them in *2-perf* formats. This is a version of the earlier film saving innovation of *Techniscope*. Instead of using the standard *4-perf* high 35 mm frame—remember, frame size is not predetermined but created by the size of the camera's film gate—the Techniscope negative used only half that. The cost savings was slightly offset by the increased cost of making the positive film *answer print*. Since all movie theaters required 4-perf projection, the film had to be blown up and elongated to fit a 4-perf format. In doing this, an additional advantage was introduced. Vertically stretching the image created an *anamorphic* frame that, when shown on a projector outfitted with anamorphic lenses capable of stretching the image horizontally, mimicked the *Cinemascope* format of ultra widescreen with an aspect ratio of 2.35:1. The very expensive and well-made lens on the optical printer responsible for blowing up the image from 2-perf to 4-perf generally surpassed any anamorphic lens that could fit on an individual camera, thus producing a very high-quality image. Its drawbacks came from an increase in grain and diminished acuity due to the enlarged frame size. In the modern 2-perf format, the film negative will never be cut. In fact, it will never be used for anything other than transferring to a high-definition digital master. This is similar to the process of producing a *DI* (digital intermediate) from a 35 mm full-frame negative.

TV image evolved to the fiercely debated 16 × 9 aspect ratio of the new high-definition format. This closely mimics the theatrical 1.85:1 aspect ratio. Unlike the theatrical 1.85 format, however, television's 16 × 9 format encodes an anamorphic image into the digital signal. This must be unsqueezed during playback.

For the film doctor, the fact that only part of the frame area is used introduces valuable opportunities. In order to produce a 1.85:1 ratio image from a square film frame, it is necessary to matte the top and bottom of the image. Because of this, the DP will compose according to the etched frame lines in the camera's viewfinder. But the additional north and south information remains preserved on the film negative. In some cases a shot can be saved by repositioning the frame lines by a field or two in order to remove a boom or to include information that was cut off, as in Figures 4.6 through 4.8.

Figure 4.6 *What the camera's viewfinder shows.*

Figure 4.7 *What the film captures.*

Figure 4.8 *What the editor sees. Note that the Avid's left Source monitor shows the original footage while the right Record monitor exhibits the image as modified by the editor, as it appears in the final cut with some of the ground removed.*

Figure 4.9 *What the audience views.*

One-Stop Shopping

Postproduction procedures that used to be the purview of labs and DPs more and more fall under the control of the editor. Though aspects such as *color timing* (also known as color grading or color correction) still find their final outcome in labs or post houses, soon everything may be accomplished in the editing suite.

Doctor's Note

Just as phones once existed merely to transmit conversations between people but now do everything from taking photos to searching the Internet, so too this computerized technology of the editing room has permeated other departments. Some futuristic prophets even predict a time without actors, without sets, without anything but an editing machine that creates all the necessary elements.

Temp music and temp dubs can also be handled on the editing machine. In fact, rather than use pre-existing soundtracks, some editors choose to write the temp music using such bundled programs as FCP's Soundtrack Pro.

Doctor's Note

Nearly 100 years ago, in the films of Mary Pickford, color was used long before Technicolor would introduce its full-color *three strip imbibition* process. Scenes were run through a chemical tint bath and colored in terms of emotional or environmental tone. Moonlit scenes were tinted blue, scenes of pain or anger were tinted red, and so on. For an excellent example, see the restored version of the 1919 film *Daddy Long Legs*, with a wonderful and lively score by Maria Newman. The film tells the story of a feisty orphan Judediah Booth, who eventually finds an education outside the orphanage through a mysterious benefactor, Daddy Long Legs. She becomes a published author, rises in society, and eventually discovers the identity of her benefactor, who, it turns out, is also the man she's fallen in love with. In this movie, a particularly disturbing scene where Judediah is punished for getting drunk on a found jug of whiskey, her finger is held to the hot surface of a stove. At that point a strong red tint pervades the scene. In other scenes flushed with sunlight, a yellow tone was used. Eastman, the premier film laboratory of the 1920s, produced a color chart with swatches composed of film strips that had been tinted during processing. These were used by filmmakers to determine the exact color for a scene. The film lab, named after George Eastman, was later known as Eastman Kodak following the introduction of a still camera whose shutter release was thought to make the sound, "kodak." Pathé, another prominent film lab at the time, offered similar swatches. The film artist, familiar with the differences in color from lab to lab, would choose the colors that best fit the tone of the film.

Decades later, deep into advanced full-color film, *wedges* became the way of selecting drastic alterations in color or saturation. These involved superimposing two separate strips of film that were produced from the original negative and incrementally altering the combined color (or lack of) and density of the two strips in order to achieve a third quality. The film *Made in Heaven* required hundreds of wedges with varying degrees of desaturation to achieve the film's tones.

Figure 4.10 Daddy Long Legs, *1919. (Reproduced by permission of the Mary Pickford Institute for Film Education.)*

Today a simple move on a virtual slider in FCP or click of a value on an Avid instantly alters contrast, hue, and saturation. This has translated to the realm of the *digital intermediate*, where the palette has increased to the point where a nearly endless number of possible color and density combinations exist. Colors that could not have been achieved through the combination of red, green, and blue on the film printer's *butterfly values* are now instantly available in the digital realm.

You Must Remember This

Film began as a truly handmade medium. Each Moviola was hand built and the films that were cut on it were meticulously assembled by the white-gloved hands of editors. Hard as it may be for today's editors to believe, since they are accustomed to hundreds of virtual buttons and commands, the Moviola had only two main switches: on/off and forward/reverse. With that device *Casablanca, Gone With the Wind, Citizen Kane, The Graduate, Raiders of the Lost Ark, Lawrence of Arabia,* and hundreds of other extraordinary films were

---

DI

The digital intermediate has replaced the film interpositive as a way of producing duplicate negatives to be used during release printing of the motion picture. The advantages of the DI lie in the fact that the original negative or high-definition master can be scanned into a computer's hard drive, manipulated to correct color, introduce effects, remove scratches, and so on, and then recorded back out to create a new 35 mm negative. One of the DI's main advantages is that, unlike the film interpositive, it does not introduce another generation of grain, which would degrade the image.

edited over the course of six decades. In recent years, the Steven Spielberg film *Munich* saw its editor, Michael Kahn, nominated for an Academy Award for Best Film Editing. Despite the frenzy over electronic editing, *Munich* was cut on a Moviola at a time when most everyone else was cutting on electronic systems—proof that it is not the machine but the filmmaker who ultimately makes the movie.

Doctor's Note

In some ways, the Avid is not an editor's tool as much as it is a producer's friend. Give an editor several strips of film and she'll splice them together to tell the best story she can. Editors will always make cuts. Producers want to make them faster and cheaper, which is what the Avid offers. But has electronic editing overcome the eternal golden triangle of "Fast, Good, Cheap . . . pick any two"? Where a film doctor used to have months to examine, analyze, and cure his patient, these days he may be given two weeks. Is the result the same? Can nine women make a baby in one month? Or are fast and cheap not as good?

R_X

- On a nonlinear editing system try assembling a scene using only the mark in, mark out, and insert functions. This mimics the original editing process.
- Ignore the inclination to add effects, make trims, or correct the color.
- Think through each cut before you make it.
- Ask yourself how each cut affects the outcome.

Chapter 5

Alternative Medicine

Nontraditional Treatments

To challenge the existing order is the mandate of youth, and the young filmmakers of the French New Wave, influenced by the popularity of French existentialism and American film noir, disrupted the traditional conceptions of cinema and, in so doing, altered the future of film editing.

Though the early Russian film school of Eisenstein, Vertov, Kuleshov, and others set down the basic principles of montage at the turn of the last century, it was not until the late 1950s that a cadre of film critics writing for the influential magazine *Cahiers du Cinéma* decided to pick up portable Éclair cameras and mount an assault on the traditional concept of narrative cinema—a classical cinema that had settled into a complacent methodology. In so doing they liberated filmmakers from the assumed constraints of style and narrative with such films as Jean-Luc Godard's *A Bout de Souffle* (*Breathless*) and *Weekend* and Francois Truffaut's *Tirez sur le Pianiste* (*Shoot the Piano Player*), *Les Quatre Cents Coups* (*The 400 Blows*), and *Jules et Jim*.

Doctor's Note

In Godard's picaresque noir film *Breathless*, while Michel Poiccard (Belmondo) is on the run, he is approached by a young woman attempting to sell him a copy of Godard's magazine *Cahiers du Cinéma*, taunting him with "Do you support the young?" Peevishly, he replies, "No, I support the old."

Godard's experiments are particularly noteworthy. He fluctuated between the extended take, such as the long tracking shot in *Weekend*, to the quick *jump cuts* in *Breathless*.

As sometimes happens, technical necessity resulted in artistic innovation. When the final cut of *Breathless* was deemed too long for a theatrical release, the director and editors began lopping out the boring parts.

The Healthy Edit. DOI: 10.1016/B978-0-240-81446-9.00005-6

A conversation between Michel (Jean-Paul Belmondo) and Patricia (Jean Seberg), filmed from behind Patricia as Michel drives his stolen car through Paris, constantly leaps forward in time, causing the locales to shift in the background due to the excised dialog. Where normally an editor would cut away to the other character—in

> ### JUMP CUT
>
> A jump cut is a discontinuous cut that leaps forward in time, thereby producing gaps in the normal sequence of actions.

this case Michel—in order to hide the gaps, Godard chose to remain on Patricia so the viewer experiences the jumps in action. Later, in Patricia's apartment, the actors dart from bed to window to the other side of the room in a series of jump cuts. These abrupt moves catch the audience off guard and direct their attention to the filmmaker's presence. Like Bertolt Brecht's epic theater where the performers consistently remind the audience that they are watching a play, the New Wave often broke the fourth wall, pulling the viewer from the uninterrupted dream state that Hollywood strived to maintain and reminding him that he was watching a movie. The Brechtian idea of allowing the actor to leave his role and address the audience was manifested in film by the New Wave. Like many innovations, it has become clichéd in recent movies and TV shows, such as *The Office* and endless student films.

Doctor's Note

As creative and clever as student filmmakers are, they are often a repository for clichés: opening a film with a character waking to his alarm, having an actor address the camera, placing a beating heart or ticking clock on the soundtrack, relying on a gun to ignite or solve a conflict, and peppering the story with excessive flashbacks and voiceovers that explain more than a Tolstoy novel.

Doctor's Note

Another example of innovation fueled by technical necessity appears in the Lindsay Anderson film *If . . .* , starring Malcolm McDowell. Frustrated by the excessive graininess of the high-speed color film they were using to photograph a low-light scene in the school chapel, the director and cinematographer chose instead to use black and white film. Intrigued by the look, Anderson decided to exchange color film for black and white in other sequences, intercutting them throughout the movie for aesthetic effect. Where in the early decades of motion pictures only black and white stock existed, with the arrival of color the use of black and white came to invoke new meanings. Consider the dramatic use of black and white in *Schindler's List*. In today's films and music videos, the mixture of film, video, CGI, animation, graphics, color, and black and white reflect the outcome of experiments such as Anderson's.

As French filmmakers experimented with the malleability of time and space as they exist in the edit, the American cinema began to adopt these practices. In editing rooms such as Dede Allen's, the once ubiquitous dissolve gave way to the straight cut as a way of transitioning from scene to scene; the typical progression from wide shot to medium to close-up fell out of order; and the shock cut overcame the traditional narrative flow. In the climactic shootout in *Bonnie and Clyde*, Allen showered the screen with cuts as quick as bullets, totaling up to 50 in less than a minute. Today Godard's jump cut has permeated every genre, from horror to romantic comedy, and from documentary to music video.

> ### SHOCK CUT
> A shock cut brings a staccato tempo to the editing that often results in the cut occurring sooner than the viewer would expect.

 Doctor's Note

Dede Allen's work on *Bonnie and Clyde* drew new attention to editing as an art form that deserved the same consideration as cinematography or directing. On this film she became the first editor to receive a single card credit on the main title.

The Match Cut

This leads us to a crucial aspect of film doctoring: the need to break rules. When it comes to telling the story, whatever fulfills the needs of the scene works. Sometimes in watching a film you might notice what you would term a "bad cut." But that bad cut might have saved the scene. It might have removed two pages of needless and boring exposition and, though it didn't match perfectly, it was damn close.

Much has been written and discussed about the value of the match cut. Directors and cinematographers strive to give their editors coverage that redundantly supplies the action and dialog for every angle in the scene. In this way each cut will transition smoothly to the next. If a character begins to rise in a close-up he will complete that action in the wide shot without apparent interruption. In a sense, the whole Hollywood filmmaking art is oriented toward the match cut.

Because of this hallowed position reserved for the match cut, an undue reverence has been attached to it. The match cut has become a tyrant. It has proliferated in editing rooms, film schools, and editing manuals. Even audiences are aware of the primacy of the match cut and will remark on the smoothness of an edit based on the fluidity of match cuts, forgetting that an edit, no matter how smooth, should not call attention to itself. The cutting should be so engaging that the audience doesn't notice the process. In analyzing an edit, the film doctor is sometimes trapped by this beast as well. Upon first examination of an insufficient cut, one may be taken by the precision of the traditional editing. One action flows smoothly into the next. There are no sound dropouts; the temp mix is superb with well-chosen music. Yet despite the evenness of execution and clarity of information, something's wrong. It's boring. There's no spark to it. It's all technique.

Because of its apparent smoothness, the film presents a challenge to anyone attempting to diagnose it. The first step is to turn off the music, since music is a band-aid for all sorts of ills. It can add fluidity and rhythm where none exists. If pacing is the issue, the next question to ask is "What is slowing the pace?"

You may discover that there was a pause in the wide shot before the actor turned his head and delivered his next line, but rather than lose the opportunity for a match edit—cutting from the head turn in the wide shot to the completion of the head's movement in the close-up—the editor waited for it. He allowed the pause so he could make the match cut. It may only be eight frames, but those are a crucial eight frames, especially when added together to the accumulation of all the other spare frames spent waiting to make the perfect match cut. The shot's value has been consumed. The viewer is prepared to move on. If the cut does not follow along with that impulse, the film's momentum lags. In general, it's best to reveal to the audience less than they expect and never more. This is when it's time to be bold. Follow your impulses and cut when you feel the need to cut. Don't wait for the permission of the match cut. Just cut.

But how are you going to make those wonderful smooth edits that viewers respond to if we refuse to be driven by the match cut? Simply by employing another time-honored editing trick: cut on action. Or go to a cutaway. Or overlap sound. The idea is to find a way to make it work. Just about anything is better than waiting for the match cut. Instead of waiting to begin an action in the wide shot and then completing it in the close-up through a matched cut, let that same action begin and end in the close-up. If in the wide shot the character completes his line, then waits a beat before turning his head, don't wait. While the editor waits, the film's energy goes on vacation. Instead, as soon as the actor completes his line in the wide shot, make the cut. But what does the editor cut to? The same close-up as before, but at the beginning of the head turn rather than in the middle of it. By starting on this action, the cut pulls the viewer into the shot, creating the appearance of a match cut where none exists. Continuity of action has been created by introducing movement at the right moment rather than waiting for the movement to carry the edit. Take control of the cut.

 Doctor's Note

Perfection is not the goal of film editing. As much as we try, humans are not perfect. When the flaws are used to an advantage, to make the film stronger, then we approach perfection. The science of metallurgy, an offshoot of alchemy, which fostered the science of chemistry as it occurs in modern medicine, relies on flaws and imperfections. Without it, steel would not exist. The alloying of pure metal with impurities creates a stronger material. So too with editing.

The perfectly cut film can fulfill all the requirements of editing principles, but fail in terms of artistry. To conclude that a film that doesn't routinely disobey the basic tenants of editing lacks vitality might not be too much of a stretch. In film schools, students are often admonished for using out-of-focus footage, yet some wonderful films, such as *Dangerous Liaisons* and *Vicky Cristina Barcelona*, have shots of questionable acuity. But those shots are important to advancing the story and characters, so the film would have suffered had they been left out. In school and in theory it is probably correct to strive for perfection, but in practice it can be fatal.

Continuity Errors

Like the match cut, continuity of place or object can be equally tyrannical. Film fans are vigilant in picking out these inconsistencies, and the Internet Movie Database (*www.imdb.com*) is full of what they title "goofs."

But most goofs aren't spotted on first viewing. Or, if they are, their impact is overrated. Look at Jason Reitman's clever satire *Thank You for Smoking*. In the film the three villains whom we love to hate—the lobbyists for alcohol, tobacco, and firearms—meet regularly at a downtown restaurant to brag about their victories, including how many lives their product has snuffed out each year. The tobacco lobbyist Nick Naylor, played by Aaron Eckhart, far surpasses the others by taking credit for an overwhelming majority of deaths. In the course of their reprehensible conversation they enjoy their quintessentially American dessert, apple pie with a slice of American cheese on it. As the scene progresses, cutting from one angle to another, something odd happens to the pie. In one angle we see Nick take a bite of it, disturbing the cheese. In the next angle the pie is back the way it was, and so on. Clearly, the performances in these different angles were valuable enough to warrant breaks in physical continuity. The scene is so well done, so amusing, that the filmmakers—who surely were not blind to this mismatch—chose to ignore the small inconsistencies in service of the greater good.

Now, imagine it another way. Perhaps the editor and director decided that the most important consideration was to maintain continuity and not potentially embarrass themselves by allowing it. They would sacrifice the delightful performances, perhaps remaining longer on a close-up or playing the scene in a wide shot in order to maintain consistency. In my experience, the danger of obsessing over such inconsistencies bears out again and again. Even though a director or producer may initially exhibit concern upon seeing his editor stoop to mismatched footage, the assurance that the audience will be more engaged in the scene by including this footage pays off.

Case Study

In *Mac and Me*, an *ET*-like story of a disabled boy, Eric (Jade Calegory), who befriends an alien who was mistakenly sucked off his own planet by a United States space probe, a variety of inconsistencies occur that are rarely, if ever, noticed. One appears in the pivotal chase scene where the wheelchair-bound boy speeds down a road with the alien on his lap, chased by several FBI agents. As the associate editor, I was responsible for editing this scene. In order to rescue Eric and the alien, Eric's brother (Jonathan Ward) and the brother's girlfriend speed up beside him in a van, open the side door, and reach out to retrieve them. Since all the necessary coverage couldn't be shot at the same time—some of the kids' close-up reactions were later picked up on a soundstage—and either no one had shot Polaroids or made a note of the costumes, some clothing didn't match. Particularly, the brother's sunglasses. As the van approaches the camera in a wide shot, we see the older brother lean out to retrieve the wheelchair with his brother and the alien. In this angle he's wearing sunglasses. Then I cut back inside the van for the kids crossing their fingers and cheering him on. Here he wears no sunglasses. Then I cut back outside where the brother is again wearing sunglasses. As the FBI closes in on them, the kids finally manage to heft the wheelchair up and into the van. By freely cutting from one angle to another, allowing the tension and pace to build, I was able to draw the audience into the scene so they didn't notice the break in continuity. I've shown this scene to hundreds of students over the years, and only a couple have ever spotted the disparity during the first viewing. The challenge is to cut the scene well enough that the audience is so absorbed by the on-screen action that their attention doesn't wander to ancillary aspects. Hence, go for the story, not for technical perfection.

When it comes to editing, good is not good enough. Editing requires serious work. By the end of the process, there exists no cut that has avoided scrutiny. The technically proficient editor, like the sloppy editor, often quits before that work is done. Having satisfied himself with the expert technique that's allowed him to construct the movie as photographed, this editor sits back and announces that the work is completed and all the elements are there. He's surprised when, having fit all the pieces of the puzzle together, a doubt is raised as to the quality of the work. The sloppy editor, on the opposite side of the spectrum, enjoys the seemingly random ability of shots to fit together and make some sort of sense, especially if accompanied by music, such as he has seen in music videos. So he's surprised that his cut, which contains a quality of vividness and excitement that's missing from the work of a more conservative and law-abiding editor, has also gone astray.

In both cases the triumph will be found in the details. When it comes down to it, what separates an excellent film from a mediocre one is the attention to detail. That pervades everything from scripted dialog, to careful and observant set design, to evocative lighting, to nuanced performances, to smart editing. There are little moments, easily passed over if one isn't attentive to them, that add life to a film. They may be as subtle as a glance, a shift in posture, or a nod of the head. Experienced editors routinely search out these moments. Think of them as The Goodies.

The Goodies

In studying the dailies, the editor considers how he or she will construct the scene. What will be the opening shot? How will the scene end? Who is it about, and so on? But also, and this is truly one of the most enjoyable parts of the process, where are the goodies? Where are the little details that make the scene come alive?

 Case Study

In *Moving Violations*, directed by Neal Israel with a screenplay written by Israel and Pat Proft and edited by Tom Walls (all of whom had worked together on the movie *Bachelor Party*), a young landscaper played by Bill Murray's brother, John—cleverly, many of the parts were played by siblings of other well-known actors—makes the mistake of tossing his apple core out the window of his truck. A storm-trooper-like cop, played by James Keach, pulls him over and issues a ticket. He goes to court and the judge, played by Sally Kellerman, condemns him to a Nazi-like traffic school to work off his violation. Here he meets a motley group of other minor violators who must endure the abuse of Keach and his female cohort. Eventually John Murray falls for a ditzy rocket scientist played by Jennifer Tilly. Since it's an ensemble piece, the audience becomes involved in several other lives, including that of a punk girl with wildly dyed hair who befriends a rather straight laced kid.

As happens with generous editors who consider themselves mentors to their assistants, Tom gave me these characters' scenes to cut. One of the more amusing episodes involved a moment when the punk-rocker girl invites the straight laced guy back to her bedroom in her parents' home with the intention of having sex. The room is decorated with posters of punk groups, a bedspread splattered with red and black paint, and so on. As they're climbing into bed, the girl happens to reveal that she's underage, and then they hear her father returning home. She springs out of bed declaring, "My father will kill us! He's a teamster," and she furiously sets to flipping her reversible room and, we glean, reversible life. She grabs a blond wig and yanks it

---

over her dyed hair; she turns over the punk posters, revealing a one-sheet for *The Sound of Music*; and finally she reverses her garish bedspread, revealing a Laura Ashley–like traditional pattern. She jumps into bed, cradling her teddy bear, while the confused boy steps to the side. When the girl's large, burly father pushes open the door to check on his daughter, he notices the slender, shirtless boy. Stammering, the boy tries to excuse his presence and states that he didn't know she was underage. The father shouts, "I will kill you!" and the boy dives out the window.

The scene went together easily, and, for the most part I managed to hit the right beats. The cut had all the elements, the setup with the two kids, the revelation of the reversible room, and the father's sudden intrusion. The timing of each moment worked well, and the scene, as written and performed, was quite funny. What took it to the next level was the director's sense of comedic anticipation and attention to detail. In reviewing the cut and dailies, he and Tom discovered an extra beat that happens after the girl has reset her room to the manner in which her parents expected it. With teddy bear clasped to her chest, she settles onto her downy perch like an innocent bird. The boy, on the other hand, settles after dashing over to the far corner of the room. These extra beats sustain the necessary rhythm to fuel the comedy. Instead of the order of shots proceeding in a straightforward progression, these extra cuts add an amusing peek at the girl's cunning and the boy's vulnerability, plus building a brief pause into the scene, creating a further moment of anticipation before the father bursts into the room.

As a side note, this is the value of apprenticeship, something that is often lacking today due to the decrease in editing room staffs. The generosity of the editor in making sure that his first assistant has scenes to cut helped more than anything to advance my understanding of the process. This information, in turn, I have passed on to my assistants, students, and readers, and it was a primary motivation for writing this book.

 Case Study

In the romantic comedy *Totally Blonde*, a singer and nightclub owner played by Michael Bublé sends a male stripper (Michael Kagan) to the office of his intended girlfriend, Meg Peters (Krista Allen). The fellow is dressed as a Canadian Mountie who has ostensibly arrived to arrest her. But instead he turns on his boombox and performs a dance he calls "The Full Mountie." The initial cut hit all the beats, making sure to reveal Meg's surprise and show the dance, but what finally brought it to life were the little details, the close-up of the Mountie's finger ceremoniously pushing the button on the boom box, Meg's confused look, the wide shot as the music begins with its strong beat, and the close-up of the Mountie bobbing his head to the beat. Once the striptease began, sprinkling in reactions from Meg and her boss (Mindy Sterling) helped propel the comedy.

Off-Camera and Off-Track

Introduction of off-camera characters arriving on the scene, usually to interrupt the present action, has traditionally employed laying off-camera sound effects or dialog over current visuals to transition the audience's attention to the new arrival. A typical illustration of this occurs in *The Princess Bride*, where the young hero and heroine, after an encounter with a large forest rodent, are about to kiss. The anticipated kiss is interrupted by the off-camera hoofbeats of the villains' approaching horses. At that point the scene cuts to a shot of the horses.

This technique has worked well for all the decades since the invention of film sound. Yet today's film-going audience is more savvy. This combined with the more energetic pacing of modern films calls for a reappraisal of this time-honored approach. While many editors today perpetuate this older technique, others have taken a more assertive approach. When a character enters the scene, we introduce him in a cut, pulling the viewer immediately into the arriving action. After the newcomer is established we cut back to the initial character's reaction, which used to occur as a response to off-camera sound. Introducing the encroaching characters in their own right, rather than as an off-camera sound, gives them greater significance. Of course, there will still be some cases where initially postponing the cutaway and allowing the sound to lead will be indicated. But the age-old habit of this approach can be curtailed. The prominence that a character must have in order to deserve a place in a scene also serves to accelerate the pace and vary the rhythm by introducing a further intercut. Additionally, it carries the audience along with the action rather than keeping them at arm's length.

Case Study

In *Mannequin: On the Move*, another tale of an enchanted princess, we introduced a character by a picture cut rather than off-camera dialog. As young Jason Williamson (William Ragsdale), in his bedroom, is about to kiss Jessie, his peasant girl lover-turned-mannequin played by Kristy Swanson, we cut back outside to find an ambulance speeding toward the house. Then we cut back inside for the head turn reaction from the two lovers and Jessie's line: "What is it?" A traditional cut would have played the sound of the approaching ambulance off-camera over the lovers, allowed for their head turn, then cut outside to see what the noise was about. Again, by today's standards, this would be clunky and dilute the excitement and immediacy of the moment.

A corollary to prefiguring action occurs in the case of interior and exterior action. Where an interior action will eventually transition to the exterior set, it helps to anticipate the exterior scene beforehand, with a brief cut to the outside before allowing the action to proceed. In *Mac and Me* the cops are trapped inside a Sears department store while an alien makes his getaway outside. By cutting from the interior with the cops to the exterior showing them through the locked glass doors, it anticipates their next move. They break the glass—interior—then rush out into the daylight—exterior.

In the action thriller *Speed*, Keanu Reeves rescues Sandra Bullock from a speeding bus that a crazed bomber, played by Dennis Hopper, has set to explode when the bus falls below 50 mph. Afterward he finds himself on a Los Angeles Metro train, again attempting to save the same woman, who now has a bomb strapped to her. She is left holding the that, if released, will detonate the explosive device. After dispatching Dennis Hopper during a classic *mano a mano* struggle atop the train, Reeves drops down into the train and, unable to stop it, decides instead to push the throttle forward to full speed. Instead of trying to disembark, he leans against the railing on which Bullock is handcuffed and hugs her while the train barrels through the subterranean tunnels. The station construction has not yet been completed, and the train leaves the tracks and tears through the construction ramp. At this point the editor, John Wright, cuts outside to establish the relative calm of Hollywood Boulevard and the boarded-up facade of the train's exit. This sets the scene. A cut back inside reveals the chaos of the train car ripping through the station. And finally a cut outside again shows the exterior street a moment before the train explodes through the wall and out onto the street barely missing a tour van.

These various approaches, ranging from the less obvious to the truly unconventional, help solve difficult editing situations.

℞

Rather than:	Try:
Thoroughly developing every action	A jump cut
Introducing a character by off-camera sound	Cutting directly to him
Transitioning with a dissolve	A straight cut
Worrying about continuity	Concentrating on story
Trying to match action	Cutting on action

Chapter 6

Genre Editing Styles I

Expectations Posed by Genre

It's all about sex. Or laughter. Or tears. It's about your life and your friends' lives. It's about genre. And, for the film doctor, his genre patients take many forms.

A surprise that confronts editors who have flourished in a particular genre is the hesitation of producers to hire them for films in other genres. Until an editor has proven himself in comedy, for instance, it may be difficult for him to land an assignment in that genre. This is a classic Catch-22. Without experience the editor may not get the job, yet how will he gain the knowledge if he has never worked in that genre? This chapter helps to supply that knowledge.

Conventions

An important first step in understanding genre resides in grasping its various conventions. These conventions are the standards that differentiate one genre from another. They exist in every fiction genre from comedy and thriller to nonfiction such as documentary, educational, and today's popular reality programming. Conventions make specific demands on the editor as they relate to his craft, particularly with regard to pace and rhythm. An action film, for instance, requires a faster pace than most suspense films, yet in both cases timing is essential.

Coming to a genre is a bit like an adolescent's search for identity. Within the genre reside needs and issues that an audience expects to participate in and, ultimately, discover resolution for. Editors and directors are often attracted to particular genres because those forms resonate with their inner needs, conflicts, or memories. A horror film director developed an affinity for the genre because his parents used to take him to horror movies as a child, well before most psychologists suggest exposing children to images of gore and violence. An action-adventure director lived much of his life roaming the African wilderness and wrangling lions and other wild beasts. A thriller director suffered an abusive home life at the hands of an unpredictable and alcoholic father. In each of the genres these individuals found inspiration in a different aspect of the human psyche.

The Healthy Edit. DOI: 10.1016/B978-0-240-81446-9.00006-8

57

From the thriller director's background, his edginess and dark outlook informed the victim-turned-victor mentality of the thriller genre. The action director's experiences in the wild inclined him toward fast-paced action and death-defying stunts. The horror director's nightmares created a proclivity for jump scares and vividly made-up monsters. Often the director aligns himself with an editor of similar disposition, one who resonates with his vision. Comedy editor Bruce Green often cuts Garry Marshall's films, such as *Runaway Bride* and *Princess Diaries*. Jon Poll, another top comedy editor, frequently works with director Jay Roach on such films as *Goldmember, Meet the Parents*, and *Dinner for Schmucks*. On the other hand, Conrad Buff, with his command of action, suspense, and visual effects, avoids comedies. His skills have helped create such exciting films as *Titanic, King Arthur*, and *The Last Airbender*.

This is not to say that an editor must work in only one genre. For some that would limit their possibilities to such an extent that they would rarely work. But it is important to find within oneself the meaning of that genre along with the genre's practical requirements and the style of a particular director. Jim Jarmusch, for instance, often employs wide master shots to tell his personal, character-driven stories, whereas Oliver Stone prefers constant cutting with a variety of angles to drive home his active style.

Crossing Genres

Although a mixture of genres, such as horror with comedy, used to be considered bad form, today cross-genre comprises a large portion of film scripts. The *Scary Movie* franchise successfully blended comedy and horror to preposterous and prosperous effect. Jackie Chan's *Rush Hour* skillfully combined martial arts action with comedy. *Slumdog Millionaire* merged dramatic suspense, action, romance, and a Bollywood dance sequence to create a deeply compelling movie. *Avatar*, upon its initial release, was billed in the movie guide for the Regency Theatres chain as "action/adventure, suspense/thriller, sci-fi/fantasy." While cross-genre stories are permissible and may someday predominate, it is important to understand the differentiation between the genres as well as the audience's expectations for each.

Doctor's Note

Though blending genres has become common, the occurrence is not unprecedented and goes back to the classic horror comedy *Abbot and Costello Meet Frankenstein*.

If film can be viewed as modern myth-making, then genre can be seen as conforming to myth cycles that ancient storytellers associated with the trickster, the hero, the lover, and so on. Today we sometimes speak in terms of formulas with regard to films that adhere to certain conventions or structures. The criticism, however, that a film is formulaic is a damning one. The challenge for modern filmmakers lies in abiding by the tenets and expectations of a genre without falling into its clichés. In the best genre films, the underlying formula remains hidden, projecting its shadow as on the cave walls in Plato's *The Symposium*.

Viewed anthropologically, it is easy to see film as enacting the rituals of particular myth cycles. While some view myth as an explanation for ritual, isn't it more likely that ritual is the driving force that has carried these stories down through the ages? Perhaps even more than Carl Jung's collective unconscious, ritual and its associated iconography have propagated archetypes throughout time and culture. Each generation discovers a way to make these archetypes relevant to its current experiences of life, love, and loss. The way that recent generations have managed this is through motion pictures. And these movies constantly evolve to carry forth, in form and content, classic messages for a current culture.

The Ritual Object

In viewing film genre we discover that each genre carries with it particular ritual objects. Anyone who questions film's reliance on ritual objects need look no further than the wedding ring in romantic comedies, the blood in vampire films, and the laser in science fiction. Who can think of a western without calling to mind the horse, the whip, the six-shooter, the sheriff's badge, the hat, and even the great outdoors, all significant icons of that genre? The editor who neglects to attend to these factors risks losing the totems' inherent power. The frequent midnight showings of the *Rocky Horror Picture Show* decades after its initial release are a testament to cinema's mythic influence and the power of ritual objects as the audience re-enacts moments from the film using rice, newspapers, rubber gloves, lights and so on.

For this reason *insert shots* exist. Insert shots allow the audience to focus for a moment on a significant object within a larger field of view. Often the film doctor discovers that an important moment loses significance because the object of concern—a gun, a watch, a gemstone, a photograph—was not given its due. Either the object was not revealed at all, revealed too late, or revealed in an angle that negated its significance, such as a wide shot.

One of the most common requests that appears on editors' and film doctors' shot lists when they request reshoots or pickups are insert shots. First-time directors are particularly prone to leaving out these essential items.

Case Study

In an indie film where the set had wrapped and the budget didn't allow for reshoots, I resorted to blowing up the film frame to center on a syringe that would play a significant role later in the movie. It had only appeared in a loose medium shot and was unlikely to be noticed by the viewer.

The only danger of this tactic is that enlarging the image increases the film grain or video noise, so the editor must act judiciously. Fortunately, with today's excellent, fine-grain film stocks and high-definition video cameras, this maneuver works better than before.

Expectations

A traditional view of a doctor is one who must also cure himself. Many doctors come to their specialty because they or someone they feel close to was impacted by an ailment that specialty seeks to cure. When viewed in this way, one begins to see the deeper meaning of an audience's expectations and the motivations of filmmakers who explore those genres. In fact, expectation fuels a significant portion of an audience's enjoyment and participation in the film experience. Audiences who attend comedies are prepared to laugh. Audiences who attend horror films expect to be scared. Conversely, films that fail to fulfill these expectations—a comedy in which people are viciously murdered and frightening events occur or a horror film where most of the action is on an even keel—disappoint their audience. With this approach to genre, we are reminded to dig deeper, to elaborate, and to consider all possibilities. A comedy writer friend used to insist that a good comedic premise has to be "sliced and diced in every possible way" in order to create a successful script. The writer has to consider the premise and its repercussions from every conceivable angle. His prescription? At least two laughs per page.

As with other aspects of editing, an understanding of story—which in the case of genre includes the underlying myth cycle—helps inform the editorial decision-making process. The following sections investigate the common myth cycles as well as editorial approaches associated with various genres. Remember, editing is not just about cutting the film but about developing an approach to the dailies. This entails advancing the story and delivering the actors' emotions. Thinking like an editor involves developing a point of view on the footage and then using that to fuel the edits.

The Western Rides into the Sunset

Watching how ritual objects play out in the course of a film adds clues to the story's significance. Lawrence Kasdan's *Silverado* begins with a dynamic homage to the many elements that make up the western genre. When the movie opens inside a dimly lit shed, the camera dollies past various icons of the genre: a wood-burning stove, a leather saddle, a whip, a pair of boots, a Winchester rifle. On the soundtrack we hear the faint crackling of embers, a horse's whinny, a hawk's cry. The serenity is interrupted by the sudden explosion of gunshots and bullet holes bursting through the walls. A rapid exchange of gunfire ensues, and finally a body tears through the roof, collapsing dead on the dirt floor. Quiet again prevails. At that point the shed's surviving occupant draws open the door and the camera leaves the dark claustrophobic surroundings, launching out into a vast frontier extending across the wide screen. In this short opening scene the director has reignited what had become a dormant genre with a barrage of iconographic images, sounds, and action.

At one time, the western held the preeminent position among genres. The film museum in Lone Pine, California, is a testament to the hundreds of films that were shot in the adjacent Alabama Hills, incorporating nearly every western star from Hopalong Cassidy to John Wayne. The museum houses much of the classic iconography, including lavishly ornate saddles, boots, and gun belts. In one corner, however, sits a display for a film of a quite different genre: *Iron Man*. Ironically, *Iron Man*'s genre came to supplant the old western. With the rise of the science-fiction film, the frontier left the valleys and hilltops of regions such as Death Valley and the Alabama Hills and migrated to what *Star Trek* describes as "the final frontier": outer space.

Case Study

My father, producer Frank P. Rosenberg (*King of the Khyber Rifles, Madigan, The Reincarnation of Peter Proud*), produced one of the last, significant early westerns. He once pointed out that, unlike many westerns that featured the Midwest, *One-Eyed Jacks* actually took place in the West, on the coast of Monterey, California. The film starred and was directed by Marlon Brando. He had replaced a director who would eventually make one of the greatest science-fiction films of all time: *2001: A Space Odyssey*.

Science Fiction and Fantasy

With *Star Wars*, audiences bid farewell to the western's domination of film genre. In this science-fiction classic, Luke Skywalker returns to find his homestead set ablaze by the Imperial Stormtroopers on the planet Tatooine. This propels him on a daring and unforeseen adventure to find a missing girl, Princess Leia, a trek similar to Ethan Edwards's in John Ford's classic western *The Searchers*. Here, Ethan, played by John Wayne, returns to find his brother's homestead ablaze following a Comanche Indian attack. This leads him on a great adventure to find a missing girl. Though the two films share a similar impetus for the hero's journey, their prevailing iconography has changed. Guns became light sabers, horses became spaceships, and the great outdoors became the endless universe.

Doctor's Note

Throughout most cultures the hero's journey is reflected in stages of initiation. Heeding the call to adventure, the reluctant initiate leaves the comforts of home, encounters guides and helpers along the way, endures ordeals, and finally claims his place in the world. Having undergone an essential transformation, he eventually returns home to share his hard-won reward or wisdom. For further investigation, see the works of Carl Jung, Arnold van Gennep, and Joseph Campbell.

Similar journeys occur in fantasy films, such as the *The Lord of the Rings* trilogy. One of the differences between science fiction and fantasy derives from science fiction's use of imaginary elements based on scientifically plausible events. Fantasy generally defies the laws of nature, displaying impossible feats in a make-believe world that may include real-life elements, such as school children, weddings, and castles. In science fiction, a genre that began in the early 19th century with Mary Shelly's *Frankenstein*, storytellers deal with technology's impact on humanity, and as creatures of technology, our impact on one another. At times technological innovation helps us; at other times it threatens to destroy us.

Visual Effects

Lifting an audience into orbit or beyond requires the use of visual effects. These photographic and digital tricks form the magic of cinema. The art of special effects began as an accident perpetrated by a stage magician, George Méliès, with a movie camera. A master of illusion, Méliès stumbled upon what became known as the *stop effect* while filming traffic in Paris. His camera jammed. When he finally got it working again, the traffic had changed. Later, when he projected the footage, he was startled to find that a bus suddenly transformed into a hearse! This delightful mistake resonated with his magician's sensibility. From that day on, he used this trick to make actors appear and disappear by stopping the camera long enough for the actor to enter or exit the empty frame, then turning it back on. Through similar techniques he performed transformations, double exposures, and superimpositions. He even invented the dissolve by rewinding the film a couple feet and then rephotographing over it.

Case Study

As a boy I used to perform magic shows for birthday parties. Occasionally I'd partner with a charming kid with a great sense of humor, Larry Wilson. As an adult Larry went on to perform popular magic shows on stage in Las Vegas and other parts of the world, and I went into feature film editing. The lessons I'd learned as a kid about sleight of hand, concealment, and timing helped inform my editing choices later on.

Like all early films, most of Méliès's movies unfolded as if on a stage without advantage of camera movement or editing. A short while after Méliès's discoveries, another filmmaker, Edwin S. Porter, introduced these essential qualities. He also tried masking out part of the frame in-camera and then double exposing it with another image to create the first matte composite. In *The Great Train Robbery*, a film billed as an accurate portrayal of real-life holdups, the train station contains a large window looking out on a moving train. The window is actually a matte.

Along with matte photography, Edwin S. Porter brought the concept of narrative editing to American film. Porter knitted together scene after scene, each related to the other by their proximity to one another, to advance the narrative. By intercutting a scene of the escaping robbers with the discovery of the bound station operator by his daughter in *The Great Train Robbery*, Porter performed the even more sophisticated trick of bending time itself.

According to Arthur Knight in *The Liveliest Art*, "the technique that Porter had hit upon in assembling this unpretentious little western provided the key to the whole art of film editing, the joining together of bits of film shot in different places and at different times to form a single, unified narrative—a principle that Méliès, with his theater background, was never able to grasp." Edwin S. Porter's use of editing eventually influenced such great filmmakers as D.W. Griffith. With *The Birth of a Nation*, Griffith became the father of the feature film, expanding upon Porter's work by freely using in-scene cutting and extending standard running times from minutes to hours. As with today's films, Griffith incorporated wide shots, two-shots, close-ups, insert shots, and so on, within the same scene.

Doctor's Note

In Méliès's time, movies were not rented but sold like cloth, by the foot. Anyone who possessed a print of a film could easily make a duplicate negative and generate endless copies to sell for his own profit. This became known as *pirating*.

Over 100 years later, the discoveries of Porter and Méliès still influence the magic of cinema. Visual effects have evolved from the early camera and animation effects of Méliès's 1902 film *Le Voyage dans la Lune* (*A Trip to the Moon*) to the stunning computer generated visuals of the recent *Star Trek* and *Harry Potter* features and the Christopher Nolan-directed *Inception*. Where *A Trip to the Moon*—a short film best remembered for its striking image of a bullet-shaped space capsule lodged in the eye of the man in the moon—accomplished its goal through in-camera photographic tricks, the evolution to bluescreen compositing and the rise of the optical printer spawned generations of science-fiction and fantasy movies. Included among these were the popular B-movies of the 1950s, which for the most part appear cheesy when compared to the CGI, motion capture, and greenscreen compositing of today's films. Each year these effects gain greater sophistication as more massive computer memory and faster processors power increasingly complex software.

Figure 6.1 *Digital compositing in* Harry Potter and the Prisoner of Azkaban, *2004. Copyright © Warner Bros. Ent.; Harry Potter Publishing Rights © J.K.R.; photographer: Murray Close. (Photo credit: Warner Bros./Photofest.)*

Case Study

In a rare step backward, Stanley Kubrick in his 1968 science-fiction classic *2001: A Space Odyssey* chose to rely upon in-camera effects rather than bluescreen compositing and opticals to create a realistic and timeless look. To accomplish his goal, Kubrick used practical, in-camera effects, avoiding the degradation that results from creating multiple film generations of an image. Kubrick's effects included front- and rear-screen projection, mattes, miniatures, and photographic movement that utilized the laws of physics. By rotating the camera and the set at the same rate, he was able to make his actors walk upside down in space. By mounting projectors inside his oversized miniature spaceships, he was able to project images of astronauts' activity through the capsule's windows. To make a pen float in the weightlessness of space, he secured the object to a large glass plate that rotated slowly in front of the lens. And to make actors float in space, he hung them above the camera to block the view of the suspension cables. Today the digital medium has turned every effect's pass into a first generation, thus removing the graininess and distortion that used to result as a film progressed from one visual effect pass to another.

Computer-Generated Images

For an editor working in the science-fiction or fantasy genre, it is important to have an understanding of current visual effects techniques. Part of the joy of working within this medium derives from the malleability of visual effects. Richard Pearson, one of the editors of *Iron Man 2*, loved science fiction as a kid. He likens the versatility of visual effects to the concept that "you get just a lump of clay (to play with)." And he then imagines, "What if Iron Man did this. . ."!

Compositing

One of the most common and effective visual effects involves *compositing*. Where previously it flourished only in the celluloid film realm, compositing now relies heavily on CG technology. In simple terms, it involves placing a foreground object, like a spaceship, over a background *plate*, like a star field. To accomplish this, the foreground object is usually photographed against a green or blue screen. The computer knows to replace all of the green or blue area with the star field.

Previously an editor had to imagine how these elements would fit together and then wait to see them married onto film by an effects house. But using nonlinear equipment, the editor can mock up a composite by placing the background greenscreen and foreground objects on separate tracks in the timeline, then applying a keying effect, such as Ultimatte. Today, new camera

OPTICAL PRINTER

The standard tool for creating motion picture effects before the introduction of digital manipulation was the optical printer. It was basically a projector that was joined to a camera, allowing for the introduction of effects when rephotographing a film image. Its uses ranged from creating dissolves and wipes to compositing mattes and titles by employing a process known as bipacking.

CGI

CGI stands for *computer generated images*. This general term refers to a plethora of visual effects, from compositing to animation, that are created by use of a computer. Originally employed in the realm of 2D compositing, CGI has advanced into the area of 3D compositing.

designs have taken this one step further. Some cameras, such as Simulcam, allow real-time compositing during filming so the director can view digital characters, designed on Autodesk's MotionBuilder, performing within live environments.

Motion Capture

Another prominent effect, *motion capture*, exceeds anything that has been achieved in the optical-effect realm. Motion capture, or *performance capture* as it is known when, rather than simply capturing an actor's body movements so they can become the framework for a CG skin, the actor's facial nuances, hand movements, and voice are retrieved simultaneously and placed into the computer. Echoing the insights of Lev Kuleshov, James Cameron's collaborator on *Avatar*, Jon Landau, pointed out in *Cinefex* magazine, "Our goal in using performance capture was not to replace the actor with our computer-animated character, but to *preserve* the actor. ... A great actor withholds information. Dustin Hoffman can sit there and do nothing in *All the President's Men*, and you are riveted. But no animator would *ever* animate a character to just sit there and do nothing."

Through performance capture the director's attention shifts from a concern about various camera angles to a preoccupation with performance. Once the best performance is captured into the system the director can choose to turn it into whatever shot he'd like—wide, medium, close and so on.

One of the main contributors to the development of performance capture is Demian "Dman" Gordon (*The Matrix Reloaded*, *The Matrix Revolutions*, *Watchmen*, and *Alice in Wonderland*). In our interview he contended that, while entirely computer-generated movies have increased in recent years, "digital actors will never replace real ones. Certain dangerous or generic action can be replaced or augmented, such as background action, or stunts, or crowd generation, but you will always need actors. Motion capture will always be an actor's medium. [On the other hand] there will definitely be more and more movies that are entirely computer generated, where some or all facets of the film occur in postproduction."

On feature films the editor plays a significant role in the motion capture process. In most cases, Gordon points out, "the capture sessions are filmed with a traditional film camera simultaneously alongside the motion capture efforts. This reference video is often cut together to make a rough edit that guides the delivery of the motion capture

PLATE

A plate is the action background that joins with foreground characters or objects, either in the CG realm—such as the digitally created dinosaurs performing in front of live action sets in *Jurassic Park*—or as live production backgrounds as in rear-screen projection.

MOTION CAPTURE

Abbreviated as *mo-cap*, this term applies to "a variety of technologies that are used to digitize the motion of real-world objects," according to motion capture supervisor Demian "Dman" Gordon. The process usually employs iridescent markers placed across the body or face. As the subject moves before the lights, the markers glow, pinpointing every movement. Recent developments replace markers with intensely bright LEDs that fire in phase with the motion capture camera. These dots are captured and stored into the computer, creating a moving skeleton on which skin, clothing, fur, and other textures can be placed.

process and provides an EDL with shot-specific timecode and shots that will be ordered for delivery from the motion capture team. In this case the editor informs everything about the delivery of the motion capture data, and the editor's EDL becomes a bible for data delivery that everyone involved follows."

As a challenge to emerging mediums, from television to video games, Hollywood has sought to capture audiences' attention with innovative formats including widescreen CinemaScope, three-camera Cinerama, 3D, multichannel surround sound, and even Smell-o-Vision. 3D, a format that comes in and out of vogue, drew audiences to theaters in the early 1950s when these films were known as "depthies" and the competition with television threatened attendance. 3D has regained favor to the point that well-respected filmmakers have declared that no film should ever again be made in conventional 2D. Nonlinear equipment companies, such as Avid, now produce specialized systems designed to handle 3D movies. Lately, however, film students, who are often a good gauge of trends, report that they are tired of 3D; they don't enjoy wearing the glasses—some even remove them during the screening—and they long for better stories over novel effects. They await the next trend—holographic movies perhaps?

Motion picture sound has followed along with innovations in picture quality and size. Early sound was monaural, confined to one track. A later innovation created stereophonic sound, employing two audio channels. Dolby, originally a noise-reduction process designed to remove hiss and other distracting distortions from the soundtrack, pioneered an encoded matrix capable of playing multiple channels. Today these analog processes have evolved into digital, with the latest Dolby 7.1 surround sound boasting eight discrete channels. Other digital sounds systems include SDDS and DTS.

3D

Any stereoscope projection system that produces a three-dimensional effect for the audience is known as "3D." Utilizing the manner in which humans perceive depth through the comparison between information perceived by two eyes, 3D processes use multiple cameras or single cameras with double lenses, offset to mimic the different angle from which two eyes perceive objects. During exhibition this double image was originally recreated by running two interlocked projectors running the same images simultaneously and later by printing the two offset images onto a single filmstrip. Special lenses, originally red and blue but later employing polarized light, isolated the separate images for each eye.

Tech Note

The new 7.1 surround sound, which debuted in *Toy Story 3*, consists of eight separate channels: left, center, right, low-frequency effects (LFE), left surround, right surround, back surround left, and back surround right. The last two channels are an addition to the previous 5.1 standard. This configuration makes it possible to pan the sound 360 degrees around the theater. Combined with 3D photography this further contributes to the immersive experience.

℞

Examine your favorite genres and determine the icons that are specific to each one.

Chapter 7

Genre Editing Styles II

The Comedy

One of the most challenging genres is comedy. Unlike other story forms, comedy requires frame-by-frame precision. A comedy editor is akin to a microsurgeon whose exactitude allows him to reattach severed nerve endings, repair vital organs, and avoid unsightly incisions. A horror editor acts more like a general surgeon, one who gets the job done but doesn't mind leaving a few scars in his path. In fact, he may prefer it. The comedy editor's work, and therefore the jokes of which he is the guardian, can live or die based on the timing of a couple frames.

Despite the demands placed on the editor by comedy's need for precise timing, the genre offers guidance in a unique way. With thrillers or dramas it is difficult to judge audience reaction. Until the movie is over and audience members are polled for their response, the editor and director have little sense of how the audience responded to each moment of the film. Comedies, however, offer a built-in and nearly foolproof measuring device: laughter. Depending on how much laughter, if any, a joke elicits, the filmmaker can judge its effectiveness.

Comedy comes in various flavors, from light romantic, like *The Proposal*, to the hard-edged and explicit, such as *The 40 Year Old Virgin* and the *American Pie* series. Some comedies are situation driven; others are character driven. The sit-com, a recurring type of comedy found in television shows like *The Office*, *30 Rock*, and *South Park*, contains characters who defy the personality arcs that dramatic characters require. Sit-com characters rarely change. Each time the viewer returns to *30 Rock*, Jack Donaghy will still be a smooth-talking control freak and, in *South Park*, Kenny will again be killed.

Comedy, like the clown, takes our human frailties and vulnerabilities and presents them in a manner that becomes not only palatable but enjoyable. Within all comedies various tenets apply as to what constitutes humor. Though what makes people laugh varies depending on geography, cultural mores, and experience, certain aspects prove universal. Even tame comedies possess some form of edginess, an irreverence that defies established authority, and, because of that, allows the viewer a delightful release. At times we hear of how a comedy has gone too far, though to some extent, that is what audiences expect from comedies: to

The Healthy Edit. DOI: 10.1016/B978-0-240-81446-9.00007-X

trespass into forbidden areas and break cultural taboos. Because attitudes and customs change, what was hysterical at one moment may lose its potency at a later time. Likewise, the pace of comedy has evolved over the years. The more leisurely comedies of the 1940s and 1950s, have given way to the often fast-paced comedies of today. In either case, that tempo is the editor's responsibility.

Case Study

When I started out in editing, the comedies of Neal Israel were very popular, and I was fortunate to work with him on *Moving Violations*, a comedy about hapless students in a traffic school run by Nazi-like cops. Today his *Bachelor Party* and *Police Academy* films are still funny, but their irreverence has, in some cases, been eclipsed by films like *Hot Tub Time Machine* and *Superbad*.

What are some of the incidents that make us laugh? Consider these:

- A person acting like a machine, as in *Modern Times*. When Chaplin repetitively continues to tighten bolts on an assembly line that has stopped operating, the mechanical quality of his actions makes us laugh.
- A machine acting like a person, as in Wall-E's amusing discovery of life's equivocal nature when the little robot of the title, having carefully organized his found cutlery into forks and spoons, finds himself confronted with a spork.
- Hyperbole plays a major role in comedy. Consider the exaggerated antics of the Three Stooges. Or the unlikely situation of the characters in *The Hangover*: waking up with a baby that is not theirs, a live tiger in their bathroom, and a naked man in the trunk of their car.
- Embarrassment also influences comedy, as in the now classic pie scene in *American Pie* or Eugene Levy's unannounced visit to his son's frat room in *American Pie 2*. There's also Michael Palin's excruciatingly debilitating stutter in *A Fish Called Wanda*.
- Bodily functions, sometimes found under the category of embarrassment, provide endless fodder for gross-out comedies such as the unexpected hair fixture in *There's Something About Mary* or the farting scene in *Blazing Saddles*.
- Absurdity, as in the Austin Powers films, makes fun of the prosaic quality of daily life, stretching it beyond reason.
- Stupidity makes us laugh because it pokes fun at the human frailties that we all share from time to time. Jim Carrey's *Dumb and Dumber* films are one example. Clowns often make us laugh because of their feigned inability to comprehend what appears obvious to everyone. Consider Steve Carell in *Evan Almighty* as he attempts over and over again to shave his beard that God has deemed will remain.

The basic structure of comedy is the *setup* and the *payoff* or *punch line*. Veteran comedy editor Bruce Green, who has edited many of Garry Marshall's "heartfelt comedies," views this structure in two basic configurations. In both cases, these approaches relate to the world's oldest slapstick situation: a man slipping on a banana peel.

In one approach the editor shows a man walking down the street, then a shot of a discarded banana peel resting on the ground ahead of him, then a cut back to the man, then to the peel, and finally to the man stepping and slipping on the banana peel. In this way the anticipation of the sight gag is set up, and the audience savors the man's approach, knowing that he's going to step on the banana peel.

In the other approach, the same man is shown walking down the street, but the editor doesn't show the banana peel. Instead, he waits for the man to suddenly slip. At that point he reveals what brought the fellow down: a banana peel. The editor has led the viewer down a road where he does not see it coming. The surprise elicits a laugh. In the context of the overall film, an editor varies this approach in order to maintain comedic interest.

In comedy, timing is crucial. Editing is about timing, and comic timing is the most unforgiving form of editing. The actor's delivery, combined with the editor's pacing, strives to generate a spontaneous release, the laughter that we enjoy in a good comedy. A good comedy film doctor knows how to take control of the actor's comedic timing.

Doctor's Orders

Take control of performance. While some may object that manipulating an actor's timing through editing destroys the integrity of the performance, a strong editor turns an irreverent eye toward that. In Bruce Green's words, "I don't believe in the integrity of anything except the audience's experience of the movie."

In conversations with another top comedy editor, Jon Poll (*Austin Powers: The Spy Who Shagged Me, Meet the Parents, Dinner for Schmucks*), he emphasized the importance of timing. In *Dinner for Schmucks* some jokes were originally getting "soft B-laughs," but in retiming and recutting the scenes, the editors brought them up to A level. As Poll puts it, "The best jokes usually have to be nurtured and helped like little children." That's the editor's job.

Through the use of coverage, wide angles, close-ups, and so on, the film doctor corrects the timing of a setup and a punch line. Coverage allows the editor to cut away to other characters, to remove space within a reading, and to arrive quicker at a punch line. If the director only films an actor's performance in one angle, then the possibility arises for the actor to place the wrong emphasis on a line or to move too slowly in setting up a line. Some actors take the opportunity to chew up the scene when the joke as written will suffice. Only the most expert comedy directors, like Mike Nichols or Garry Marshall, have the luxury of limiting their coverage to a single wide shot if they chose. Referring to *The Birdcage*, its editor, the late Arthur Schmidt, explained how in the instance of one of the early kitchen scenes the director chose to limit Schmidt's editorial choices by supplying him with only a single wide angle of much of the scene. Of course, when confronted with the likes of Mike Nichols and Robin Williams, the chance of such an approach failing is greatly diminished.

This is one reason that comedies are often talent driven, designed for known actors and comedians with extraordinary track records. Audiences recognize that these performers have made them laugh in the past and expect them to succeed on subsequent occasions. Star talent also helps promote this genre overseas where jokes may not translate as well. Bruce Green mentions the use of Hector Elizondo in most of Garry Marshall's films. In *Runaway Bride* Elizondo was hired because he could best deliver the line where Julia Roberts escapes her wedding by hopping a ride on a Federal Express delivery truck. When someone asks where she's headed, Hector's character replies, "I don't know, but she'll be there by 10 tomorrow morning."

Jon Poll, who has worked successfully as a director (*Charlie Bartlett*) as well as an editor, views performance issues from two points of view. As an editor he watches dailies by placing himself in the position of an audience member. In this regard he constantly hopes the actor will give him what he needs. "It's all about judging performance, talking out loud, and hoping the character will do the line in a particular way." But as a director, Poll found himself on the set and able to ask for what he wanted. Directing with an editor's sensibilities can be an advantage because he can visualize additional coverage that would be useful in the editing room where others might be satisfied and move on. Ultimately, however, Poll concludes that the editor probably has the greatest influence on a film.

Surf the Laughter

If certain jokes don't land well, they can affect the entire film. In this regard Poll suggests that the editor has to "surf the laughter." Like a surfer waiting out the small waves in anticipation of a great ride on a larger one, the editor finds that "sometimes it's worth losing little laughs in order to get to bigger ones with more momentum."

In this regard, different comedies rely on different approaches to humor. In the *Austin Powers* films, the filmmakers came to rely on where each laugh would fall. The exact positioning of the jokes became crucial and required fine-tuning, whereas, on character-based comedies, like *Meet the Parents*, the editor becomes more accepting of laughs arriving at different or even unexpected moments. Much of this depends on reaction shots. In *Meet the Parents*, for instance, if Poll didn't get the expected laugh on De Niro's shot, he might get it by cutting to the reaction on Stiller or vice versa.

Sight Gags

Another significant aspect of comedy editing is the sight gag. Like the banana peel joke, the sight gag relies on physical humor with visual setups and payoffs rather than on dialog. Even in a smart comedy like *The Birdcage*, which excels in pithy verbal humor, the sight gag works as a potent accent to dialog scenes. These moments often benefit from a wide shot following a series of tighter shots engendering the comic tension. In *The Birdcage* the sudden climax in the wide shot reveals a physical stunt, such as when Robin Williams drops an ice bucket or the butler trips and falls.

Goldmember, the popular comedy from the *Austin Powers* series, creates a hilarious scene primarily composed of sight gags. In search of Doctor Evil, Austin Powers clandestinely boards his ship, disguising himself as one of the officers cloaked in a long white coat. Beneath the coat, however, he rides on the shoulders of Mini Me.

The image of the unusually tall Austin toddling through the ship makes for a good laugh. When Austin enters the sick bay, he's asked to give a urine sample. Since no one—except the audience—is looking, Mini Me fulfills the request by spitting apple juice into the specimen cup. Later, a shocked sailor watches as Austin's silhouette behind a white sheet appears to give birth to an oversized baby, umbilicus and all, which is actually Mini Me released from a pack on Austin's chest. All excellent sight gags.

There are many other factors that also influence comedic response. To promote these the editor draws upon other editorial tools, including the sound mix. Sound effects, if inappropriate or excessive, can be funny. If the setup line to a joke is not loud enough to be heard, it can ruin the joke. In that case, the line needs to be pushed up in the mix so the audience can hear it. Such manipulation may be subtle, but a couple decibels can make the difference between getting a laugh and not.

The structure of comedy remains fairly traditional, altered only by the outlandishness of a new plot and characters and by the crafting of performance, as seen in the Jud Apatow (*Superbad*) type comedies. These have found, or created, an audience that was not present or, at least, not ready for it in earlier years.

Romantic Comedy

Romantic comedies end with a wedding exemplified by the classic *The Philadelphia Story*. Even if there is no actual wedding there is a promise that such an event will occur in the not-too-distant future. Romantic comedies, of course, are a subset of the larger genre of comedy. Rather than relying on the machine gun effect of firing off one laugh after another, they delve into the world of relationship, of boy meets girl, boy loses girl, boy marries girl. Unlike most other comedies, there is often a poignant moment near the end that elicits tears rather than laughter. The editor's timing of a particular look is often the point separating a release of genuine feeling from something that will feel forced. Again, it is important to keep in mind that it is what the audience brings to the image that imbues it with such power. Because of this, it is often the subtext or even the silence that sustains the great well of emotion.

Time and again what works in dialog in a script often becomes overstated on film. At that point it becomes appropriate to trim out some dialog and let the juxtaposition of the actors' faces, perhaps accompanied by music, build the scene's emotion. Remember that the more neutral or unloaded the images, the better the chance that the audience will see themselves in the experience. The psychological concept of identification and projection is a potent factor in creating strong characters, because the characters are ultimately aspects of ourselves.

Action Adventure

The next genre has undergone huge transformations over recent years. The shift in camera design and editing techniques has changed the action film from the spectator sport of such brilliant films as *Raiders of the Lost Ark* to a more immersive approach where the audience is swallowed up by the action. With the advent of new digital 3D systems, the opportunity for an enveloping experience has grown even further. A film like *Avatar*, while more traditional, even conservative, in its narrative approach and editing style, benefits greatly from the leading edge technology incorporating motion capture, CGI, 3D, and other effects.

The action scenes that comprise an adventure film are an editor's playground. In cutting action the editor takes the most liberties and freely employs his or her inventiveness. Action is often covered by multiple cameras in order to give the editor a wide range of choices and to guarantee that difficult and potentially unrepeatable shots are captured from as many angles as possible. This increases the quantity of footage, but manyfold. Conversely, the quality is inconsistent. A move that might look large and impressive from one angle might be dwarfed by another angle. One camera may only glimpse part of an action, while the other camera might register the entire action. Consequently, the editor must comb through thousands of feet of film looking for those gems that will make a scene work. Often, action scenes need to be cobbled together from many pieces, but those pieces are what give the scene its dynamism and vitality. Remember the Editing Triangle? Nowhere are shot selection, length, and juxtaposition more obvious than in an action sequence.

When it comes to the position of shots, it is important to keep in mind that action, like conversation, is dialectic. In action, instead of opposing opinions or ideas, the clash occurs between the physical manifestations of different aims. This is conveyed through images and sound effects rather than words. Where the back and forth conversation between two characters in a dialog scene reveals the story, in an action scene the dialectic is created by intercutting visuals.

Action is the essence of film. It is immediate, visceral, and requires no translation or interpretation. Perhaps this is why the action genre remains the largest revenue generator for studios. It is also why exposition generally stands out like a boil. The audience, caught up in the excitement, does not want the momentum interrupted by long speeches. Even the fantastic chase scene in *The Rock* bumps when the pursuing FBI agent explains to us that Sean Connery is "running into things to try to slow us down."

Action films revolve around the deeds of the hero, such as Batman in *The Dark Knight* or Neo in *The Matrix*. In Hollywood they are often big men with big egos. But at some point we get a glimpse into their vulnerabilities, such as cocky Indiana Jones's (Harrison Ford) fear of snakes. Either way they risk their lives in battling to the finish with evil. The opponent's villainy must be commensurate with the hero's goodness. The greater the antagonist, the stronger the hero. But mere black hats and white hats aren't enough these days. The hero must have a bit of an edge or instability, while the villain needs to display some humanity, if only as far as a rationale for his misdeeds.

In constructing scenes with the hero character, the editor needs to find those moments that imbue him with charm, humor, and daring. It can be a glint in the eye, an extra beat before a reply, or a slick, well-practiced move. Consider the quirkiness of Robert Downey Jr. in *Iron Man*, the stunning physicality of Russell Crowe in *Gladiator*, or the confident charms of Sean Connery and Pierce Brosnan in the Bond films. Film critic Betsy Sharkey, in her *Los Angeles Times* article "How to Build a Better Action Hero," suggests that aside from the obvious aspect of a great physique and daring, "it helps to be a little crazy. . . . The crazy we like comes with an unhinged look that never leaves their eyes. . . ." Other pluses include "a passion-fueled intensity," a boy-next-door appeal, and a funny side.

Guideposts

Two significant structural issues permeate most action films. One is *temporality* and the other is *geography*. For most of film's history, action has supplied audiences with thrills and chills. Part of what makes an action sequence effective involves the audience's orientation toward place and time. In a chase it is generally important to know where the pursuer and the pursued are in relation to each other. If the pursuer seems too close to the pursued, then the challenge of the chase is diminished. If the pursuer is too far away, then the tension lessens. By incorporating *guidepost shots* the editor manages to subtly clue the audience into the timing of the pursuit. If the escaping vehicle passes a palm tree on its way out of town, then the audience is able to gauge the distance between the vehicles by noting when the following car also passes the same palm tree. Employing these landmarks, as well as occasionally cutting wide, helps orient the viewer and establish the temporal and spatial distance between the two vehicles.

Lately, however, a more expressionistic approach has emerged. This allows that in the tumult of action, where swift responses predominate and chaos enters the fray, a certain amount of disorientation is appropriate. In this vein, films like *Crank* and *Quantum of Solace* rely on an extremely fast, selectively nonlinear structure that overrides the viewer's ability to digest all that occurs in front of him. It becomes difficult to decipher time and locale. In this approach, extreme and short-lived close-ups flood the screen. These tighter shots, by virtue of the singular and narrow information they communicate, reveal only a glimpse before being overtaken by the next shot. Because the surrounding terrain appears only in occasional glimpses, the impression becomes wrenching and chaotic. Adrenaline rises, pulses race, and attention focuses. The disadvantage of this approach is the risk of losing the audience and plunging the ensuing events into a dissociated morass where the audience loses interest in the overall movie.

While geographic and temporal relationships still matter in order to keep the audience oriented, their significance has diminished in the new editing room. Orientation is sacrificed for the sake of disorientation. The visceral feeling of actually being immersed in the action with its wild, unfettered thrill holds precedence. One need look no further than a film like *Quantum of Solace* to witness the new approach to Hollywood's longest-running franchise: James Bond. The opening chase sequence is cut so fast, employing such quick and disorienting shots, that the

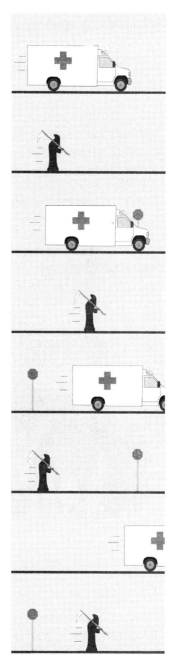

Figure 7.1 *The guidepost shot.*

audience perceives little more than the pure adrenaline rush of the car chase. Its editor, Richard Pearson, already a veteran of other popular and sprightly edited action films such as *The Bourne Supremacy*, confided that he had already assembled the scene with vigorously paced cuts when the director, Marc Forster, asked him to throw the whole scene into overdrive with shots of even shorter duration. Rather than go with the usual white car chased by three black cars, Forster chose to change it up—a gray car chased by three black cars. According to Pearson the goal was to present this installment of the franchise "more like an art film," including making the chase "much more impressionistic." Many loved the unique and innovative approach, but some diehard Bond fans were disappointed. They didn't like the attempts to alter a formula they had grown familiar with.

On another sequel to a hit movie, Pearson encountered similar issues. *Iron Man 2* arrived in Pearson's editing room with similar demands based on the original. The editor, he explained, "can't deliver exactly what the audience wants, yet fans are disappointed if (the film) diverges too much." Such is the effect of genre and its sequels.

Figure 7.2 *The opening chase scene from* Quantum of Solace, *2008. Copyright © Sony Pictures.* *(Photo credit: Sony Pictures/Photofest.)*

Doctor's Note

According to *Motor Trend* magazine, Bond's Aston Martin in *Quantum of Solace* was "painted in a new, darker, and positively elegant shade of gray called Quantum Silver...." The new car boasted none of the usual gadgets, such as oil slicks, machine guns, or ejector seats.

As an editor, one sifts through footage like a beachcomber hunting for lost treasures. Among all the grains of sand one discovers an unexpected coin, a silver ring, or fragments of a gold chain. Likewise, the editor discovers moments that the untrained eye would ignore or discount. In action, the jarring bump of a camera, a flicker off of chrome, an unintended swish pan as the camera finds its mark all add up to glimpses into the whirlwind of a chase or fight scene. These, coupled with quick close-ups of the drivers along with cutaways to wheels, speedometers, stick shifts and so on, increase the excitement. In such cases a reference shot or quick cut to a wide angle will supply the only orientation the audience receives.

Crank

Another popular action technique derives from the use of slow motion, or *slo-mo*. *Overcranked* footage—running the camera at a higher than normal speed—has exemplified and amplified violence as far back as Sam Peckinpah's *The Wild Bunch*. In this groundbreaking film, Peckinpah photographed the action scenes using multiple cameras, each running at a different speed. Later, in the editing room, he and his editor, Lou Lombardo, interspersed the various slow-motion angles with normal speed.

Today, after *The Matrix*, film motion bends to and fro, accelerating wildly and then suddenly decelerating. Time is manipulated and achieves plasticity. Overcranked footage gives way to undercranked footage. The film *Crank*, appropriately named considering its highly accelerated pace, crams an immense amount of fast-paced fights, car chases, and explosions into its slim 88 minutes. In the dynamic opening scene of Wayne Kramer's *Running Scared*, the director accomplished a wide variety of speed shifts by using a specially modified camera that he could crank faster or slower depending on the desired effect. The editor, Arthur Coburn, then accentuated the violent shoot-out between drug dealers and corrupt undercover cops with short, fast, well-placed cuts.

> **UNDERCRANKING**
>
> A method of accelerating on-screen action by slowing the film's movement through the camera. In the early days of film, cameras required manual cranking rather than electric motors to drive the moving parts. Undercranking decreases the number of frames per second. Action that was photographed at 12 frames per second will appear to double in speed when played back at normal 24 fps.

While undercranking and overcranking effects are often created within the camera, most nonlinear editing systems offer the ability to alter the action by precise increments, with varying degrees of success. Overcranking, for instance, works better when produced in-camera, since actual frames are created. On an NLE system the effect is achieved by multiplying existing frames. New high-speed digital camera cards, such as class 10 SD cards, process images fast enough to produce the slo-mo effect that used to be produced solely on film.

Undercranking generally works better than overcranking on NLE systems, since it involves removing existing frames. A chase sequence can be enhanced by speeding up the cars by using the computer's motion effect. If a motion-altered sequence is later conformed back to film, however, a film effects house must *skip print* or, in the case of slo-mo, repeat print the film frames to achieve the desired effect. Since film is a discrete form, some motion effects will not carry over from digital to film.

Doctor's Orders

When finishing a movie on film, be sure to calculate motion effects so they translate into a film environment. Unlike interlaced video, for instance, there are no half frames in film.

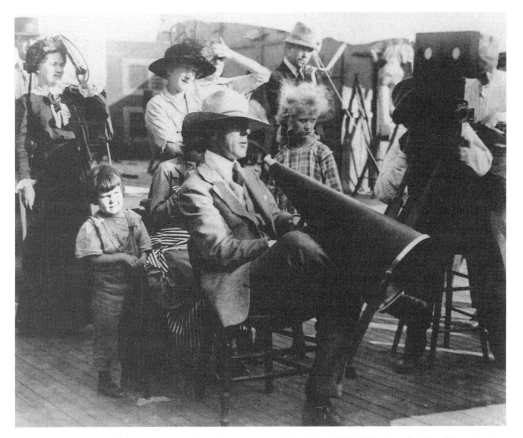

Figure 7.3 *D.W. Griffith directs. (Reproduced by permission of the Mary Pickford Institute for Film Education.)*

Doctor's Note

According to film historian Kevin Brownlow, the early films of D.W. Griffith were limited to one full reel. Wishing to extend his limited ration of film stock, Griffith experimented with slowing down the camera's cranking rate to as little as 12 fps. In this way more information was imprinted on the film. Projectionists were instructed to playback the movie at the reduced speed in order to maintain realistic motion. Fearing that the flammable nitrate film might catch fire, projectionists often ignored this request. When the film was played back at standard speed on the projector, the action appeared to have speeded up.

Emphasizing an Action

Like the dynamic editing found in documentaries and later infused into music videos, the pacing of action editing benefits from the use of jump cuts. The action leaps ahead or doubles up through the use of jump cuts. In this regard, some events and stunts call for more attention in order to create their full impact, such as explosions. In reality, explosions are short-lived events. In films they often hold a pivotal position, culminating a scene or changing the course of the plot. In order to give them their due, editors may choose to slow them down either by using overcranked footage or by incorporating the three-step pattern. In this case the explosion begins, but before completing the eruption, the editor cuts to the same or different angle with the burst slightly retarded from its last position. The editor allows it to grow past the last position but not to full bloom. Again, a cut is made, and again, the action rewinds several frames earlier before it is finally allowed to crescendo as a full eruption. This technique, while effective in action scenes, can provide emphasis in myriad editing situations.

In *Poison Ivy: The New Seduction,* Jaime Pressly's character Violet strips off her thin robe in preparation for taking an early-morning swim before the prying eyes of her girlfriend's father peering surreptitiously from the upstairs window. As Violet peels off the diaphanous gown, the cut resets to frames earlier where the gown has just begun to leave her shoulders, allows it to progress further in its removal, then resets again— this time deeper into the action—and finally plays out until the silken garment falls completely away, revealing her naked form. In *The Rock*, Nicholas Cage, roaring across the screen in a yellow Ferrari, pursues Sean Connery, who drives a borrowed black Hummer. When Connery appears to be evading him, Cage takes a shortcut through a warehouse. He's confronted with a gigantic plate glass window. "Oh, why not?" he asks himself and throws the car into gear, bursting through the glass. If the moment were allowed to play out in a single, temporally correct shot, it would lose much of its impact. Instead, the editor, Richard Francis-Bruce, chose to break the action into thirds, allowing the Ferrari to emerge through the glass three times in an exterior shot that each time resets slightly to the earlier phase of the action.

Doctor's Note

A danger that editors confront when cutting action comes from the plethora of images that audiences have become accustomed to seeing in modern films. With such a wide selection to choose from, it is easy to forget the primary throughline of the story and character. When multiple ancillary characters populate a scene, the editor may neglect to focus on the character whose scene it is, therefore giving even treatment to all. The protagonist gets lost in the shuffle. Ultimately, while it is important to keep secondary characters alive, the torrent of images should not condemn the protagonist to obscurity among the crowd.

When the editor has finished his cut, he will want to add some temporary sound and music to help enhance it. This is especially important in action scenes, where much of the footage may have been shot without sound. Prerecorded sound effects can be downloaded from the Internet or from CD libraries. Your goal isn't to replace every sound in the scene—that's the job of the sound effects editors as they prepare for the final mix—but to hint at what sound will occur there. In a car chase it is helpful to put in temporary effects of roaring engines and skids but only those sounds that are most essential to telling the story. If a character leans out of a car, points a shotgun at the vehicle beside him, and fires, you'll want to hear the gunshot. Later, the sound effects editors may find a better gunshot or even record one using that same gun, but for now, to tell the story, you have temporarily placed the appropriate sound there.

℞

In film doctoring comedy, editor Jon Poll offers three basic aims:

1. Milk the comedy. Find moments that are missing and discover if there's anything more to squeeze out of a joke.
2. As fast as possible, get through anything that's not getting good laughs.
3. Find moments in the characters that an audience will remember after they leave the theater. These are the human, relatable moments.

Chapter 8

Genre Editing Styles III

The Horror Film

The horror genre addresses our concern with the weaknesses of the flesh. Human mortality and decay occupy the images in this genre. Interestingly, serious directors in this genre often remain engaged to horror for their entire careers, such as Dario Argento, John Carpenter, Wes Craven, and Jack Sholder. These directors have a passionate commitment to the blood and gore that has permeated the modern visions of horror films. More than anything, however, the horror film is devoted to the monster. Whether it is a block-headed behemoth with bolts in his neck or a transient sporting razors on his hands, the horror genre asks us to look at our own monsters by manifesting them on screen in the guise of various personages. The characters of earlier times, Dracula, Werewolf, and Frankenstein, join Freddy Krueger, Michael Myers, and Jigsaw in more recent fare to populate our nightmares with ghastly creatures.

Fear of death, fear of dismemberment, and fear of pain permeate the horror film. The editor in this genre is treated to a host of bizarre and otherworldly images. Various monster shops, of which Rick Baker's was one of the most prominent for decades, supply the latex masks and quirky appliances that make monsters unique and captivating. Unlike comedies and action films, the horror film can sustain itself on the blood of lesser-known actors. Also, these films can be produced on a very low budget. The grosser, the better remains the adage of some horror directors, and audiences devour their films along with popcorn and hot dogs while watching late-night reruns.

Case Study

The oddest review I ever received appeared in *Variety* with regard to a horror film I edited called *The Convent*, starring Adrienne Barbeau and Coolio. The reviewer, intending to pay a compliment, announced that the editing was "much better than it needed to be." In saying this, he reminded the reader that the horror genre is, at times, the least discriminating of all genres. On the other hand, the time and attention that the director and I put into constructing the film are probably what helped send it to the Sundance Film Festival and into theaters around the world.

The Healthy Edit. DOI: 10.1016/B978-0-240-81446-9.00008-1

Doctor's Note

Why we enjoy a good scare and why in high school we coaxed our dates to late-night screenings of *Creature from the Black Lagoon* in the 1950s, *Night of the Living Dead* in the 1960s, *The Exorcist* in the 1970s, *Friday the 13th* in the 1980s, *Scream* in the 1990s, and *Saw* in the new millennium, answers an intriguing psychological puzzle. Teenagers seem to suspect that scary movies can lead to hook-ups with the opposite sex, even though it seems counter intuitive. But it works. Frightening situations lead to arousal. Arousal leads to attraction. And what better way to create arousal than to take one's date to a horror movie?

Psychologist Arthur Aron from the State University of New York has spent years deciphering human attraction. A while ago, he performed an experiment on the Capilano Canyon Suspension Bridge in Vancouver, British Columbia. The rickety five-foot-wide, 450-foot-long bridge hangs 230 terrifying feet above rock-strewn rapids. Halfway along its swaying and wobbly length, Aron and his research team positioned an attractive young woman prepared to ask bogus survey questions of unsuspecting young men between the ages of 18 and 35. She also offered her phone number in case they had any subsequent comments or questions. On a sturdy bridge farther upriver, and suspended only 10 feet above a gentle stream, Aron repeated these encounters using the same young woman. What he discovered was that the young woman appeared more attractive to the young men crossing the scary bridge than to those crossing the nonthreatening span. Half the men who crossed the scary bridge phoned the young female researcher afterward. Only two men from the sturdy bridge called. "People are more likely to feel aroused in a scary setting," Aron concludes. In this regard, horror films satisfy a significant desire of the human psyche. Who would have guessed that horror could be classified with the romance genre?

Because of the horror film's potentially low-budget status, flexible story structure, and tolerance for one-note performances, it has thrived as the mainstay of the independent film world. Upon its turf resides a fertile ground for young filmmakers, from directors to editors to DPs, to launch their careers. The comparatively small initial investment has made it attractive to investors who at times reap huge returns from films that gain a large, or even cultish, following. *The Blair Witch Project* and, more recently, *Paranormal Activity* have grossed millions of dollars despite budgets that linger in the thousands. Horror films also reproduce like viruses. It is not unusual for the initial film to spawn sequels numbering five, six, or even seven. Yet, despite its kinship with low-budget producers, the horror film also attracts studio-size budgets and production value. Recent films of Sam Raimi, such as *Drag Me to Hell*, sport more sophisticated story structures, fine acting, and well-honed picture and sound editing.

In terms of editing, the horror genre relies on the jump scare. A sudden motion or a loud sound is nearly guaranteed to make an audience jump. Adding a jump cut to catapult the suspended action, usually from a wider shot to a frenetic close-up, heightens the effect. Precede this with creepy music and a good helping of suspense and you are likely to have an audience so on edge that they are ready to bolt for the exits. If the editor and director can further take the audience off its guard, such as in the final moments of Brian de Palma's *Carrie* where the dead girl's hand juts up out of the cemetery soil and grabs her foe, then the thrills are increased. *Drag Me to Hell* capitalizes on the jump scare, scattering it liberally throughout the film to the point where it becomes almost numbing. The movie's superb sound of the cyclonic force of evil scattering props left and right aids the action.

Doctor's Note

Though the horror film employs an effect that runs contrary to the suspense film, each borrows from the other. Hitchcock contended, and rightly so, that between suspense and surprise, suspense was preferred. A surprise is like the cheap trick your brother or sister plays by jumping out as you pass down a deserted hallway. The ensuing start satisfies a certain emotional thrill, but it is short-lived. Working on a purely primal level, surprise requires minimal skill to accomplish. Suspense, on the other hand, must be set up. Rather than walking unsuspectingly with the character down the hallway, the audience has an inkling of something terrible about to happen. In a cut the editor has shown the villain waiting around the corner. The anticipation of what he will do and when he will do it keeps us on the edge of our seats. Where, in horror, the editor relies on a quick, loud cut to illicit a scare, in suspense she slows down and milks the moment, stretching it until the last, unbearable second. Then she unleashes the final punch.

Sometimes tracking the main character in a sustained wide shot, devoid of cutaways or other angles, builds the suspense. Sometimes a tight shot—which precludes the audience's opportunity to notice a threat lurking in the shadows—becomes the best strategy. Essentially, the lengthening of time by allowing a shot to play out proves an effective means of maintaining suspense.

Blood Suckers

Starting in 1922 with F.W. Murnau's *Nosferatu*, a silent movie based on Bram Stoker's novel *Dracula*, the vampire has lurked in the dreams and nightmares of filmmakers and their audiences up through the present day with the popular *Twilight* franchise. The telltale fang marks that first appeared in *Nosferatu* reappear in *Dracula* starring Bela Lugosi, in Francis Ford Coppola's *Dracula*, in *Twilight* and in *Let Me In* based on the Swedish cult film *Let the Right One In*. This iconic image, along with garlic, smoke, crosses, bats, coffins, mirrors, and many others, reflects the realm of the vampire. Recently, the *Twilight* series has attempted to deconstruct almost all of the popular conventions associated with the vampire, yet the prevailing strength of the genre, rather than being sapped of its energy, has been revitalized. Like the creature itself, the vampire legend appears to be eternal.

Part of the vampire's attractiveness lies in his duality of a charismatic refinement combined with an animalistic lust for blood, particularly that of virgins. The eroticism, power, and mystery associated with the vampire challenge the decent though repressive mores of civilized society. On the surface, the film *The Servant*, written by Harold Pinter, is a domestic drama about an upper-class Englishman, Tony (James Fox), who hires a manservant (Dirk Bogarde) to maintain the order of his London flat. Eventually the tables turn and the servant gets the better of Tony, unraveling his respectable existence and figuratively sucking the life out of him. Though rarely identified as a vampire film, *The Servant* clearly has its roots in that genre. Mindful of this, the filmmakers placed subtle hints throughout the movie, including braids of garlic in the kitchen, mirrors that glimpse partial reflections, smoke, and even crosses formed from masking tape on the new glass windows.

The Thriller and Mystery

Like the mystery genre the thriller genre often involves detection of the evildoer who must finally be brought to justice. It deviates from the mystery genre, however, in many ways. In fact, mysteries and thrillers often present antithetical story cycles. Since editing's primary purpose is to the tell the story most effectively, it is important for the editor or film doctor to understand the distinctions between the genres so as to avoid missteps. For instance, thrillers often demand that the protagonist go *mano a mano* with the villain at the end. It should be a fight to the death, where the outcome is uncertain. All the hero's resources must coalesce to take down the evildoer. An editor who is cutting a thriller where this doesn't occur should, in collaboration with the writer and director, rethink the ending.

Likewise, understanding the difference between the two genres will help in the decision of what to reveal and when. In a mystery it is a good idea to hold back the shot that reveals too much, gives away a clue too soon, or reveals an identity. In a thriller, however, the editor wants to reveal certain items early on. Through a cutaway, for instance, the editor will reveal a killer waiting around the corner as the protagonist wanders down a dark alley. The aim here is to expose information that the audience, in knowing, will feel intense concern for the hero.

When to reveal information through a cut pervades many a thriller editor's concerns. Again, timing is everything. Show an action or character too soon and it dissipates the momentum; show it too late and you have sacrificed the thrill of the audience's anticipation. One of the most gripping features of this genre derives from the audience's close identification with the hero and the ensuing dread that something terrible will befall him or her. If the audience lacks the necessary information, such as location, intent, or abilities of the antagonist, then the tension is diluted.

Where obscuring information is important in a mystery, the need to supply information is tantamount in a thriller. The one essential piece of information that is intentionally left out of the thriller involves the true perpetrator. Sometimes the character we believe to be the villain isn't, and the one whom we were most comfortable with, even believed we could trust, turns out to be the betrayer. It could be a close friend, a relative, a trusted doctor, or even a priest. In *Angels and Demons*, one of the stronger aspects of the film is the handsome young camerlengo who, on the surface, appears to save the day. Near the film's end, he hops on a helicopter and ferries a container of stolen antimatter safely away from the Vatican before its magnetic containment shield shuts down, setting off a devastating explosion. His heroic deed is certain to earn him the position of pope. The audience suspects that one of the older cardinals is to blame for multiple trespasses, since he appears to have an overzealous ambition to be the next pope. Yet, moments before the end, we discover that the charming camerlengo was responsible for stealing the antimatter. He's the actual villain. In these cases misdirection helps to enhance the story.

The mystery presents a protagonist who starts life generally with more confidence, strength, and know-how than the thriller's protagonist. The detective fulfills a power fantasy since he enters the story already capable of taking on the challenges before him. The protagonist in a thriller, however, starts out at a disadvantage and must learn the skills required to defeat the antagonist. The mystery's protagonist is proactive, like Hercule Poirot, Miss Marple, Adam Dalgliesh, or Sherlock Holmes. The invitation to the audience is to use their brains, follow the clues, and solve the mystery. When it is coupled with the action genre, the mystery creates spy movies such as the James Bond franchise. The hero, searching for the clues to smuggled gold in *Goldfinger* or a downed NATO bomber carrying a nuclear payload in *Thunderball*, must battle vicious adversaries in order to solve the mystery. In the recent, cross-genre *Sherlock Holmes* film with Robert Downey Jr., the previously retiring sleuth jumps into the fray with fisticuffs and weaponry.

The protagonist of a thriller is rarely so daring. Rather, he or she has been thrust into a situation for which he is ill-prepared. He is a victim who becomes an unlikely hero. Cary Grant's character of Roger Thornhill in Hitchcock's classic thriller *North by Northwest* is an innocent bystander whose mistaken identity embroils him in a deadly game of international espionage. He ends up fighting for his life as he's chased across America by a gang of ruthless spies. Clarice Starling (Jodie Foster) in *Silence of the Lambs* is an FBI cadet who's not prepared for the treacherous manipulations of Dr. Hannibal Lecter (Anthony Hopkins). By enlisting Lecter's help to find a serial killer, Clarice ends up nearly losing her own life.

Suspense films grip an audience like no other. Even *Rope*, that experiment in nonediting, sustains because of its suspenseful story. In *Rope*, Alfred Hitchcock introduces the audience to two killers—upper-class rogues from Ivy League colleges who, for the challenge of it, have constructed what they believe will be the perfect murder. As the story evolves, we discover that one, Brandon, possesses more daring than the other. He is so pompously sure that his scheme will succeed that he has invited the deceased's parents and fiancée over for dinner. Not only that, but he has moved the dining room tablecloth over to the settee—which houses the dead body—and sets it for dinner. At each turn the story raises the ante, adding greater and greater jeopardy.

A less successful attempt at repeating this experiment, the film *Russian Ark*, with its tediously long tracking shots and contrived story, reinforces *Rope's* masterfulness. *Russian Ark*, which was shot on high-definition video and has the advantage of no splices, since the filmmakers employed a full-length videocassette, repeats Hitchcock's experiment in color and with the fluid movement of a Steadicam. Photographed at St. Petersburg's Hermitage Museum, the film is a production designer's dream. The lavish sets and costumes, the large cast, and intricate camera moves make it worth viewing. But the meandering story, beginning as a sort of mystery with a disembodied narrator wondering where he is, makes for a less intriguing experience. It is further diluted by lovely but not very dramatic stage and orchestral performances within the confines of the Hermitage. Here, the superiority of suspense over mystery again becomes clear.

Family Films

The family film is another genre that implies various conventions. Though such films can be formulaic, they must never expose their formula. It is generally easy to identify the ones that are constructed by committees along the lines of various precepts garnered from film schools or story seminars and those that spring from the wringing of the writer's heart. In art, feeling has precedence over technique, though good technique helps to express feeling in a meaningful way. Rather than building outward from a formula, the filmmaker is best to build from the inside and then check the structure against outer conventions.

Family films often highlight conflicts within relationships or over the concept of family. Ideal differs from real, and along with way the audience finds an insight into those issues. Whether we deny family or celebrate family, the fact of our relatedness to people we may or may not choose as friends remains. A film like *Family Man* shows the conflict many young men experience about transitioning from their ego-centered, successful bachelorhood to a world of family and commitments. In this case, Nicholas Cage plays a Wall Street broker with a Ferrari who, by an act of magic, wakes up one morning with a wife and children. One endearing scene finds him walking in on his wife (played by Téa Leoni) in the shower and then guided by the older child into diapering the baby. He continues to insist, "This is not my life," only to find out at the end that it is the life he needs and ultimately wants.

Characters in these stories often believe they know what they need and are set on achieving it. Though they may not achieve their original goal, they find something else that is more valuable and enduring. As the philosopher Martin Buber once observed, "All journeys have secret destinations of which the traveler is unaware."

James Joyce's term *epiphany* describes the ah-ha moment that these characters often experience in the third act of the story. Without these transformative moments, the family film, while perhaps entertaining, does not rise to the potential of its genre. In *Prancer*, the epiphany of the father's and daughter's acknowledgements of their love for each other is further reinforced by the physical manifestation of their newly shared faith in each other and in the magic of the season—the reindeer flies!

The Documentary

The documentary is a genre that most vividly represents the editor's influence on filmmaking. It has evolved from the early newsreels to travelogues and nature movies to cinéma vérité to reality shows to features like *The Cove*; *Food, Inc.*; and *An Inconvenient Truth* that confront political and social issues. Initially a collection of seemingly unrelated images, the documentary has grown to include re-creations, visual effects, and surround sound.

There are basically two kinds of documentaries that confront the editor. One is what National Geographic regularly produces. The subject matter, based on a historical, cultural, or scientific topics, has been exhaustively researched. The research eventually renders a script divided into two halves, one representing what will be seen and one representing what will be heard, video and audio, with accompanying timecode. In many cases a re-creation of an event may be portrayed. Visual effects help to explain complex concepts or illustrate what cannot be shown. On the soundtrack, narration intersperses with interview sound bites.

At first the editor may record the voiceover himself, but later it will be replaced by a trained actor or voiceover artist. Footage-wise, the editor is supplied with interviews from experts or those who have experienced a particular event. This is accompanied by *B-roll*.

In this case the editor proceeds in a fairly circumscribed way. First, he may string together what is known as a *radio cut*. The radio cut, as the name implies, is an audio portrayal of what comprises the

> **B-ROLL**
>
> A B-roll originally referred to the tape deck that housed the supporting material that was to be played to reinforce information from on-camera interviews. This deck was labeled B, while the primary deck containing the interviews was A.

movie, built from the temporary narration and a *head bed* of interviews or talking heads. Through digital nonlinear editing, the construction of these tracks has become much easier. Where previously producers and editors constructed their cuts from timecode logs, known as *paper cuts*, the computer allows a graphic representation of the various cuts that can be easily moved around, repositioning them for the best effect. On the timeline the individual video cuts sit directly above the individual audio cuts, and, to a certain extent, it is possible to invoke the old-school paint-by-numbers approach. For every audio cue the editor need merely find an accompanying video clip to illustrate those words. Though the tendency is to ignore this seemingly prosaic approach, the result of not yielding to its time-honored effectiveness generally produces a confusing story.

There are plenty of places to get creative and supply expressionistic or impressionistic images to overlay an abstract concept such as love or beauty. But it is often advisable to show a volcano when the narrator refers to a volcano or to show a three-toed sloth when the interviewee mentions his encounter with such an animal.

Playing with Blocks

Editing a documentary is a bit like playing with blocks. In this case the blocks appear as rectangular chunks of color on the computer's timeline. They can be expanded, contracted, transposed, and moved around at will to configure the best sequence to tell the story. The *drag and drop* feature found on some NLE systems makes this kind of shuffling easy. Some editors like to string shots together one after another along a single video track. Others like to stagger the blocks over multiple stacks of video tracks, keeping in mind that only the uppermost ones will be seen.

DRAG AND DROP

A nonlinear editing feature for moving clips from bins into the timeline and from one position on the timeline to another.

Tech Note

Drag and drop is one of most efficient features found on Final Cut Pro. By clicking on an icon in the Browser window, a clip can be dragged into the Viewer window, where marks or in and out points may be added. The clip can also be dragged directly from the Browser onto the Timeline. When adding it to the Timeline, the editor guides the pointer to a faint gray line on the video track. Placing it above the line yields a forward-facing arrow, designating an insert edit. Placing it below the line reveals a down-facing arrow, which signifies an overwrite edit.

On video tracks only one shot predominates at a time, unless the editor creates some sort of transparency, such as titles with *alpha* channels. This is not the case with the audio tracks. Audio tracks are like team builders who include everyone in their game. Audio tracks are inclusive rather than exclusive. Many NLE systems allow the construction of up to 99 audio tracks, though monitoring them may be limited to eight tracks at a time.

Documentary editors use video track exclusivity to their advantage. Take, for example, a head bed of interview subjects excitedly chatting about their field of interest. At some point, probably fairly early on, the talking head is going to become tedious to look at. Before that happens, the editor splices in a shot of the snow monkey he is talking about. If you are editing on a single video track, you use the overwrite function to replace the dull talking head with the cute, dynamic shot of the snow monkey. Meanwhile, the audio track remains unchanged, supplying a voiceover narration.

On the other hand, if you use multiple video tracks, you have the option of preserving the entire talking head shot so you can refer back to it by turning off the video tracks above it. If after that you decide that you should have allowed another six frames before going to the snow monkey, you can shift the clip above it six frames later. When you turn all the video tracks back on, you'll now have the cut you wanted. A lot of editors like this approach. Others find it confusing to have so many clips running on so many tracks, with only some of them showing up when the sequence plays. Presumably, if you have thought about your cut, you probably will not have as much juggling to do. In that case, the editor should follow the mindset of the old-school paper cut editor who calculates everything ahead of time.

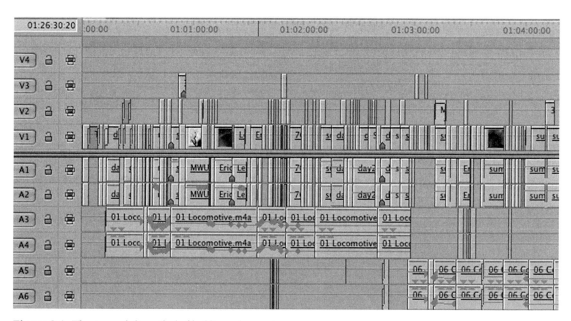

Figure 8.1 *The staggered clip method of building a documentary sequence.*

While these methods may seem too prescribed to pique the innovative interest of a creative editor, they actually rely heavily on the editor's skills and artistry. The narration and interviews are only the starting point, and the choice of shots as well as the flow and pacing of the story depend upon the editor. As he proceeds through the material, it will become evident which concepts and images best reinforce the story and which ones are superfluous or confusing. This fuels a sort of dialog between editor and writer/producer/director where the narration will be reworked to conform to the needs of the cut. This approach is not open ended, however, and depends on production schedules, air dates, and required or contracted running times.

Tech Note

Regarding running times, it is appropriate to say a brief word about two forms of time-code: *drop* and *non-drop frames*. Editors and others are often confused by the two different kinds, and some even assume that the choice is arbitrary, as long as it is not altered in midwork. In practice, the distinction is simple—one denotes actual running time and the other denotes actual length. Because of the nature of video, it is necessary to drop or remove occasional frames every second in order to produce a length of video that is time accurate. If no frames are removed, the time that might read 30 minutes on standard, nondrop frame timecode (00:30:00:00) would actually run longer than that. With the frames removed, the drop frame time-code 00:30:00:00 will provide an exact measurement of the production's running time. In setting the timecode, a colon between the numbers (00:00:00:00) usually means nondrop frame, while a semicolon (00;00;00;00) designates drop frame.

While National Geographic strives for accuracy and employs researchers to maintain its integrity, other documentary filmmakers design their movies to support or refute various political or social agendas with less regard for facts. Their stories and influence become the primary concern. Even the news, it is important to point out, is based on stories. In many cases the events depicted have nothing to do with where we live or people we know. Yet they are captivating as they unfurl insights into the human condition, the lengths some people will go to seek revenge, gain a fortune, or make a name for themselves. While National Geographic's aim is to present a factual and unbiased account, other documentary filmmakers find their power in exposing corruption or challenging existing ideas or mores.

Case Study

The first time I worked for National Geographic, I was surprised to find that a significant portion of the material, while accurate, wasn't purely documentary but a re-creation of an event. But documentary is not *cinéma vérité*. Did Robert Flaherty, perhaps the greatest documentary filmmaker of all time, ever cheat his audience by allowing artificial means? Look at *Nanook of the North*, the ruggedly Spartan tribute to a fading way of life in the frozen north, portraying the innocent Inuit Nanook eking out his harsh existence. How did Flaherty get those amazing shots inside the igloo? Is there enough light to film in an igloo, especially with the slow emulsions they used to use? And if you did have the options of electric lights, wouldn't it melt all the snow and defeat the movie's integrity? In fact, the igloo was a sort of a set, constructed in situ but with the top open to the sky to take advantage of the sunlight. Even those World War II newsreels with the shaky camera, often shot handheld on a 35 mm Bell & Howell Eyemo running on one-minute loads, were sometimes staged by the filmmaker. Smart field correspondents learned very quickly that it was better to wait until a battle was over and then ask the troops to fire off a few fake rounds reenacting what they'd been through than to stand out in the open and become a potential target.

(Continued)

Case Study (Continued)

And to take it even further, all these films were edited. The fact that they were edited and various images juxtaposed with others meant that the filmmakers were altering reality. They were infusing actual events with the story they wanted to tell. In physics the concept of the Observer Effect reigns as one of the great revelations of science. To put it in general, unscientific terms, it reveals that it is impossible to be completely objective. The fact that we are present, that an observer is watching the action, implies that the action will be different than if there were no observer. The witness influences the event witnessed and therefore alters the event.

A corollary of this approach is exemplified by the documentaries of Ken Burns, who has capitalized on topics dear to the hearts of Americans—baseball, jazz, national parks, and the American Civil War. His films use massive amounts of still photographs, some of which are animated with zooms or pans, to illustrate the words of prominent and unknown participants of that era. The familiar voices of various celebrities read from historic papers, letters, and books. Because of the effective and pervasive use of his approach, the term *Ken Burns Effect* has entered the documentary vernacular.

Both the Ken Burns approach and the National Geographic approach require a huge amount of research and preparation. They tend to aim toward a particular audience and venue so the running time and viewer sensibility are figured in. Other types of documentary, notably the feature documentary, issue forth with less restrictions and greater risk. The muckraking documentaries of Michael Moore (*Fahrenheit 9/11, Sicko, Capitalism: A Love Story*) highlight some recent achievements in the field, similar in aim to the poetic works of Pare Lorentz and his 1936 film about the environmental mismanagement that led to the Dust Bowl, *The Plow That Broke the Plains*. Cross-genre documentaries mix humor, horror or social commentary with questionable reality in such films as *Borat, Exit Through the Gift Shop, The Blair Witch Project* and *I'm Still Here*. These quirky offshoots are variously referred to by such terms as mockumentaries, crockumentaries and prankumentaries.

The Auteur Editor

The world of the feature-length documentary is wide open. In some cases, those who have money and the ambition to become part of the entertainment arena find an entry in this way. Though most documentaries require extensive research, it is possible to mount a film by collecting interviews pertinent to a subject and then shooting accompanying B-roll. Since some of these documentarians are not initially filmmakers but individuals with a passion to be heard, they must rely heavily on the editor to mold their collection of images and words into a coherent and compelling whole. In this realm the editor is given an opportunity to flex his muscles and employ all the skill and creativity at his disposal. The caveat is whether he or she is up to the task. While stringing together interviews and beautifully shot images may at first seem deceptively simple, the requirement to tell a story that will sustain for 90 minutes or two hours is hard to fulfill. It requires a full understanding of structure, pace, rhythm, and character.

When confronted with the initial disorder of unscripted, seemingly random footage, it is important to create careful logs preferably with transcriptions and timecode. If the logs are inputted into the editing machine, it is possible, using the search function, to type in a key word, such as "toad" and instantly locate references to a toad and the corresponding timecode. Using the timecode, the editor can jump immediately to the corresponding shot. In the case of projects where the editor must determine some kind of throughline by linking related footage, a starting point can seem daunting. Where does one begin? What images or sound bites does one look for out of 100 or more hours of footage? Since drama demands some sort of conflict or dialectic, a good place to begin is with contrasting images or conflicting opinions. Instantly the audience is thrust into the conversation, compelled to take sides or, at the minimum, wonder at the validity of each side. Challenges beget interest and interest sustains a movie.

The 1980s film *Koyaanisqatsi*, translated as *Life Out of Balance*, is a brilliant exposé on the deterioration of the natural environment and the rise of corporate mechanization—all without a word spoken. Its initial slow pace, where one pristine natural image amplifies the one before it, eventually leads to a striking contrast in the accelerated pace and tarnished appearance of overpopulated human society. Here the filmmakers have used comparison and contrast, along with a gradual progression, to build their message. The editor's pacing combined with Philip Glass's score, carries the film to its captivating conclusion.

℞

To help gain an understanding of genre conventions, select a favorite film of a particular genre and then rewrite a scene by placing it in another genre. For instance, what would the opening of *American Pie 2*—where the college couple's parents arrive unexpectedly while they're having sex—look like if it were played as a thriller, a western, or a drama?

Chapter 9

Internal Medicine

Coverage

One of the delightful aspects about professional editing is how each morning or afternoon a package will appear on the doorstep of your editing room. Contained within it are toys for you to play with. It is probably as close as you can get to nursery school as an adult, and also be paid for it. Those toys are the previous day's *coverage*.

Coverage is what an editor has to work with. As the name implies, coverage is achieved through the variety of angles that the director captures in order to cover all the necessary action and dialog contained within a scene. From this range of possibilities the editor must select the best candidates to construct the film. In features, the coverage arrives each day of production in the form of *dailies*, or *rushes*, the collection of scenes and takes from the previous day's shooting. Traditionally, lab cutoff is midnight, which means that the raw negative must be delivered to the film laboratory by midnight or else miss the opportunity for developing and printing or for digital transfer for the next day's viewing. Where shooting a million feet of film used to be an extremely rare occurrence, today studio productions often consume from 500,000 to a million feet.

Though technology has made the editing process accessible to more and more students of the medium, it has introduced another aspect that rarely existed in the past. That is the issue of substandard coverage. Apprentices and assistants in the past were constantly exposed to professionally shot footage and, though they may have complained ceaselessly about every little gaff, they had the advantage of seeing footage that met professional standards. Today, though coverage is more plentiful than ever—probably more digital images are created in a day than were previously photographed in the course of a year during the celluloid era—the overall quality has diminished.

The contemporary student editor or independent film editor, some of whom may also wear the hat of writer, director, or cinematographer, often deals with limited coverage, takes that end too soon or don't hold long enough on the subject, arbitrary compositions, poor lighting, and sparse setups. Confronted with this paltry coverage, the editor, at best, learns to rely on ingenuity to overcome deficiencies but, at worst, fails to develop an appreciation for well-shot material and the demands that it entails. When possible, some

The Healthy Edit. DOI: 10.1016/B978-0-240-81446-9.00009-3

neophyte filmmakers hire experienced professionals to help bridge the gap in terms of obtaining well-shot coverage. Others, enamored of the auteur approach but forgetting that most auteurs had extensive experience on other filmmakers' projects before taking the helm, prefer to perform most of the functions themselves with mixed results.

But what are these different angles that make up the coverage? A close-up seems fairly obvious, but what's a master, or a cowboy, or a pickup? As with most pursuits, film has nomenclature for common objects and activities. Probably it has more than most, and some are quite colorful due to the creative nature of the business. Following is a brief review.

The Master Shot

The *master shot* generally contains all the dialog and action in the scene. It can require sophisticated blocking in order to choreograph the actors' and camera's movements throughout the course of the entire scene. In that way it becomes the editor's road map, along with the script. In subsequent coverage this *long shot* will be broken down into its constituent parts to supply multiple angles for the editor. In some cases the master shot becomes the sole coverage for a scene, such as in the previously mentioned opening of *The Bonfire of the Vanities*. Other master shots that play well without a cut include the Halloween CarnEvil scene from the 2009 remake of *Fame* and the roving, 360-degree master from Kenneth Branagh's *Hamlet*. Early films, as far back as the 1930s, often relied on static master shots to tell the story. Today that approach is generally considered too stagey and runs counter to the needs of editors.

Many directors expend a lot of time and attention ensuring that they get a superb master shot. Some have limited experience in the editing room and rely on heavily choreographed masters to fulfill the function of a scene. Directors who have worked as editors know that master shots will generally be chopped up and intermixed with other angles.

The Establishing Shot

The *establishing shot* identifies a locale and places the viewer in the physical context of the scene. Too often this shot is left out of the coverage, resulting in a claustrophobic feeling, as well as making it difficult to perform a smooth transition from one scene to another. The establishing shot may be the exterior of a building, a panorama of a city or landscape, or an otherworldly locale.

The Wide Shot

The *wide shot* allows the viewer to place the objects and characters in the frame. It can vary between a *medium wide shot*, where

Figure 9.1 *The wide shot.*

actors are recognizable, to *extreme wide shots* that give a sense of place without identifying the actors within it. While master shots often contain wide shots, wide shots are not necessarily master shots. When composing a wide shot the director must attend to populating the frame with compelling, well-lit, and well-composed information. Darryl Zanuck's concern with CinemaScope, his studio's great technical achievement, was that it showed too much. This has been proven time and again when wide shots appear sparse.

The Medium Shot

The *medium shot*, sometimes known as a *cowboy* when it is framed loose enough to include the holster in westerns, supplies a valuable transition between the restrictive framing of the close-up and the expansive view of the wide shot. When coupled with a dolly move, the medium, cowboy, or medium wide shot works well to follow conversations while actors stroll, jog, or sprint toward the camera. Sometimes the camera tracks directly backward as the actors approach. In other setups the camera may favor one actor over the other, in a sense creating a moving *over-the-shoulder shot*.

Figure 9.2 *The medium shot.*

The Close-Up

In some regards the *close-up* is the most important shot in a scene. Through it the audience is allowed entry into the character's inner life through the corridors of expression, reaction, and nuance. Traditionally, it is also the shot for which actors save their best performances. When reviewing close-ups in the first day's dailies, the director and editor should evaluate the lighting to ensure that the eyes, those windows to the soul, are lit well enough to evoke a character's emotions. Unless designed for a particular effect, extreme close-ups tend to overpower a scene and, in the case of wide angle lenses that distort the face, will add a strange or quirky dimension that may not be desirable.

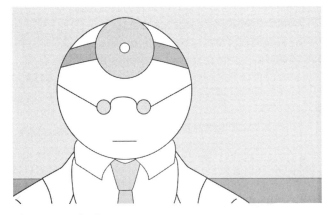

Figure 9.3 *The close-up.*

The Over-the-Shoulder Shot

Though often used in dialog scenes in a role similar to the close-up, the *over-the-shoulder shot* allows a tie-in of the two characters. By framing the on-camera character with the shoulder of the character to whom he's speaking, the director helps reinforce the physical proximity of the actors within the frame. The over-the-shoulder is one of the main shots to which the *180-degree rule* applies. By observing the convention of placing the camera over the shoulder of each actor on one side of an imaginary line, screen direction and eyelines are maintained.

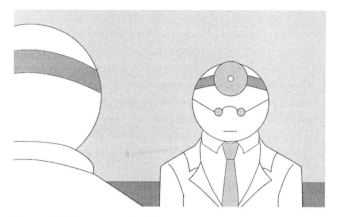

Figure 9.4 *The over-the-shoulder shot.*

The 2-Shot

As the name implies, the *2-shot* displays two actors, usually seen in profile, facing each other and framed in a medium shot. This angle is useful in dialog scenes where cutting to a wide shot would be too extreme. The shot's size remains intimate while allowing some breathing room and depicting the physical relationship of one actor to another. Leaving the 2-shot in order to return to a close-up can sometimes appear awkward. One solution is the *springboard*. Character A speaks, and then, as Character B begins her response, the editor springboards off of Character B's dialog into her close-up where the line culminates. In this way the transition from medium or wide 2-shot to a tighter shot is accomplished.

The Reverse Angle

Though the most interesting shots are usually those that play on the actor's face, sometimes a complete reverse is called for. In this case the camera sits 180-degrees away from its original position, giving us an alternate view of the set and the characters in it. *Reverse angles* prove useful in action and dance scenes, where their presence adds reality, variety, and clarity to the scene.

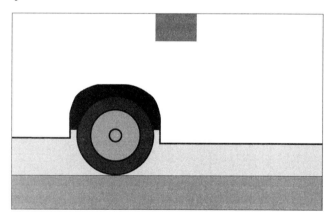

Figure 9.5 *The insert shot.*

The Insert Shot

Perhaps the most neglected of all coverage, the *insert shot* can contain essential information without which the scene might not make sense or the audience might feel cheated. Because of this the *insert stage* was invented, a small set where significant props could be photographed for inclusion in the final cut. Objects of all kinds, from guns to syringes to handwritten letters, end up on the insert stage.

Such are the basic angles that make up the daily footage.

Sync

Tech Note

In the not-too-distant past, the dailies arrived in cardboard lab boxes about the size of an individual pizza. One was issued from the sound lab that was responsible for transferring the quarter-inch tape from the *Nagra* recorder or the *DAT* tape to 16 mm *fullcoat* (the magnetic emulsion covering the entire celluloid strip of film) or 35 mm *single stripe* sprocketed sound film that would run through the Moviola or KEM flatbed. The other element was the film workprint, which was produced by contact printing the original camera negative, or *OCN*, onto positive stock. The negative was then stored in a vault for safety. Using the clapper slate to align and synchronize picture and sound, the assistant then drew corresponding start marks on each of the two film strips. These were used as reference points to code the film strips with identical numbers occurring at one-foot intervals. When placed beside each other, the picture and sound *edge numbers* maintained sync. Today the same OCN is transferred, by way of electronic *telecine*, to a digital medium such as digital videotape like *Digibeta, DV, HDV,* or *DVC-HD* tape, or directly to a hard drive, disc, or memory card. Today the best-quality sound is still achieved by recording *double-system*, using a separate microphone and track, then synchronizing the sound and picture through Avid, Pro Tools, or other digital audio system.

The digital delivery medium is constantly evolving based on improved engineering of digital memory. In the case of the film print, an assistant has the task of breaking the film down into scenes and takes, removing the unusable material that consisted of lab waste or long pauses before the slate. In all cases the useable material lives somewhere between the slate where the ubiquitous striped sticks clap together before the director calls, "Action," and the flash frame that appears when the camera stops, and its open shutter allows light to burn out the frame following the director's call for "Cut."

Doctor's Note

Savvy directors, who are sometimes wary that some of their coverage had been cut short by the film lab, will ask to see the flash frame, which tells them the true ending of the take.

With improvements in high-definition cameras and digital recording devices (see Figure 9.6), the need for processing of film negative and its overnight stay at the lab is changing. Most Hollywood films, however, are still shot on 35 mm celluloid.

Figure 9.6 *Various digital recording and delivery formats.*

From Chaos to Order

Most importantly, whether the film was shot on 35 mm film or high-definition video, whether it was printed onto film or transferred to a digital medium, the dailies arrive in the editing room in a completely disorganized form.

What does that mean? Didn't the production crew take care to meticulously arrange each shot? Didn't they keep records of each of those takes? Didn't they make an effort to get all the coverage the editor would need in order to tell the story? Of course they did. But life on the set is different from life in the editing room. And the order in which events occur on set is different from the order that must be established in the editing room.

Case Study

The first film I worked on as an assistant suffered from the malady of chronic disorder. Even though the assistant had been in the industry for many years and claimed to have worked for top studios, he had organized the film in a way that made it endlessly cumbersome to access.

He had arranged everything by shooting order. At the time, movies were coded with edge numbers that the assistant printed in ink on the side of the film, using a special coding machine. In this case the code represented the day the film was shot. In order to understand what scene the daily footage belonged to, one had to go through a complex series of investigations, not unlike deciphering the Da Vinci Code. The numbers on the film referenced to a hand-written code in a book on a shelf in another room. And that code referred to the scene and take number. But why not code the scene number on the film rather than the day it was shot? After all, what does it matter what day the film was shot? That's going to vanish as soon as the film is broken down and integrated with other scenes. What mattered was that when you found a stray film clip you could read the code on its side and instantly know what scene it belonged to. This was the suggestion of the film doctor who eventually took over the film. If the film clip said 023 2319, that meant it belonged to scene 23 (**023** 2319) and that it could be found on the second roll of dailies for that scene (023 **2**319—or 023 **1**319 if the numbering scheme began with zero), and that it resided 319 feet down (023 2**319**) in the thousand-foot roll. Even though this type of coding is rarely used today, it teaches us something about the importance of scene order over shooting order. This is important because even our modern, high-definition digital editing systems will foil our best attempts if we organize our bins and clips in a haphazard manner.

Figure 9.7 *Final Cut Pro's bin folders (left) as compared with Avid's frame view bins (right).*

Finding Order

How does the editor establish the necessary order? First by keeping in mind that, beyond all else, he is there to tell a story. That is what it is all about. It cannot be overemphasized how important it becomes to organize the scenes and takes in story order, not shooting order, which is the way they arrive. Directors do not have the luxury of doing this. On the set they have other priorities, such as getting the best performances, placing the camera in the most effective position, and making their day (i.e., completing all shots scheduled for that day). In this regard, it becomes necessary to shoot the movie out of order—not just out of scene order, as the scenes appear in the script, but also out of shot order as the shots appear within a scene.

In lighting a set it might be easier to start with close-ups while everyone is fresh and while the time-consuming task of lighting the entire set is underway. But close-up dialog doesn't necessarily begin a scene. The scene might need to begin with a wide shot, but the wide shot is scheduled for after lunch. So the shooting order becomes a matter of expediency and convenience and a hundred other factors, few of which pertain to story. Because of this, the shooting order inevitably varies from the story order. And this conflicts with the proper organization of the editing process.

An example of shooting order follows. The boxes represent *circled takes*. Circled takes are the takes that the director prefers. In the case of film, they are the takes that will be printed or transferred by the lab, saving the costs of materials and time. In the case of video transfer, all the takes are often included since the cost of selecting circled takes would overtake the cost of transfer time and stock.

23 – 1, ☐2☐, 3, 4
23A – 1, ☐2☐, ☐3☐
23B – 1, 2, 3, ☐4☐, ☐5☐
23C – 1, ☐2☐
23D – 1, 2, ☐3☐
23E – ☐1☐, 2, ☐3☐, 4, 5, ☐6☐
23F – 1, 2, 3, ☐4☐

In this case the first number, 23, is the scene number as it appears in the shooting script. The letter—identified as Apple, Baker, Charlie, Denver, and so on—signifies each new setup or camera position. Scene 23A might be a close-up, while Scene 23B might be a medium shot. The last series of numbers to the right are the take numbers. Every time the director calls for action, he creates a new take. And so the shooting proceeds, in alphanumeric order. This information is transferred to the slate so the camera records the information that can later be viewed at the head of each take. This, at least, is how it occurs in an ideal world. Remember the list of trials and tribulations enumerated on the set? Sometimes in the rush to get a shot, the slate is forgotten or, if remembered before the take is over, placed at the end instead of at the beginning. In that case it is referred to as a *tail slate*, and the board is turned upside down to designate this.

On all studio shoots a script supervisor sits beside the camera. Even low-budget and indie films, realizing the significance of this role, often include the script supervisor in their budget. The script supervisor is one of the editor's best friends. She or he is responsible for logging all the pertinent information that applies to each and every take. That includes the scene's duration, the lens used, the circled takes, and a brief description of the action and any problems that are encountered. The script supervisor also creates a new document, known as the *lined script*.

Editors, thankfully, are not usually privy to the mishaps, complications, and logistics of the set. In this way, they are like children who blithely play with the toy dinosaur they received for Christmas, unaware that their parents had to work to get money to buy the toy, pay the mortgage for the house where the dinosaur and child will live, cook the meals, and so on. They take all of that for granted. Editors have to concentrate on one thing: telling the story in the best way possible. Again, what better method to organizing the dailies than in story order rather than shooting order!

Yet many editors miss this point and thereby introduce disorder into the process. When this happens, the end result suffers. It requires a certain amount of patience to carefully review each set of dailies and organize them into story order before starting to cut. By proceeding in this way, the editor and her assistant have begun the editing process at the moment they begin to organize the dailies. In both film and digital editing rooms, the assistant becomes an integral part of the storytelling process

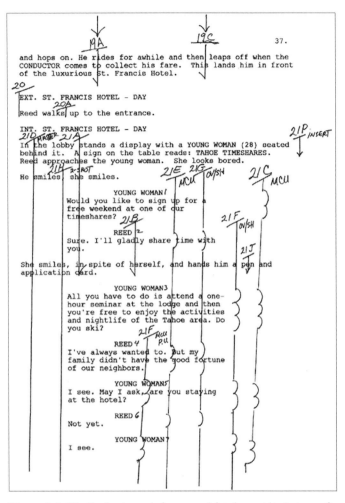

Figure 9.8 *The lined script reads from upper left to lower right. In terms of order, the topmost notations have priority over those farthest to the left. And the left has priority over those to the right.*

when he or she must think and carefully consider the order used to build the material.

Doctor's Orders

It's important for the editor to confirm that he or she has all the footage that was shot and printed. The best way to do this is to compare the information on the back of the

(Continued)

Doctor's Orders (Continued)

lined script, known as the *script supervisor's notes*, to the information on the camera, sound, and *lab reports*. If all these correspond with the footage you received, most likely you're in good shape. This rarely happens 100% of the time, so it's important to check. Occasionally, there will appear a take or two that was circled by the script supervisor but missed by the sound or camera department. Or maybe the lab neglected to print or transfer it. This problem will become less prevalent as more and more movies are shot on digital and all takes are available all the time.

Story Order

We have proceeded from the writer's original screenplay to the shooting script that contains scene numbers and *colored pages* (signifying changes to the shooting script) and finally to the script supervisor's lined script. This progression mirrors the translation process referred to earlier: from story to dailies to release print. Even for those whose shoestring budget precludes the employment of a script supervisor, it remains important to understand the role of the lined script and how it functions. Following this approach will benefit every filmmaker, from those whose budgets surpass $250 million to those who managed to find a few thousand dollars to shoot a low-budget indie. Even if the editor does not have a lined script, he can decipher the order by carefully studying the footage and plotting out the shot arrangement. Generally, establishing shots and master shots are placed first, followed by medium shots, and then over-the-shoulders, close-ups, and finally inserts. In this case the order might look like this:

    23B – 4, 5
    23A – 2, 3
    23 – 2
    23E – 1, 3, 6
    23C – 2
    23D – 3
    23F – 4

Notice that only the circled takes were printed, transferred, or included.

In constructing the scene bins or folders, the editor clicks and drags the clips around the bin until he has achieved a satisfactory order. This is reminiscent of a storyboard layout. Once the reordering is accomplished, all the takes will be available and in correct sequence each time the editor opens a bin. From this point they are ready to be loaded into the Viewer or Source window and played back. Final Cut Pro editors often stack folders labeled with scene numbers in the Browser window and within these folders display the text version of each take. This saves space when working with only one computer monitor, but it restricts the editor's view of the material. Most Avid editors and some FCP editors prefer to use two monitors and organize the shots as images. Since editing involves visual memory cues, it generally helps to look at pictures rather than text. Consider it a right brain verses left brain issue. Placing all the daily bins on the left computer monitor frees up room to work in the timeline area on the right computer monitor.

Tech Note

On Final Cut Pro, by right-clicking in the Browser, the editor can expose a menu that offers small, medium, or large icons. Further, the opportunity exists to select a frame that best represents each take by using the Get Poster Frame function, found under Mark. On Avid one need merely play the clip contained within the particular frame until arriving at the best representative image. The machine remembers that image and always displays it as the frame corresponding to that scene and take. The frame icon may be resized by selecting Edit > Enlarge Frame or Edit > Reduce Frame. There's also a keyboard shortcut where holding the Ctrl (in Windows) or the Command key (in Macintosh) and pressing L will enlarge and K will reduce the frame size.

Some editors, particularly those who started out by cutting on film, such as Richard Chew, the editor of *Star Wars* and *Risky Business*, have told me they build their dailies as if on KEM rolls. In other words, they string the takes together into a continuous sequence that can be played back as one roll. Using the scroll bar on the Avid, the editor can rapidly scan forward or backward through the dailies and select what he needs. From this he may build a *select roll*, a sequence that contains only the favored shots.

Other editors, such as Richard Pearson, have their assistants lay the dailies out into the scene bins. In the case of action scenes, he will build large select sequences in scripted, or perceived, story order. In dialog scenes he sometimes strings together every take of a particular line reading. This allows him to compare in order to find the best one. This has also proven to be a useful tool when working with directors who might have questions about which was the best reading.

Another useful tool is Avid's ScriptSync. It produces a graphic representation of the lined script. By touching a particular text line, the editor can locate and play a corresponding take. This also allows immediate access to all takes that match a line of dialog.

Some editors, including Pearson, like to have the script right in front of them and reread each scene before diving into it. They also feel it helps to read the script supervisor's notes beforehand to see if anything unusual came up on the set. It also allows the editor to make a case for why he didn't use a particular take, if it ever comes up.

Conrad Buff, on the other hand, minimizes the value of the script during the editing process: "I've read the script and have the story down, but so much is dependent on what the director gathers and what the actors do." Through their interpretations and the fact that some of the material usually gets rewritten, the script becomes less potent than the actual dailies that are in front of the editor. As a result there are new issues that he must recognize and somehow solve.

Doctor's Orders

Arrangement is crucial! Organize your dailies according to the lined script.

Case Study

A while back I was speaking with a professor who taught Final Cut Pro. The approach that he and others recommended to their students, based on several FCP manuals, was to organize the shots by angles and take advantage of FCP's coloring function to color code the folders in which they resided. In the case of wide angles, all wide-angle shots were placed in a blue folder in the Browser window. Close-ups were placed in a green folder, medium shots in a red folder, and so on. Though this might work for a certain kind of documentary, it could be disastrous for fictional narrative. In effect, the editor was adding confusion by tossing an array of shots into a folder where their only relationship was based on their size. It would be like trying to build a house by tossing all the nails, screws, staples, and hooks into a box marked *fasteners*. The carpenter would spend much of his day searching for the correct screw. Just because we've become more advanced technologically doesn't mean we know better how to accomplish the task at hand. Rather than simply ordering the dailies by lined script, we now have the option of color coding them; turning them into icons of various sizes; logging them by day, tape, or hour; and so on. In fact, with more choices and possibilities, the potential for mismanagement has increased.

Reducing Bloat

Encountering the large volume of material that an editor is often faced with may seem daunting at times. Documentaries can accumulate over 100 hours of footage, and some feature films will shoot over a million feet of negative. Even when you are careful to watch all the dailies and make detailed notes, it is difficult to recall everything you have seen. What is the best way to keep track of all the best footage? The answer is *selects*. Or what I think of as *The Goodies*.

When combing through thousands of feet or, as it often translates these days, hundreds of minutes of footage, editors can cull out the best material and string it together as a selects roll or sequence. Editors used to preview the copious footage with grease pencil poised to tick off the beginning and end of a shot. This would then be handed to the assistant, who would physically cut out the favored pieces and attach them one after the other to form a select roll. Today the selects can be built as the editor views the material, leaving out the interim step—and, unfortunately, the assistant.

Tech Note

A valuable feature of Final Cut Pro resides in the marking system that allows the editor to place colored markers with notes at the beginning of preferred sections. Once the scene is filled with markers, it can later be opened in the Browser by clicking the disclosure triangle and exposing the entire list of preferred portions along with identifying titles and notes. This works particularly well on documentaries where the use of video has allowed takes to run up to an hour long.

In Final Cut Pro a marker is generated by pressing the "M" key or by scrolling from the toolbar under "Mark," where a variety of marker options exist, including the ability to edit the marker using color and text. In Avid the preferred moments can be identified by colored markers, known as *locators*. FCP's marker system also allows for the creation of subclips, where the marked sections can be transformed into separate clips as subsets of the original, larger clip. This is accomplished by dragging the marked-up file into a new folder. FCP understands this as subclipped material and performs the task of breaking off each piece into separate clips designated by the clip icon with ragged ends.

Tech Note

What in film was known as a *select roll* translates in electronic editing as a *select sequence*, a series of preferred clips built into a sequence that the editor can draw from in creating the rough cut. Where FCP falls behind is in the editor's desire to mine useable pieces from a previous sequence of selected shots. With Avid, a new sequence is easily constructed by loading the select sequence into the Source monitor, clicking the Source/Record toggle icon, and locating the desired shot within the timeline. After that the editor makes an insert or overwrite edit in the same way he would when working from the original dailies.

Figure 9.9 *Avid's sequence toggling feature.*

While a similar method can be used with FCP, it currently lacks the opportunity to view the timeline corresponding to the Viewer window. The closest approximation uses multiple tabs representing various sequences in the Canvas's timeline and then copying and pasting between them.

The Gap

Once the dailies are properly organized, the editor screens them, usually with the director. In previous times—not too long ago—the standard method involved projecting the celluloid dailies in a screening room on the studio lot or in a makeshift space on location. Some filmmakers still value this approach. On the film *Inception*, director Christopher Nolan insisted on screening 35 mm dailies with his DP, Wally Pfister, and editor, Lee Smith. This old-school approach complemented the latest digital technology to allow nonlinear editing alongside 35 mm screenings. This permits the best evaluation of the film image while taking advantage of nonlinear editing.

According to *Film & Video* magazine, *Inception* "did not get digital dailies or go through a digital intermediate. The editors were working with an HD telecine made from a film print (not a negative), and the director was screening dailies in 35 mm scope every night plus Avid screenings of the evolving cut, through a Christie 2K projector, every Friday." After cutting the telecined footage on the Avid, the editors conformed the cut back to a 35 mm workprint so it could be screened in the theater.

Discussing his approach to dailies, editor Conrad Buff points out that running dailies in the traditional manner (often using nontraditional technology, such as HD projection) allows him to "see all the ingredients available in a logical order, compare takes for visual and performance reasons, and also try to determine if something is missing that would be great to have." After that, the editing process begins. Here, the editor's approach to the material becomes crucial.

Says Buff, "Having talked with the director to get any notes he or she may have, I make my own choices of where to begin a scene, what takes or portions of takes I like, and I usually find that when I can determine where I want to start the scene, the rest just evolves naturally. The big questions for me are what do I want to see or what do I need to see next? I put myself in the position of the audience, and things seem to roll along in a comfortable way."

But what if, in putting the film together, the editor discovers gaps in the story, coverage, or character development? This is one of the crucial aspects of film doctoring. Curing this involves, as for any doctor, a careful examination of the patient.

Examinations

Along the road from script to dailies to final cut, new items enter, unnecessary ones leave, and questions are raised. What made sense on the printed page suddenly jumps out waving red flags in the editing room. Or what seemed sufficient, even miraculous, on the set, suddenly pales before the detached and questioning gaze of the editor. Editors are generally people who are good at asking questions. They are not satisfied with what lies before them. They take nothing for granted. What may have seemed obvious to the writer or director or producer makes no sense to the editor. In this regard, an editor who has a strong command of story as well as aesthetic and technical expertise will be well suited to diagnose and ultimately cure the problems of incomplete coverage.

The Puzzle

Remember the jigsaw puzzle referred to in the first chapter? Students were asked to work collaboratively to build the puzzle. What they didn't know was that a piece had been left out. Their job evolved from fitting the pieces together to using their imaginations and surmising exactly what that missing piece should look like. This is the editor's job.

In the world of filmmaking, there are many options for filling that gap. Often the editor steals shots from other scenes. Or she moves around existing coverage within the scene. Sometimes she might order *stock footage* to create an important establishing shot or to fill out a montage. If there were lifts, she might retrieve the lifted footage and reincorporate it in an altered form. If the budget allows and the producer is willing, a time-consuming and expensive approach involves additional shooting. These *pickups* might be handled by a second unit crew, sometimes assigned to the editor's supervision, or by the director. These may be as simple as an insert shot of a particular prop or action, or it might entail shooting a whole new scene. In each case the shots can be tailored to fit exactly what the editor and director feel is needed.

Saved in the Editing Room

It is important for the aspiring filmmaker to realize that these gaps occur in every film—to greater or lesser degrees—and not just on low-budget productions. One notable example is the Antoine Fuqua film of *King Arthur*. This film, with a budget of approximately $100 million, was shot on location in England, Ireland, and Wales. Much of the pivotal action takes place during a battle on a frozen lake. At one point in the skirmish, the surface cracks, large shards of ice rise up, and the attacking army is swallowed by the frigid water. It is an ambitious scene and one that plays out magnificently on the big screen. But, according to the editor, Conrad Buff, it wasn't always that way.

> **STOCK FOOTAGE**
>
> Stock footage is material shot by a third party who is not associated with the film's production and licensed based on time and usage (such as worldwide rights in perpetuity).

Figure 9.10 King Arthur, *2004. Copyright © Touchstone Pictures. Photographer: Jonathan Hession. (Photo credit: Touchstone Pictures/Photofest.)*

The production "was troubled due to a lack of time and some politics between studio and director." The entire scene, a major setpiece, was assigned to two days of production. In Buff's opinion it would have required at least seven to ten days to shoot properly. The first day was consumed with mainly panoramic shots of the approaching armies, filmed from a mountaintop. After that, there was only one day left to capture all the needed coverage, including vital close-ups. By the time the second day wrapped, there wasn't enough coverage to fully tell the story. "The initial dailies I received were essentially all master shots with some coverage of principal actors," says Buff. But a scene of this magnitude required more comprehensive coverage than was supplied. "It was a battle, and it needed much more detailed and specific shots of archers firing arrows, men dying, ice breaking. . . . It was pretty much impossible to tell the story with the material [I'd been given]."

Back in the editing room, Buff reviewed the dailies and pieced together a preliminary cut that included place-holders for the missing pieces of the puzzle. "I therefore with [the director's] blessing indicated where I thought a close-up of Arthur or any other character was needed and where any POVs were required. The first unit would get time later based on the first cut to shoot actors against greenscreen for which we'd add backgrounds. A second unit was able to get very specific pieces on a stage in Pinewood Studio water stage with extras and stuntmen. Of course, this sequence was eventually turned over to the visual effects team, who transformed many details and backgrounds into a beautifully executed winter reality. I think this is an extreme example of what editors can encounter and help solve with the 'magic' of editing."

> **POV**
>
> A POV, or point of view, is a shot filmed at an angle that portrays the scene through a character's eyes.

Shot List

Surprisingly, many directors do not shoot to edit. They shoot to create interesting shots, to give the actors something to do, or to accumulate footage. But a director's shot list is the beginning of the editing process. As David Mamet noted in his book *On Directing Film*, "The work of the director is the work of constructing the shot list from the script."

There are probably as many directors who have no idea how the material they shot is going to fit together as there are directors who feel they can sit down and edit it themselves. At opposite ends of the spectrum both do themselves a disservice. A director's job is to generate footage based on the characters' objectives. A director is not required to put the film together. He or she is responsible for creating the raw material for the cut. One of cinema's greatest directors, Stanley Kubrick, offered the notion that "everything that precedes editing is merely a way of producing film to edit." Of course, talented directors accomplish this in a unique way. In conjunction with their production designer and cinematographer, they fashion a compelling look or style. But the essential energy and pulse of the film remain in the editor's hands.

As the early Russian filmmakers discovered, it is not an image on its own that is responsible for creating meaning but the collision of images. Like atomic particles smashing into one another, they liberate a new element, which carries the meaning of the scene. Over a century ago, Russian director Vsevolod Pudovkin revealed how each shot exists in a sequence to communicate one piece of information. Just one. Sequences are built "brick by brick" according to Pudovkin. This is an essential point. Yet it is not as obvious as it seems. All filmmakers forget this from time to time, and some never learn it.

Sergei Eisenstein's revelation, based on an understanding of Japanese calligraphy where the combination of characters creates the meaning, added to Pudovkin's concept and fueled his theories of montage. The pictograph for crying, Eisenstein realized, was made up of two images: one for eye and one for water. Rather than merely placing them together, the combination spawned a completely new idea: that of crying. This marrying of previously unrelated images to generate a new meaning is what editing is all about. It is as true today as it was at the beginning of the art, even as the length of a particular shot has changed and the pace generally increased over the decades.

In this sense, the director needs to consider each shot as having something unique to say, but only one point to make at a time to forward the story and character. In my production classes I ask students to create a complete shot list before greenlighting their projects. Most start out by imagining the coolest camera moves they can come up with but neglecting the importance of a shot's meaning. Instead they are asked to create a list of neutral or, as Mamet advises, uninflected, shots based on their characters' objectives.

Take something as simple as a guy who wants to get the attention of a girl in his class without the teacher noticing. Rather than asking each shot to fulfill multiple functions, we follow, as Pudovkin advises, a design for one—and only one—action. Here's a possible shot list:

1. WS teacher writing on the board
2. CU girl looking forward
3. CU boy staring in girl's direction
4. CU girl turns toward boy
5. CU boy smiles
6. CU girl smiles
7. MS teacher turns away from board, facing class
8. MCU boy looks down
9. INSERT boy's hand writes on paper
10. WS teacher turns back
11. MCU girl looks toward boy
12. MS boy folds note into paper airplane
13. OV/SH boy aims plane at girl
14. MS teacher continues writing on board
15. MCU boy throws paper plane
16. CU plane lands on desk
17. MS large, muscular student looks at the plane resting on his desk
18. CU boy staring
19. MCU muscular student opens the note
20. CU boy
21. CU girl watching
22. MCU muscular student reads the note
23. CU boy
24. CU muscular student looks up, throws a kiss
25. CU boy puts his face in his hands

Through this series of shots the story becomes clear. Yet the shots, taken singly, explain nothing. Only when placed next to the other shots do they take on meaning and forward a story.

Once the shot list is formed based on the characters' objectives, it is possible to consolidate all the similar shots into a master shot list. It would look like this:

Wide shot (WS) teacher
Medium shot (MS) teacher
Medium close-up (MCU) girl
Close-up (CU) girl
Medium shot (MS) boy
Medium close-up (MCU) boy
Close-up (CU) boy
Over the shoulder (OV/SH) of boy on girl
Medium shot (MS) muscular student
Medium close-up (MCU) muscular student
Close-up (CU) muscular student
Insert boy's hand writes on paper
Insert plane lands on desk

As you can see, only about half the number of angles would be required. All the shots from the original shot list are subsets of these shots. These would become the dailies. From these shots the editor will find all the individual components he needs to build the whole scene.

Whether organizing shots into bins, as in Avid, or folders, as in FCP, the important issue is to make sure you do it in a consistent and orderly fashion. How is this achieved? First, consider the work you have set out to do. All the fashionable dressings of color and labeling are fine, even aid efficiency, but they are not the point of why you're there. First and foremost, you are there to tell a story.

R̶x̶

When writing a prescription, medical doctors know that *bid* means *twice a day*. Film doctors need to know the abbreviations for a scene's coverage.

- CU = close-up (or MCU for medium close-up or ECU for extreme close-up)
- ESTAB = establishing shot
- MAS = master shot
- MS or MED SHOT = medium shot
- OV/SH of (name of character) on (name of character) = over the shoulder shot
- WS = wide shot (or EWS for extreme wide shot)

Chapter 10

Surgery

What Goes and What Stays

One of the most challenging aspects of the editor's job is as trauma surgeon. Deciding what goes and what stays when the pace lags, the story grows convoluted, or a performance falters requires a discriminating eye and ear. Two primary terms describe the surgical approach to film editing: *trim* and *lift*. A lift is the more invasive approach. It involves excising an offending scene or part of a scene, the sort of item that might end up as a deleted scene under a DVD's special features. It is also known as an *outtake*. The removal of this portion of the film is sometimes thought of as one of the editor's primary functions. The old-school image of filmstrips on the cutting room floor reflects this. In fact, as with surgery, total removal of a diseased organ is rare. The most common and frequent surgery performed by editors is the trim, removing portions rather than wholes.

Doctor's Note

Again, we should differentiate between traditional film terms and their altered meanings in the electronic realm. Where a *lift* typically refers to the deletion of part or all of a scene, Avid altered the term to mean a type of cut where a shot is removed, leaving a gap of the same length. Though it is possible to lift an entire scene, editors generally use the *lift* function to remove a single shot. Either way, a gap remains behind. On Avid, using the *extract* function removes a shot and closes the gap, much like the *ripple delete* function in Final Cut Pro. To return an excised shot to another position in the timeline, the Final Cut Pro editor uses *paste*, which is what Avid refers to as *overwrite*. To insert a shot between two others, FCP editors use *paste insert*, which Avid refers to merely as *insert*.

The term *clip* also has multiple meanings. The confusion probably comes from the vernacular "to screen a film clip," which in that case meant showing a portion of a movie. But *clips* can also be short pieces of film. To avoid confusion, a portion of a shot will be referred to here as a *trim* rather than as a *clip*.

The Healthy Edit. DOI: 10.1016/B978-0-240-81446-9.00010-X

Practical Considerations

A trim involves shortening a portion of a shot that resides within the body of the cut sequence. Sometimes the trim can be as small as a single frame. When working with celluloid, the editor had to carefully consider the move before applying the scalpel. Once the trim was removed, it could not be reattached to the film without leaving a mark. Originally, it required glue or, subsequently, transparent tape to reunite it with the original shot.

Today, trimming has become so easy it has negated any hesitation before applying the blade. Using the Trim tool in Avid, Final Cut Pro, Premier Pro, and other nonlinear systems, the editor can instantly remove or add frames to any shot in the movie. Since no physical splicing is involved and the images appear by accessing virtual addresses that link to the media, this leaves the original media intact so the process can be repeated over and over until satisfactory. In fact, one approach to trimming allows the editor to loop the section of the cut that requires attention so it plays over and over while he adds and subtracts frames until the shot looks right. It should be noted that until one reaches the trimming phase of the process, an experienced editor cutting on a Moviola, paperclipping his shots together for an assistant to tape later, could assemble a film almost as fast as an editor cutting on a modern digital system. The notable difference occurs when one enters the trim function. Trimming is infinitely easier on an electronic system.

There are four basic trim functions that mirror processes used by editors cutting on celluloid. In Final Cut Pro these are known as *Roll*, *Slide*, *Slip*, and *Ripple*. Once they are understood, these functions make life easier, though gaining command of trim operations remains one of the biggest challenges for editors learning a new system. As with film, trimming applies to the audio tracks as well as to the video tracks.

Tech Note

In Avid, the Trim Mode icon consists of a single button that toggles between the standard Source/Record editing mode and the Trim mode. The image on the button looks like a 35 mm film cartridge for a still camera, where pulling on the film would unspool it from the cartridge and turning the spool's nib would rewind it back into the cartridge. This graphically suggests the manner in which trim modes work, extending or contracting the amount of material to be shown.

To enter any of the trim functions, the editor simply clicks on the Trim button. Once in Trim mode, a pair of pink rollers appear over the cut. Depending on which way the cursor draws the rollers, the shot will extend into the preceding shot or over the incoming shot. In the Double Roller mode, the shot will *overwrite* whatever is ahead of it or behind it. To *insert* more material, the editor clicks on only the left or right roller, selecting a single roller. The single roller will allow material to be added (or subtracted) to the beginning or end of a shot without altering the surrounding shots. It will, however, alter the sequence's duration. Lastly, it's possible to change the beginning and end point within a shot without affecting the length or altering sequence duration. This is useful, for instance, in syncing a frame to a particular beat of music or sound effect. The single icon activation with the use of rollers allows the editor to work in the same area and quickly switch between trim modes.

In Final Cut Pro the editor must select from four different trim icons that launch from a separate tool bar or else use keyboard shortcuts (such as "r" for Roll). These perform similar functions but must be selected separately from a variety of complex-looking icons. In practice the system works smoothly once the editor becomes accustomed to the functions.

The first function is *Roll*. Roll is like the double roller function on the Avid. It overwrites or lifts and does not affect sequence duration.

In *Slide* mode the length of the shot doesn't change, but as the shot slides forward or backward, it alters the length of the preceding and following shots.

In *Slip* mode the internal length of the shot doesn't change, but the in and out points shift. If the shot begins 10 frames earlier at the head of the shot, it will end 10 frames earlier at the tail of the shot. This is the same as double-clicking on the rollers in Avid.

Figure 10.1 *Final Cut Pro's trim functions accessed from the Tool palette.*

Ripple is analogous to the single rollers of the Avid. As the Ripple tool is dragged forward or backward across the cut, it alters the sequence duration by adding or subtracting footage to the existing shot.

These are the practical considerations that editors must master, however, the aesthetic decisions comprise the most important part of the process, whether today or 70 years ago. What are the aesthetic choices that precede the physical act of trimming or lifting material from an editor's cut?

Tech Note

The revelation that allowed nonlinear editing systems to exist and to function as smoothly as they do runs counter to the traditional method of shot selection. Where the editor used to actually affect the physical media of every cut, marking with a white grease pencil the beginning and end of the shot, severing it from the whole with a splicer, moving it around, and attaching it to another strip of film, the nonlinear editor doesn't impact the actual media at all. In this system, the editor is only altering addresses that tell the machine where to find the media so it can display the various images. These addresses are the timecode numbers that relate to each frame of video. By altering the addresses, the order of images changes.

Before the friendly interfaces of Avid, Final Cut Pro, Premier Pro, Media 100, Vegas Pro, and others, the editor was compelled to type the beginning and ending timecode as well as the shot's duration for each and every shot in the entire movie. For instance, a desired shot might begin at 00:46:38:21 and end at 00:47:40:28. Its duration would be 00:01:02:07 or one minute, two seconds, and 7 frames. Mistakes occurred when the editor accidentally typed a wrong number, which was easy to do considering how many numbers there were! This was the case with the early Editflex or CMX editing systems. Since these systems couldn't store media on their hard drives, the numbers that were entered into a cut list referenced timecode on videotape or laserdiscs located on various decks. As the deck located the shot, it would record it onto a separate tape, where the sequence was compiled.

(Continued)

> **Tech Note** (Continued)
>
> What made subsequent systems much easier to operate was replacing videotape decks with hard drives and then adding virtual buttons or keystrokes representing mark in and mark out. When pressed, these virtual buttons capture the timecode that corresponds to the desired point in the scene. To play the scene back, the machine simply reads through the list of addresses and displays, in sequence, the corresponding images and sound. The fact that these simple text addresses can be stored in a minimum of space, using hardly any memory, provides an added advantage. Aside from making it easy to back-up or save the cut after each session it allows the editor, if he has identical dailies loaded into his home editing system, to work remotely between the studio and home. The days of an editor working in a dark little room are ending.

Trimming for Health

When we speak about trimming, we're not going to concern ourselves with one or two frame changes. Except in very specific instances, mostly involving comedic or musical timing, one frame doesn't make a difference. Beginning editors, and some directors, often obsess over whether to trim a shot by one frame or not (see Case Study, page 114, 115). We are going to think in terms of the overall performance or pacing.

> **Doctor's Note**
>
> Richard Pearson has likened the trimming process to moving Jenga pieces around. The more you can take out, the better off you are, but if you take out too many, it collapses.

In dialog, trims are essential because they help communicate the inner meaning of what is said. As will be discussed further in Chapters 11 and 12, the length of a character's reaction can communicate more about the dialog's meaning than the actual text. Consider Natalie Portman's revealing pause in Wes Anderson's *Hotel Chevalier*, a short film preceding *The Darjeeling Limited*. Jason Schwartzman's character, Jack Whitman, has been holed up in a fancy Parisian hotel for over a month when he gets an unexpected visit from a former lover, played by Natalie Portman. Later, as Jack sits on the bed undressing her, she asks, "Have you slept with anyone?"

"No," he replies. "Have you?"

After several beats she finally answers, "No." In that hesitation Jack and the audience realize that she's lying. "That was a long pause," he tells her. As their lovemaking continues, he finally says, "I guess it doesn't really matter." Immediately she replies, "No, it doesn't," and they tip back onto the bed. The lack of pause preceding "No, it doesn't" reinforces her anxiety to move past her previous fib and on with the matter at hand.

Likewise, in creating subtext through shot placement and length, the editor determines the precise moment to cut away to a reaction as well as the amount of time spent on that reaction.

In action, trims are important because they add to the scene's excitement. When cutting action, the editor's initial feat involves mapping out the movement so it makes sense throughout the course of the scene. After that he trims and trims until the desired pace is achieved.

Trimming involves a sense of timing. Every shot in the movie has an effect on every other. While the juxtaposition of shots remains one of the most potent aspects of editing, it is not everything. It is possible to have the correct sequence of shots, each perfectly placed beside the other, and still have a plodding cut. This is because another point on the Editing Triangle has been neglected. That is length. The length of a shot affects its meaning as well as the meaning of the shots around it. It also impacts the overall pace and rhythm of the film.

> ### FILM TIME
>
> Russian director Sergei Eisenstein realized that, through editing, the usual perception of time can be altered. He called this concept *film time*. A classic example occurs in his Odessa Steps sequence from *Battleship Potemkin*, where the Cossacks' murderous advance on the crowd extends well past the time their actions would actually take. Through this expansion, Eisenstein emphasized the pain and suffering of the populace.

Eisenstein's greatest theory, that of *film time*, directly depends on the trim function. In a sense, time is all that human beings have. How we spend it determines the value of our days. But chronological time is different from psychological time. Time as determined by a clock varies greatly from time as perceived by our minds. Our thoughts include the memories and experiences that affect how we perceive the world and our experiences within the world. Eisenstein's revelation that real time does not matter as much as perceived or psychological time informs editors' decisions to this day. The fleeting time one experiences over moments of great joy as compared to the seemingly endless time that weighs upon us when we're forced to endure an activity we despise or to suffer pain or sorrow reflects this notion.

In film, the increase or diminishment of tension and emotion relates directly to this sense of time. This is affected by the length of shots that in turn relates to the use of the trim function. The plasticity of film time exists due to the ability to extend or contract a shot or to add or lift multiple shots in a scene.

Tarantino and Time

Quentin Tarantino is one of the modern masters of manipulating film time. The opening scenes of films like *Pulp Fiction* or *Inglourious Basterds* succeed in part due to Tarantino's ability to extend the prosaic and seemingly neutral moments leading up to impending doom, thus creating excruciating suspense. In *Inglourious Basterds* the deceptively leisurely pace of the opening scene where the kindly dairy farmer Perrier LaPadite (Denis Menochet) is visited by the mild-mannered Nazi SS officer Colonel Landa (Christoph Waltz) goes on and on, far beyond the endurance of most scenes. Yet we cannot turn away from the frightening prospect that the Jewish family the farmer has sequestered beneath the floorboards will be viciously exterminated as soon as Colonel Landa finishes the second glass of milk he has so blithely requested from his host.

Later, the tables are turned as The Bear Jew (Eli Roth), a baseball bat–wielding executioner, is summoned to kill a captured Nazi officer who refuses to divulge the whereabouts of soldiers waiting to ambush the

Figure 10.2 Inglourious Basterds, *2009. Copyright © Universal Studios. Photographer: Francois Duhamel. (Photo credit: Universal Studios/Photofest).*

crew of Lt. Aldo Raine (Brad Pitt). Employing Kuleshov's juxtaposition of neutral images, Tarantino creates tension by cutting between the officer's paralyzed expression and vacant shots of a dark passageway where only the increasingly loud sound of a bat tapping against the brick walls captures our attention. What makes these scenes work is the juxtaposition of uninflected images and sounds combined with critical choices in terms of shot length. Too short and the effect is lost. Too long and the tension dissipates as the audience becomes comfortable with the image. The precise timing of each shot, determined by trimming, is what torques the tension to unbearable levels.

This approach has been variously misinterpreted, leading to what some refer to as "cinema irrité." In other words, rather than heightening the tension and propelling the scene onward, some directors and editors have achieved the opposite effect by heaping gobs of trivial and pointless chatter over a scene.

Case Study

I once had the disturbing experience of walking into the editing room of a director who'd been cutting alongside his editor. The producer had given him his own editing room, perhaps to get him out of the way. The sight that met my eyes was a large, wide fellow with meaty hands hunched over a flatbed editing machine with hundreds of single frame clips taped to the walls, windows, and trim bins. He'd been working on the same scene for weeks, cutting out frames here and there and then putting them back in, reminiscent of the torture of Prometheus. Ultimately, it didn't make much difference, and what he eventually presented as a fine cut was taken away from him by the studio who hired a film doctor to recut it. Obviously, there were bigger issues at stake than a frame or two.

Years later, when a film I'd edited was being conformed in order to make release prints, a visit to the negative cutter finally drove the point home once and for all. I'd stopped by on an emergency mission from the director to remove a scene before the film was sent to the lab for printing. I had a workprint with me as a guide so I could match the key numbers on the negative with their printed-through counterparts on the print. Also, since it was film, I could compare the images and scene changes on the negative with those on the celluloid print. After locking the workprint, negative, and soundtrack together in the synchronizer, I carefully began rolling down to the middle of the film where the designated scene lay. Long before I reached that point, however, I noticed something that sent a chill through me.

The negative was a slightly different cut than I'd submitted in my locked reels. At first the images on the negative had corresponded exactly with the images on the workprint. Then suddenly the cuts shifted. The shot on the negative ended a frame earlier than the shot on my workprint. And the next shot began a frame earlier. As I continued to roll through the reels, I found that periodically, throughout the course of the film, shots would end a couple frames earlier or later than my version. But by the time the next scene appeared, everything was back in sync. What had happened here?

The negative cutter had recut some of my footage! She was considered one of the best in the business, so I figured there must be some explanation. That, or she had secretly been recutting, improving upon editors' work like some elf in a workshop. I called her and asked what had happened. Because we were friends and she didn't want to lie to me, she told me the truth. She'd messed up and cut the negative a frame early. With a negative, unlike a positive print, you can't simply reattach it with a piece of tape. With a negative you lose a frame every time you make a cut in order to hot splice it to the next shot. The only way she could fix it and still maintain sync was to add a frame to the incoming shot. So now two of my shots were different from what I had originally produced. Since this happened periodically throughout the course of 12 thousand feet of film, there were numerous places where she or her assistants had performed repairs in order to rescue the flub.

Was this particular to her? No, she told me. All negative cutters do this. It's the law of the negative cutter's jungle. Nobody's perfect. But no one knows it because, to be frank, nobody ever notices a one-frame trim, not even the editor who cut the movie . . . unless, of course, he happens to put the negative and the workprint next to each other and compare!

The Lift

Letting go of good material can be a painful experience for filmmakers. Directors expend major portions of their lives getting a project greenlighted, conceiving the shots that will go into it, and executing those shots. One director, when asked what one item he'd want with him on a desert island, replied without hesitation, "My dailies." Yet some shots, and even scenes, do not belong in the final movie despite the fact that a director works tirelessly to achieve them. Nevertheless, this labor impels some directors to become overwhelmingly attached to their creations, like a parent to a newborn. For that reason, working with a trusted film editor is essential.

Doctor's Orders

When making a lift, be sure to save it in a bin, properly labeled.

Like doctors whose compassionate feelings have brought them into the profession yet must maintain a certain detachment in order to function effectively, the film editor works to remain objective. In terms of deleted material, the editor's and director's choices to make a lift are more drastic and less subtle than a trim. In a sense, a lift can be considered the gross adjustment on a microscope, while the trim is the fine adjustment. But why lift?

Wasn't this all worked out beforehand in the script? Wasn't it clear which scenes worked and which ones didn't? If we look back at the script where original scenes were laid down, we find that every scene and portion of a scene was deemed essential, probably after months of rewriting and polishing. So what changed when the film reached the editing room? The act of visualization. The moment the text gained texture through the visual medium, things changed.

Case Study

After months and months of receiving editorial first aid, a comedy had lapsed into a coma. Instead of improving with each cut, it was growing closer and closer to death. During the initial consultation the director revealed the following about the patient. Her initial approach was toward a zany comedy with lots of fun action, over-the-top quirky characters, and a good pace. She'd agreed to take the project because it offered challenges in terms of action and character even though there were some pretty stupid jokes, as well as gaps in the story that defied logic. By the time she'd completed her director's cut, she was feeling less than enthusiastic about the whole endeavor. A test screening reinforced her concerns. The recruited audience found the humor to be forced, the pace slow, and the story slightly confusing. A frantic and time-consuming return to the editing room unleashed a new version several weeks later. This scored even worse.

The audience found the comedy lame, the pace unbearably slow, and the story incomprehensible. At this point the director met with the producers, who were wary that they would lose their investment, and decided that while they liked the current editor and had promised to credit him on the film, they had to let him go. He could share the credit with the film doctor they'd brought in.

The film doctor's first action was to watch the film. Sure enough, the test audience had been correct. This editor sat down in the editing room with the director and asked her about the film. The director pointed out some of her chief concerns. In this meeting the editor discovered the following information—just as a doctor or detective might divine various clues that might not be obvious to the layperson. First, the director was aware of the film's slow pace. She'd intended for it to be a spirited romp, not the plodding disaster it had turned into. In an attempt to alleviate this condition, she tried some home remedies, as it were. Considering that the film was too long and too slow, she surmised that removing scenes would both pick up the pace and shorten the overall running time. After all, unlike action films or dramas, comedies usually clock in under two hours, generally between 90 and 100 minutes. So she bit the bullet—a phrase, by the way, that derives from old-time surgery without anesthesia where the patient held a bullet between his teeth rather than risk biting off his tongue from the pain. She combed through the film and lifted scenes that weren't absolutely essential. These were stored in a separate bin, labeled *lifts*.

In theory, this should have helped. In practice, it worked against the film. Why? Because as those scenes were removed, they took with them important story and character points. Just as removing a diseased kidney might save a patient's life, removing two kidneys would end it. Other scenes had been removed for the opposite reason. They had some amusing jokes, but they did little to forward the story. But without jokes it wasn't much of a comedy. So, in the hopes of improvement, the film's overall health had suffered. The viewer was left with all sorts of unanswered questions about the plot. Once the audience got lost and lost interest, their perception of the film changed. Even though physically shorter, the film's apparent length was much longer.

The solution came in the form of trims, not lifts. Since each scene contained either important story information or humor, they were all reinstated. But then the editor went through and trimmed everything he could. Entrances and exits disappeared. Pauses before and after speech disappeared. Redundant actions or dialog disappeared. Hesitations in order to allow perfect match cuts disappeared. And after a while the scenes gained new vitality. Instead of standing out like blemishes, they merged nicely with the overall complexion of the film.

Then the editor went back to the beginning and, starting from the very first frame, examined each and every cut, finding where he could nip and tuck. He trimmed until the overall film was not only shorter but faster paced and peppier. The increased energy fueled the jokes and performances, and soon the film played as a comedy should. In the next test screening it scored exceptionally high, a response that everyone had pretty much given up on ever seeing.

Sometimes it is hard to remain objective and unattached, especially after working on a film for a year, balancing your actions between everyone else's input and your own intuitions. One enters a "forest for the trees" state, where the editor, in a sense, becomes the film. One trick is to make notes during the first reading of the script. Often several questionable plot points, lines of dialog, or character motivations will jump out. After months in the editing room, sometimes it helps to check back with those early notes and see if the problems you initially spotted have been solved. If not, you have fresh questions with which to approach the material.

Another trick is to temporarily flop every shot in the movie. This alters the viewer's perspective, giving a fresh look to the film. Since all shots receive equal treatment orientations such as eyelines are not affected.

The Way of the Lift

A technical note about lifting scenes. In days before digital editing, a scene was removed intact, with both the workprint and the soundtrack rolled together and labeled with the scene number and a brief description of the lift. This was stored in a separate box on the film rack along with the film dailies and cut reels. In some cases, the lifts were duplicated onto black and white film (known as a *dirty dupe*) if the editor felt the scene might need to be revisited after the constituent parts were reconstituted into the original daily rolls for use elsewhere.

Today, it is still advisable to maintain this kind of order. Since nonlinear editing systems allow us to make as many versions as we like—a questionable advantage—it becomes possible to save the previous version without altering it. After backing up a previous version, however, it is a good idea to use the new version in the manner common to editors working on film. That is, make lifts in the new version and store them in a separate bin. This way you can keep track of every scene you removed without having to compare versions. If at some point you decide to add back certain footage, you have the luxury of the previous saved version as a reference.

Lift and Separate . . . or Not

Accomplishing these kinds of lifts requires not only the notion to do so but also a sense of how to create smooth transitions that weave one scene with another. Editor and post-production supervisor Norman Wallerstein views editing as a marriage. In good marriages, even if the couple is from opposite backgrounds, they find a way to make it work. In editing, you are often required to unite disparate shots or scenes that, while they want to be together, may not fit easily. The editor's job is to make the marriage work smoothly.

As noted before, a lift raises issues of attachment to good material. This is one of the reasons that directors who are fully capable of editing their films should not. Despite best efforts to remain objective, a director finds it hard to part with material, especially if it shines. On the other hand, some directors are all too willing to dismiss material, usually out of impatience. Where the camerawork or performance falls below their expectations, their immediate response is to lift it out. In this case the film doctor is sometimes confronted with a film that is unengaging as well as confusing. It is the film doctor's job to revive the patient.

Rx

Make a lift, and be sure to save it.

- Create a separate bin or folder labeled "Lifts."
- Mark in and out for the section to be lifted, choose Duplicate from the Edit menu, and drag the lifted scene into that folder.
- After the copy has been placed in the folder, press the X key or the Extract icon (on Avid) and remove it from the new sequence version.
- Some programs, such as Final Cut Pro and Media 100, use the cut function more like a word processor, in which case it's not necessary to duplicate the section before placing it in a lift bin. Instead, the marked section can be removed and then pasted into the lift bin.
- Whichever way you achieve this result, you'll know exactly what you'd removed from the first cut, if it ever becomes necessary to refer back or reinstate a deleted scene.

Chapter 11

Psychiatry of Character Disorders—Part I

Dialog

Well-written dialog evokes a sense of reality, even though it is, in essence, unreal. Where people in everyday life may speak on and on, in movies their dialog usually confines itself to one or two sentences at a time. In a sense, dialog is more about the listener than the speaker, since most of us, most of the time, don't listen well to anything that doesn't immediately impact us. Tell someone about how your day went, a dream you had, or what you did on vacation, and his attention drifts in and out. Tell that same person that the tests came back positive and they only have three weeks to live, and you have got his full attention.

With dialog we become distressed when too much information is crammed into one character's speech. As an audience we prefer to discover the betrayal, the attraction, the panicked warning through the back and forth pattern of conversation. In editing we also want to reinforce that enjoyment of making this discovery.

In the area of dialog cutting, digital nonlinear editing has produced several surprising developments. Even though other aspects of editing, such as action cutting, have also experienced a paradigm shift brought on by the digital dawn, their evolution has proceeded pretty much as could be expected. In the section on action editing we saw how instant access to diverse takes, a highly effective trimming system, and the ability to mock up effects, such as motion ramping and greenscreen compositing, have kicked down the doors of the traditional action sequence. It has fostered even faster chases, more daring escapes, and heightened devastation. But in the realm of dialog editing, the progress has been subtle, though perhaps of greater significance.

In the days of editing on film, a common deterrent to a well-cut dialog scene was the editor's unwillingness, uncertainty, or incorrectness in determining the overlaps. In a dialog scene, an overlap occurs when it becomes necessary to shift the audience's attention from the speaker to the listener. At the moment when Character A proclaims something of importance to Character B, the audience wants to see Character B's reaction, even while Character A is still speaking. What occurs in that character's reaction often tells us more about the scene and about the character than what the character has stated. If the character says, "Luke, I am your father," we want to see Luke's reaction.

The Healthy Edit. DOI: 10.1016/B978-0-240-81446-9.00011-1

The timing of the overlap with the reaction is crucial to the audience's understanding of the scene and the characters' involvement in it. While action scenes supply the excitement and thrills in many films, dialog scenes reveal the deeper meaning. To understand how film dialog communicates meaning, we first need to examine the value of subtext.

Subtext

Good writing, like good editing, is about relaying complex and even conflicting information in a subtle and interesting way. This is generally the realm of subtext. In the case of anthropology, the concept is known as metacommunication, the visual and auditory signals that we telegraph each other—wittingly or unwittingly—that underlie the stated message. *The Invention of Lying*, a comedy about a world where everyone says exactly what is on his or her mind, intrigues us because it runs counter to typical social interaction. In most cases, even a simple "Hello" can project all sorts of complex or hidden messages, as reflected in Dorothy Boyd's classic line from *Jerry Maguire*, "You had me at hello." Suffice it to say, how an actor delivers a line, how the other character reacts to the line, and how the editor places it in the scene are the essence of effective dialog.

Take another simple greeting that projected a much larger meaning in *Hotel Chevalier*. Jack Whitman reclines indolently on the king-size bed in his Parisian hotel room when the phone rings. In the wide shot he puts down his newspaper and picks up the phone. "Hello?" he says. A female voice on the other end says, "Hi." As the single syllable crosses the cut from the wide shot to Jack's tight profile, the drastic change of angle signals us that the caller holds far greater than passing significance for him.

The end of the Diane Keaton/Mandy Moore romantic comedy *Because I Said So* exemplifies the use of subtextual dialog to subtly communicate meaning. In it Diane Keaton plays an "overprotective, overbearing, over-the-top mother" and caterer with three grown daughters. Determined to find a good husband for her youngest daughter Millie, played by Mandy Moore, she resorts to all sorts of meddling, including interviewing perspective husbands whom she recruits through an Internet dating service. The story's middle revolves around two particularly eligible suitors, a successful and charming architect and a kind, devoted musician with a young son and little money. The audience senses that Millie really loves Johnny, the musician, even though her mother would prefer to see her with the wealthy architect. Eventually, she falls for Johnny, while maintaining the relationship with the architect to satisfy her mother. Everything goes fine until both relationships fall apart.

In the end, a heartbroken Millie is again alone, conducting a cooking class for the love-lost geriatric set. As she explains, "When you're cooking for one, it's important to look forward to the end result." At that point an off-camera voice, which we recognize as Johnny's, interrupts to say, "What if you want to make it for two?" The scene cuts to Johnny standing behind Millie's students. Then it cuts back to Millie as she replies, "It's a little more complicated, but it can be done." After that, Johnny approaches her, and they embrace and kiss. Though more overt than the subtext in a dramatic scene, this dialog displays an amusing and basic use of subtext. Rather than Johnny appearing and professing his love to Millie—perhaps after admitting he was wrong to leave her even after she'd admitted her love for him and explained why she'd been with the other guy whom she didn't care about—it's more satisfying to use the cooking analogies to fuel the meaning beneath the lovers' statements. "Cooking for one" obviously refers to Millie's lonely life. Here she is even teaching a cooking class to elderly people who have grown old perhaps without finding Mr. or Mrs. Right. Johnny's question about cooking for two offers the possibility that he and Millie might be together. Millie's final response, "It's a little more complicated, but it can be done," acknowledges the difficulties of being in a relationship but her awareness of its value and her willingness to commit to Johnny.

One of the best examples of good writing and dialog editing resides in the Mike Nichols film *The Birdcage* based on the play *La Cage aux Folles* and edited by the late Arthur Schmidt. Here, the editor's use of reaction shots injects the subtextual dialog with added meaning. In the long but compelling climactic scene, every character has something to hide. This scene epitomizes a wonderful exaggeration of life's subterfuges and stands out for its use of subtext and reaction.

Robin Williams and Nathan Lane play a gay couple, Armand and Albert, who own a thriving drag club in Miami's South Beach. The film opens with a musical number performed to the pointed lyrics of "We Are Family," before introducing Albert in the guise of the drag queen star, Starina. Initially we are introduced to the flamboyant, fussy, and colorful life of this successful gay couple. They're not prepared for the announcement by Armand's son Val—a child he fathered 20 years ago during a brief heterosexual relationship—that he's getting married . . . to a young woman. And not just any young woman; he's marrying the daughter of the ultraright-wing Senator Keeley played by Gene Hackman, a devout supporter of family values and cofounder of the Coalition for Moral Order. We learn that he has no sympathy for homosexuals, Jews, or liberals. Armand and Albert fit all three categories. This forms a perfect dramatic, as well as comedic, setup, bringing together characters from opposite ends of the social spectrum.

Figure 11.1 *Guests arrive for dinner in* The Birdcage, *1996. Copyright © United Artists. (Photo credit: United Artists / Photofest.)*

As the story progresses, Val pleads with his father to help make the meeting of the two families a successful one. In his mind that goal can be accomplished by portraying their household as a typical God-fearing, heterosexual American home, supporting the values that the senator holds dear. But at this point in the story a dark spot has already appeared in the senator's half of the yin yang. His colleague, Senator Jackson, has been found dead in a prostitute's hotel room. The Republican contingent, of whom Senator Keeley appears to be the most outspoken, is busy doing damage control. The senator welcomes the opportunity to get out of town with his wife and daughter and drive south for a dinner with his prospective in-laws in Miami.

As the senator makes his escape, avoiding the hungry reporters waiting in the snow outside his home, the action cuts back to Armand, sweating in the heat of South Beach, as he agrees to compromise for the good of his son. He'll portray himself as a typical male dad married to a typical female mom. He even goes as far as to enlist the help of Val's biological mother, whom he hasn't seen in 20 years, ever since the ill-conceived tryst that led to the boy's conception. Armand's live-in lover, Albert, who raised the boy, grudgingly agrees to make himself scarce and to allow Val's birth mother to take his place at the dinner. Further, Armand removes all suggestive objects, wall hangings, and books from their home, creating a sparse, spartan-like environment centered on a large cross hanging from the wall, despite the fact that he is Jewish. He has even agreed to alter the pronunciation of his last name, Goldman, to the gentile Coleman. All in all, the preceding action is a brilliant setup to the mayhem that will follow.

In the climactic dinner scene, the conflicting elements—liberal-conservative, gay-straight, loose-uptight, cold-hot, muted-colorful—all come together. As the evening proceeds, with the forces of deception hard at work, the tension burrows under each character's calm facade, and the audience delights in knowing what others do not. This knowledge, fueled by the reactions of the characters, unleashes an outrageously comical, barbed, and enjoyable experience. Early in the dinner scene, a long and rambling speech by the senator about his and his wife's car ride from the north to the south highlights the awkwardness and distance between the two families. It is told mainly in cutaways to the reactions of his listeners. The actual dialog is as neutral and prosaic as can be, but the characters' reactions tell an oblique and compelling story.

As the dinner proceeds and the senator pontificates about his concern for upholding family values, various incidents threaten to upset the well-planned evening. The pretend wife gets caught in traffic and will arrive late, the drag queen-turned-butler stumbles around and screws up the cooking, and reporters from the *National Enquirer* figure out where the senator has escaped to and follow him. At each tear in the fabric of deceit, the audience shares in the delightful suffering of the characters. At one point in the dinner, the quasi-butler has neglected to observe the dinnerware and serves his inedible soup in bowls decorated with Greek images of young men copulating. Though we never see what hides in the bowl, and the senator, having misplaced his glasses, thankfully can't make out the image, the audience, through the reactions of Armand, his son, and the son's fiancée, realizes what is depicted beneath the puddle of murky soup. When Albert, who's been sequestered in another part of the house, can't stand it any longer and finally prances onto the scene dressed in full drag, portraying Val's mother, another round of humorous reactions ensue. As Albert exuberantly introduces himself, even correcting the senator who calls him Mrs. Coleman rather than Goldman, Armand, the son, and the future daughter-in-law struggle to maintain the deception. Throughout the film the strategic use of overlapping dialog and reaction shots creates the subtext that fuels the scene.

The Overlap

But how does the editor know when to cut away from one character to another and how to overlap one character's dialog over the reaction of another character? For many, this process has evolved as a somewhat arbitrary decision. Convinced of the necessity to supply overlaps in order to maintain a scene's momentum, inexperienced or less expert editors will determine these moments based on whim, chance, or guess. The dictum to overlap is so deeply ingrained that many will not proceed to the next line of dialog without first considering an overlap. Yet this is one of the primary ills that film doctor encounter. In previous forms of linear editing, the condition was exacerbated. In the case of videotape, as mentioned previously, it was necessary to build the cut by laying down one shot at a time. This was accomplished by playing back the desired shot so it could be recorded onto a fresh roll of tape encoded with SMPTE timecode. Since the audio and video tracks were laid down separately at predetermined timecode spots, it gave the editor the option of inserting the video at a different position in relation to the audio, creating what is known as a *split edit* or *L-cut*. The tendency for editors, producers, and directors working in this manner to make *paper cuts* on a notepad, and then build the edit based on timecode notes meant that overlaps were built in as the cut developed.

Moviola editors working in film had a slightly different workflow, more akin to what would become known as nonlinear editing. The Moviola editor viewed individual takes by running individual rolls of workprint and soundtrack through the machine, marking the selected areas, and then cutting the film and attaching it to the previous shot on a roll. As mentioned earlier, experienced editors actually paperclipped the selected picture and track sections together to be assembled later by an assistant. Only after the film was physically spliced together did the editor see the outcome of his decisions. The discipline required a mindset similar to someone making paper cuts on video or to a chess player calculating many moves ahead so as not fall into checkmate.

To save time and to avoid making too many physical cuts in the film, many Moviola editors worked with a synchronizer by their side, building in the dialog overlaps as they went. Likewise with the linear-based KEM editor who was inclined to take a similar approach. With the introduction of digital NLE systems, it became even easier to build in overlaps along the way. But some of the best editors knew that the most effective way to cut overlaps on the first pass of a dialog scene was to not do so at all.

Why is this? Because overlaps supply emotion, feeling, and response. How can an editor accurately gauge the feeling of a scene and, by extension, the character's response without viewing it in the context of the overall scene? In this regard, it is better to cut the whole scene first before supplying any overlaps. This is particularly easy on a NLE system where subsequent trimming is easier than ever. Because of this, cutting dialog is the easiest and hardest procedure an editor can perform. It is easy because all one really needs to do in a two-person dialog scene is checkerboard the cuts onto the non-linear system's timeline—in other words, cut straight across without thought of overlapping back and forth from Character A to Character B and so on. Cut just before the character speaks, without extra air, and then cut out as soon as the character stops speaking. Proceed in this manner, back and forth, for each character until reaching the scene's conclusion. If using only one take per character, you can even expedite the process by cutting all of Character A's lines and assembling them like railroad cars. Then go back and cut all of Character B's lines, interspersing them with those of A. Using this approach it is possible to cut an entire dialog scene before lunch.

Of course, it is not quite as simple as it sounds. Each selection requires an evaluation of performance—a decision as to which take best serves the purpose of the scene. In this regard, many editors comb the variety of takes in search of the best reading for each line in the scene. Others, touting the integrity of performance, will settle on one take for each character and use that throughout the scene. The problem with this approach is that if the actor's intensity is particularly strong in one take, there may be moments, particularly at the beginning or end of the scene, where you need to ramp up or ramp down that intensity. If the actor has started at full throttle, in comparison to the scene's overall energy, the performance may seem one-note after a while. Regardless of the approach to selection, most of the editing time should be devoted to determining which performances best fulfill the needs of the story. Once this is clear, the pieces fall into place.

After the checkerboard is complete, it is time to sit back and watch the scene. Let the scene speak to you. This is where the next phase of cutting occurs. As you watch, you'll be struck by impulses that tell you *this is where to cut, this is where we need to overlap.* Watch carefully and trust your feelings. Maybe the actor says, "What do you think? Should I take the offer?" and your inclination is that you'd like to see the "you" he's referring to and see what he's thinking before he responds. So after the word "think," you cut away to the listener while the rest of the dialog, "Should I take the offer?" plays over the listener's expression. As the overlapped dialog finishes, the actor responds, "Sure. Go for it." But by the time he says this, the audience will already have a sense of his true feelings and the motivations for his response. This is the magic of overlapping.

The editor also encounters other issues of clarity in reviewing the scene. For instance, what if the actor in close-up says, "Someone sent me this photo of you. Can you explain who you're with?" It's an opportunity to cut wide to see the hand reaching into the purse and taking out the photo. Or maybe you don't need to establish where the photo resided and an even tighter shot, an insert of the hand holding up the photo, will work best. Or perhaps cutting the dialog too tight misses a needed beat that would allow the viewer to question the speaker's integrity or sympathize with his plight. By laying out the basic foundation for the scene, it becomes much easier to evaluate its needs and prescribe the proper audio and visual cues.

With the advent of digital nonlinear editing this highly linear approach to cutting dialog has been infused with new life—and almost by default. Because extending or shortening a clip in the timeline requires a separate procedure—an activation of the trim mode functions, whether in AVID, Final Cut Pro, or Premier Pro—the editor's tendency now is to proceed in the checkerboard fashion just described. Because the access to and selection of the material happen so swiftly, it is possible to throw together an initial cut in a matter of minutes. Often, without appreciating the underlying wisdom of this approach, the editor is compelled by the nonlinear system to cut the first pass in this manner, using straight cuts without overlaps. But generally it helps to understand why one is doing something, in the editing room as well as in life.

By discovering the underlying premise, one can carry the procedure through all times and places. In this way the insightful editor maintains the ability to address a variety of situations on various films rather than finding himself foiled by dependence on the elusive and unreliable pattern of habit. Yet, as in previous years, many novice editors still feel compelled by the urgency to overlap dialog and begin the procedure before laying down all the cuts. Again, this leads to confusion and, potentially, disaster. In viewing scenes constructed in this premature manner, an audience senses that something isn't quite right, even if they can't articulate it. In many cases, because they have the advantage of viewing a completed scene with no preconceptions, the audience unconsciously anticipates certain moves that, when they aren't forthcoming, frustrate their involvement in the movie.

Granted, at times it is advantageous to outwit the audience's expectations, as David Lean did with the clever cut in *Ryan's Daughter* where the audience fully expects the character of the British officer-turned-illicit-lover, Randolph Doryan, to commit suicide by igniting the dynamite and blowing himself up. But the scene ends before the anticipated explosion. Only in the next scene, from a distance, do we hear the powerful reverberation from across the landscape of a detonation. At other times it is best to jump ahead of the audience's expectations and, in a sense, beat them to the punch or surprise them. But in emotional scenes, where the realm of human emotion makes everyone an expert, generally it is best not to mislead the audience.

Exposition Infection

To the other extreme from good subtextual dialog lies excessive exposition. In dialog, the film doctor must beware of this particularly noxious infection. Once it begins to spread, it can take over and destroy its host in a matter of scenes.

What do we mean by exposition or expository dialog? Basically, it is dialog that explains what has happened, is happening, or will happen. The old tenet in television of "Tell them what they're going to see, tell them what they're seeing, and then tell them what they've seen" reflects this approach. Such a prescription posits that the audience is so stupid, presumably because only someone without much intelligence would buy the products advertised, that they had to have it all laid out for them like a TV dinner. In recent years, the proliferation of cable channels, including those that carry feature films; more film-savvy audiences; and greater competition have forced broadcasters to elevate their approach to TV writing. As the writing becomes more subtle, producers find that audiences gravitate toward shows like *Mad Men*, *House*, or *30 Rock*. On the other hand, purposely confounding an audience or keeping them guessing about essential bits of information can be deadly as well.

Show, Don't Tell

The often pronounced prescription of *show, don't tell* is particularly important with regard to a film story. What a viewer sees with his own eyes holds much more validity than what he's told. Experiencing a boxing match is much more satisfying, informative, and memorable than having it described to you. Even spectacular, highly visual films like *Avatar* have to wrestle with excessive exposition. The concept of the avatar, a host body possessed by a person's psyche, becomes clear when Jake Sully (Sam Worthington) enters the scientist's pod and finds himself transported among other avatars and, ultimately, among the Na'vi as one of their own. Yet a lot of dialog is expended explaining what the audience can easily glean through the stunning visuals.

If we look back at the earliest films, we are reminded that those filmmakers didn't have the luxury of sound to tell their story. Generally, these silent movies were accompanied by a musical score played live before the audience. The essential information that had to be communicated in words was displayed on title cards, some intricately drawn, some simple white text on black background. Even films like Charlie Chaplin's

Modern Times, appearing in 1936, a decade after sound had entered the arena, relied more on visuals than on sync dialog, even to the point of presenting title cards in place of some on-camera dialog. Either way, these filmmakers knew that if they piled on too many cards, it would interrupt the story's flow and disrupt the audience's involvement. The early Chaplins, Pickfords, Keatons, and others used these sparingly. The images on the screen had to tell the story.

The arrival of the talkies offered a great privilege to filmmakers, and some used it wisely, often enlisting the talents of great playwrights or novelists to craft the dialog. Others did not. Some silent film stars, who had grown accustomed to miming their way through a movie, had a hard time adjusting to sound. It revealed their unattractive voices and unconvincing speech. Silent film directors also struggled with the unforgiving demands of sound. Occasionally, it would go awry, as in the intriguing though overly long monologue at the end of *The Great Dictator* where Chaplin explains his philosophy to the audience. We must remember that as valuable as a message may be, it will mean more to an audience if they experience it for themselves. Filmmakers today would be well-served to consider the effectiveness of early silent films when deciding how much exposition they need to tell their story. (For more about expository dialog see Chapter 13, Page 145).

New Territory

Aside from bringing into common practice a process of dialog cutting that had been the purview of a select group of editors, digital editing has also made way for a sophisticated new dialog technique. For practical purposes, this method couldn't have existed before now. It involves the selective use of multiple dialog takes for multiple characters within a single shot. Where the option of multiple takes has always given a dialog editor the chance to select and craft performance throughout a series of close-ups or over-the-shoulder shots, computerized editing allows the determined editor to shape performances within a stationary 2-shot as well. One of the early proponents of this approach is the comedy editor Bruce Green, who has spoken about it on a number of occasions for my students. He originally used this technique in the Mark Waters film *Just Like Heaven*.

Generally, the shot consists of two characters engaged in conversation. Each actor depends on the other's performance as well as her own to make the scene succeed. Until now, if one character's performance is spot on but the other's is not, the take is either rejected or used with its compromised performance. But today the offending performance can be removed and a better performance substituted for one character while not affecting the other character in the shot. This is accomplished by splitting the screen in half and employing a different take for Character B than was used for Character A, while retaining both within the same frame.

Obviously, this technique can only work if the camera is locked down so all the takes are identical in terms of subject matter, framing, and camera steadiness. With the use of *motion control*, where a computerized camera mount repeats the exact movement, such as a pan or tilt, for each frame, conceivably the editor could combine different takes with identical camera moves within the same scene.

As this technique makes clear, the computer's ability to alter the frame through such effects as picture-in-picture, cropping, scaling, repositioning, warping, flipping, flopping, and so on affords the editor seemingly limitless control over the once immutable frame. Where previously any effects had to be produced by a film laboratory according to the editor's specifications and optical counts, now the editor can experiment freely, altering the frame at will. What he produces falls well beyond the means of earlier laboratories and postproduction facilities. In the coming years, with increased resolutions and decreased processing and rendering times, the picture editor will be able to output the final product directly from his editing machine, ready for screening. Currently, successful experiments, such as the combining of takes within one frame, must still be mimicked and the quality enhanced by a laboratory so the material can be used in a final theatrical release print. The main requirement, as in all film editing, still involves the aesthetic sense and skill to determine what constitutes a good performance.

$$R_x$$

- Dialog overlaps require a change in shot length.
- When you add to one character's shot, you must take away from the other character's shot in order to maintain sync.
- Film requires measuring the exact amount of frames to be added on one side of the cut and removing the same number from the other side.
- In nonlinear systems a sync change appears in the timeline as an offset in frames. Using the overwrite function avoids sync changes.

Chapter 12

Psychiatry of Character Disorders—Part II

Performance

Having discovered how best to arrange a dialog scene, one is still left with the overriding concern of performance. There are many decent actors, but a few are truly spectacular. Some are basically self-directed, while others benefit from the determined and dedicated attention of the film's director. A film consists of many characters, and some are better realized or better performed than others. Once the scene is in the can, it becomes up to the editor to make sure that the best performance is obtained. Some actors deliver their lines with amazing consistency. They've studied their part and know exactly what they're going for, beat by beat. In that regard, they've mapped out the entire scene so they know what they're feeling at each moment, from the beginning through the middle and into a new realization by the scene's conclusion. This, coupled with the director's choice of angles and camera movement, knit together to form the dialog scene. In *I Am Sam* Richard Chew utilized erratic, disjointed cuts combined with handheld camera work and the intense performances of Sean Penn as Sam Dawson, a developmentally disabled father of a smart daughter, and Michelle Pfeiffer, his pro bono lawyer, to project an impression of their tumultuous but sympathetic relationship.

Tracking the Beats

Actors often aim for actions that they want to accomplish in order to fuel the emotional life of a character. For instance, in one scene the actor may attempt to kill with words. In another she may want to seduce, or frighten, or hurt. The performance is like a road sign, signaling the editor to turn left here, slow down there, and stop here. When film composers construct a musical score, they not only think in terms of the rhythmic pulse of a composition but in terms of the story's plot beats. These alter the composer's tempo or melody at various junctures in the scene, just as actors take their cues from the story's twists and turns.

But what about less experienced or talented actors? What about performances that go awry for various reasons, such as poor directing or clumsy writing? For whatever reason—and the reason is of little concern to the editor—editors must sometimes deal with performances that fall wellbelow optimum. How does the editor craft a lackluster performance into something worthwhile, even moving, and if neither of those,

The Healthy Edit. DOI: 10.1016/B978-0-240-81446-9.00012-3

something that isn't laughable or obstrusive? There are many approaches to saving performance. These include substituting dialog readings, rerecording new readings, minimizing impact by shot size and selection, trimming or removing pauses, trimming or removing exposition, and so on.

Case Study

There are also the Hollywood factors that ignore true abilities in service of other considerations, such as hiring the producer's brother or the director's girlfriend. In *One-Eyed Jacks*, the lead actor who happened to be the biggest star in the world at the time, Marlon Brando, had a girl-friend. Her name was France Nuyen, and he expected to recruit her as his ingénue in a romantic role. When, among other initial suggestions for the role, the star tossed in her name, the original director, a young Stanley Kubrick, retorted, "Her? She can't act," which, in short, is why Stanley Kubrick didn't direct *One-Eyed Jacks* and Marlon Brando did.

Substitution

The tendency among actors is to give their finest performances in their close-ups. Some professionals strive for the best possible readings no matter what the camera angle. But once in a while an editor will decide that the wide shot best conveys the information needed at that point in a dialog scene. Along with effective camera angles, the actor's body language and movements also play an important part. But the line reading in the wider angles may fall far below the performances in the closer shots. In this case, it is wise to determine the very best reading of the line, no matter what angle it was shot at, and then use that reading to replace the lesser quality performance in the wide shot.

This serves two purposes. First, it enhances the overall condition of the acting by preserving only the best performance. Second, it creates consistency in audio quality. Since wide shots are often recorded using shot-gun microphones mounted on a handheld boom placed outside camera range, the sound quality has a slightly different resonance to it than those where the microphone is close to the speaker's mouth. In some cases this isn't disconcerting because the audience anticipates a certain shift in ambience when the view widens. On the other hand, a threshold exists where the sound's deterioration becomes distracting.

Doctor's Note

Lavaliers, those tiny microphones hidden beneath an actor's clothing around the chest area, are popular because they can supply superior sound when sent through radio transmitters. But they risk distortion from clothing movement or radio interference, and the editor must attend to that.

In the case of close-up dialog that is employed in a wide shot, the editor is almost guaranteed better sound quality and performance, and any slight perspective shift can be supplied in the final mix through the use of reverb and equalization. To accomplish the substitution, the editor relies on the consonants in the speech.

Since letters like P, G, K, and so on contain an innate percussion, they become the oral clapper sticks for a sound edit. What does this mean? Traditionally, in syncing sound to the picture, the editor locates the sharp snap of the sticks closing on the slate with the visual action on the film. At the moment the two sticks meet, he places the corresponding sound. Once these two are locked together, everything after the slate will be in sync until the end of the take. With sound effects, a door slam or gunshot is also placed right at the moment of impact or ignition. Dialog works the same way. In dialog, a consonant forms a specific shape on the lips. P tends to pucker, G tends to unfurl the lips and expose the teeth, and K separates the teeth. When the corresponding sound is placed next to this image, this acts as a reference point. Everything after that will fall into sync. To accomplish the task, editors become adept at lip reading.

When cutting on celluloid it is necessary to mark the consonant on the sound film and then mark the corresponding frame on the workprint, then line up the two, backspace to the beginning of the line, and then cut straight across, substituting the new sound film for the old soundtrack. Once this is accomplished, the two can be locked into step using sprocketed wheels as in a synchronizer or the KEM. On a nonlinear system it's even easier. As with the previous method, you locate the strongest consonant sound in the Source monitor, locate the same sound on the Record monitor, lock them together using the gang function, and cut straight across.

The Cutaway

One of the greatest saviors of dialog editing is the cutaway. Normally conceived of as an overlapping line of dialog combined with a reaction shot, a distinction arises based on intent. Where a simple overlap of dialog is standard procedure with well-shot, well-performed footage, in the case of film doctoring the cutaway to a reaction becomes the tool for salvaging poor material.

An example of this occurs in poorly trained or poorly rehearsed actors who forget their lines, thereby stumbling through them. Or it can arise in the case of well-trained actors who incline toward weighty, meaningful but deadly pauses and excessive emphasis. One time I had the privilege of producing and editing a film involving an Academy Award–winning actor who was along in his years. He still brought the same charm and color to his performance, but he experienced difficulty remembering his lines and had to pause frequently, often requiring a cue from the script supervisor. In editing his performance my opportunity to cut away to other actors or even to the environment made all the difference. While the actor was on track, I would stay on him, but the moment his performance began to waver, I would cut away to the listener. Then, while the speaker was off camera, I was able to cut out any pause and tighten up the reading or replace a misreading with a proper one. Since this surgery occurred invisibly, one might even say arthroscopically, by virtue of the fact that the words didn't have to sync with the speaker's lips but were hidden behind another's reaction in the cutaway, the sense was one of total fluidity. Once the actor was back on track, I returned to his coverage.

Proceeding in this manner created a surprisingly fine performance, and no one ever knew the difference. Of course, the only drawback came from the fact that the editor was compelled to cut away based on the need to dodge problems rather than motivated by an emotional need to see a reaction. It was rather like the difference between driving in smooth flowing traffic and driving where people are intoxicated. If you're alert, you have a good chance of making it to your destination, but you've had to do a lot more work along the way. Fortunately, in this case it was possible, by combing through multiple takes and readings, to bring the emotional need and the technical requirement into alignment.

In less drastic instances, this process of hiding dialog trims behind cutaways to another's reaction remains an excellent way to enhance a scene's pace. If possible, it is advisable to let the actor's performance influence the scene's rhythm, especially when working with well-trained or experienced actors. On the other hand, some well-regarded actors only come off well because of the editor's involvement.

Words Like Skin Tags

Another odd trait that crops up now and again is the tendency for actors to add a word or two to the beginning of a dialog line. Ancillary words such as "You know," "Well . . . ," and so on don't usually appear in screenplays because they're considered superfluous and time wasters. But some actors insist on adding them. They are as useless as skin tags and potentially as dangerous and should be excised. As with their biological counterparts, their removal makes for a smoother feel. For some actors the added words give them a running start, so by the time they hit the actual line, they're up to speed or into character. For the most part it is important to cut these out. I have known some directors who, aware of how these false starts can aid a performance, actually give an actor a word or even a sentence to say before the important scripted line. Again, in this case, the editor should refer to the script and cut out what shouldn't be there, unless specifically instructed to leave it in.

Improvisation

Improvised readings are a different case. Here, in an attempt to develop or enrich an emotion, to free up the actor's delivery, or to experiment with something new and unexpected, the director will encourage the actor to improvise the lines based on an understanding of the scene's overall meaning and intention. Some directors, especially those who are also writers and know the effort involved in finding just the right word to convey information, reject any attempt at improvisation and will even remind actors, "Just read what's on the page."

In the case of improvisation, it becomes the editor's task, sometimes in consult with the director, to determine the best approach and build a coherent scene from the various takes. The beautifully cut driving scene in Antoine Fuqua's *Training Day* where a veteran narcotics cop, Alonzo Harris (Denzel Washington), initiates his partner Jake (Ethan Hawke) into an acceptance of the law's gray area consisted, according to its editor Conrad Buff, of frequently improvised footage that had to be tailored to fit the scene.

An issue that comes up when cutting improvised dialog is the drastic variability of performance from take to take. Here it becomes important to determine beforehand where you want to end up and fashion the scene so it contains a natural arc, rather than flatlining with one emotion or erratically jumping from peak to valley throughout. With this in mind, it sometimes helps to cut the end of the scene first so you'll have a target to aim toward. Knowing how the scene will end informs where it will begin. If a scene needs to end on a high emotional note, then it might be best to start with more restraint. If a scene will end in a quiet, romantic kiss, maybe it should capitalize on a more fiery or impassioned improv in the beginning.

Bingeing

Another dialog challenge originates with the script. Screenwriters occasionally introduce extra character description and even dialog because they want to supply the reader with a vivid sense of the characters and their intentions by taking advantage of this literary component, aware that much of the information will later be clear through visual representation. Convinced that this material will enrich the script's marketability, writers sometimes binge when it comes to supplying conversation. Some writers expect that portions of dialog will be removed later on as the text is transformed into the visual medium of film, although they are often at a loss to tell you exactly which ones they'd cut out. Others, by virtue of tight deadlines that restrict revision time or who are not good enough editors, will pile on extra dollops of dialog. In some cases it may reflect the writer's state at the time. In the process of conceiving a scene, the writer allows the dialog to unfold until it encounters the essential part of the scene, which is probably where it needed to begin in the first place. In such instances, the film editor slogs through scenes that, while they make sense, are tedious. They hover around an idea or central conflict without diving into it. Here, perhaps in consultation with the director, the editor begins the task of trimming or rearranging excessive dialog.

Case Study

One example that was presented at a forum at the Sundance Film Festival following the film's presentation involved one of my earliest editing experiences on the film *Horseplayer*, a noir-like thriller directed by Kurt Voss. The dialog, an otherwise outstanding feature of the movie with its sparse, realistic tone, paled in one particular scene when compared with the others. In the scene preceding the one in question, the antagonist (Michael Harris), hunching over his drawing table with cigarette in mouth, orders his girlfriend, Randi (Sammi Davis), to fleece Bud the horse-player (Brad Dourif) of $2000. At first she resists, but eventually she submits to the artist's exhortations. Upon her agreement the artist leans over and plants a kiss on her lips, a payment for her loyalty. The next scene opens with Randi seated beside the horseplayer in his old car at the L.A. River. They're engaged in small talk. She asks him if he comes here to think, and he says he does. She asks him what he thinks about and he says that he doesn't know, he just zones out, and so on. Not terribly dramatic. The true substance of the scene occurs a page later when Randi says, "I want to ask you something," and requests two thousand dollars. At that point Bud reacts, surprised and chagrined. Initially he states that he doesn't have the money. Eventually he succumbs and says, "But I can get it." Like the previous scene, this one ends with the reward of a kiss.

The challenge in editing such a scene was that even though the director and producers agreed that the opening dialog didn't fulfill a crucial purpose and therefore could be eliminated, cutting directly into the middle of the scene would've appeared too abrupt. Upon considering this, I realized that the kisses could act as a transitional device. Why not steal the kiss from the ending of the L.A. River scene and place it at the beginning of that scene? This way it would create an associative cut, a smooth transition from one scene to the other. Since we'd seen the couple in bed together in a previous scene, there was no need to save

(Continued)

Case Study (Continued)

the kiss until the end, as one might in a story arc where two people fall for each other and finally give in to corporeal desires. Placing the kiss at the beginning meant that the girlfriend kissing her boyfriend segued to the girl kissing the horseplayer. Visually, it said much more than any dialog could. It created symmetry with the other scene by associating the ending of the last with the beginning of the next scene. It reinforced the conflict between the world of the horseplayer and the world of the artist. And it placed the girlfriend in the middle of the conflict. After deciding on this course of action—all before making even one cut—the only remaining challenge was to pull the couple apart following the kiss. After all, that's where the dialog would now begin. Since the kiss was originally designed to end the scene, there existed no coverage of Bud and Randi completing the kiss, then pulling apart in order to begin their dialog.

This was remedied by reversing the action. In one of the kissing shots, playing it backward supplied the necessary pull apart. In this way the scene began with a 2-shot through the car windshield of the couple kissing, mirroring a similar pose to the couple in the previous scene, then cutting in tighter to an over-the-shoulder shot of Bud kissing Randi. This was followed by a cut to an over on Randi. Since her shot had been reversed, the static part of the kiss played as normal, but after a moment she eased away and looked into Bud's eyes. (In the original shot, it began with a look, then leaning forward, she plants a kiss on his lips.) At that point, before it would continue to reverse and give away the trick, I cut to Bud's look and then to Randi's line, "I need to ask you something." With this revised opening, the sense was that they'd come down to this questionably romantic spot on the seedy shore of the L.A. River to make out. After the initial foreplay—a much more interesting prospect than idle chatter—she popped the money question. After that, the scene evolved exactly as written, ending with another kiss and finally a wide shot of the car framed by the urban river's graffitied concrete abutments, accompanied by the wonderful saxophone score by Garry Schyman (*Lost in Africa* and video games *Dante's Inferno* and *BioShock*) wailing over it. In the end, the two kissing scenes played very well together, and no one could imagine that they hadn't been originally conceived this way.

Tech Note

Today, on nonlinear systems, reversing action is easy to do. One merely accesses the motion effect or motion tab, places a minus sign in front of the 100% speed allocation, hits "enter," and watches as the clip runs backward. On film it's harder. If one were to turn the film around, splicing the foot of a shot where the head normally goes, the film would run backward, but the image would appear upside down. Only by handing the material over to a laboratory where the film frames can be rephotographed—but in reverse order on an optical printer—can this be accomplished. Either way, reversing the action through editing can solve some problems.

In Good Shape

The ability to shape performance remains one of the main attractions of feature-film editing. Commercials, music videos, and documentaries generally do not offer this aspect of craft to the editor. Their requirements vary, offering intriguing challenges but usually not the depth of feeling. For those who feel drawn by character and a character's relationship to story as it emanates from the internal and external struggles of human beings, the narrative film holds precedence. When considering character it is important to realize that the drama springs from three main conflicts.

First is the conflict between man and man, as in many martial arts films at the most basic level, where the characters actually go *mano a mano* with each other. Most action films present this sort of conflict. In *Taken*, for instance, a distraught but well-trained father fights human traffickers to gain the safe return of his daughter. *Star Wars, Quantum of Solace*, and even *Avatar* capitalize on this kind of conflict. More subtle and complex issues also arise from this kind of conflict, such as in *No Country for Old Men*. By extension this can include man against machine as in *Transformers* or man against monster as in *Alien*.

Second, another hotbed for conflict, is man against nature, as seen in such films as *2012, Into the Wild,* and *The Perfect Storm*. In these films the natural world challenges the adventurer or the one who has not heeded nature's demands.

The third main category is man against himself. Many dramas deal with this sort of conflict, such as *The Aviator, American Beauty,* or *There Will Be Blood*. While most popular films deal with the first two types, no good film is immune to the third type. Even if it is not the main plot focus, this inner struggle should manifest within the film. In this regard, *Star Wars*, with Luke's struggle to overcome the dark side and use the force to guide him, or Clarice's struggle with the uncertainties that have caused her to fall prey to Hannibal Lecter's influence in *The Silence of the Lambs* brings deeper meaning to these engaging stories. In fact, the inner struggle has found its way into films that in the past neglected, for better or worse, to deal with this aspect, such as the James Bond series. Part of the joy of film editing derives from finding those superb inner moments, subtle yet revealing, when a character shows us a glimpse into his or her inner life.

℞

When cutting improvised dialog, the editor must attend to shifts in tone, emphasis, rhythm, and structure. Unlike scripted dialog, which often has the advantage of careful rewriting and attention to detail that connects with the overall story, improvised dialog tends to go off on riffs and tangents, like well-played jazz. Its advantage resides in its spontaneity and originality.

Chapter 13

Genetics

Story Problems Inherent in the Screenplay

Film is a translation process. Each of the main creative participants has his or her approach to the material. The writer envisions the story from a blank page. She populates it with characters tormented by deep needs and overwhelming obstacles. She drives the plot toward an exciting climax and resolution. She gives birth to the beast. The director and director of photography transform the writer's words into performance and images through well-conceived camera work. The actors and settings bring life to the dormant words upon the page. And the editor takes all those images, all the action and dialog, and shapes them into a compelling structure propelled by a strong pace and rhythm.

Romeo and Juliet

One of the best and most blatant examples of this is Baz Luhrmann's version of William Shakespeare's *Romeo and Juliet*. Using the classic text of the timeless love story that was written for the Globe stage over 400 years ago, Luhrmann reenvisioned the opening scene to take place in a gas station among gangsters who wield mean-looking guns called Swords (to correspond with the bard's line "put down your swords"). The ensuing confrontation is described in Shakespeare's first folio with merely two words: *They fight*. Luhrmann, along with his production and costume designers, Catherine Martin and Kym Barrett, took those two words and developed a spectacular array of primary-colored costumes, pimped-out cars, fast-moving cameras, chilling images, and powerful performances.

The editor, Jill Bilcock, took the raw footage and built it into a highly compelling scene—a cascade of sights and sounds incorporating live action, titles, graphics, music, and sound effects. The sound editors, sound designer, and composer reinforced those cuts with dramatic sound and music. The crunching of a steel boot heel against a wooden matchstick resting upon cement is a particularly stunning and simple piece of sound design. The images fly past, the pace intensifies, and the cutting erupts with the same explosive quality as the on-camera explosions.

The Healthy Edit. DOI: 10.1016/B978-0-240-81446-9.00013-5

Through a scene such as this we see how the translation process nurtures the film, coaxing it through various stages of development like a child growing into an adult. Finally, it is released into the world.

Inherited Traits

When it comes to human ailments, scientists remind us that many maladies are caused by bad habits, such as smoking, overeating, and lack of exercise. But a significant percentage of all disease has nothing to do with lifestyle issues. Unfortunately, some people can eat a vegan diet, run five miles a day, and never smoke, yet still contract heart disease, cancer, or other afflictions, often the same as their parents or grandparents. These hereditary ills are passed down through the genes, encoded with defective chromosomal structures that tick like a clock waiting for the moment when they will burst onto the scene. Where do these come from? It is hard to say, maybe back in the dark recesses of one's ancestry. We all, to a greater or lesser extent, benefit and suffer the influence of genetic traits. In terms of filmmaking, the screenplay is the heritage for all narrative motion pictures.

In the chromosome-like words dispersed across the screenplay page, the structure of the future living film is determined. If something goes amiss here, it will eventually have repercussions somewhere else. That is why it is crucial to have a well worked out screenplay before the cameras roll. It is also why the shooting script often looks different from the original script, which had good characters, a unique premise, compelling action, and a satisfying ending. It worked well enough to be sold and to convince producers and distributors that it was worth investing immense amounts of money and time. Then, as other creative people became involved—the actors, director, cinematographer, production designer, and so on—new ideas began to emerge. These ideas became colored pages, first blue, then pink, then yellow, and so on until many revisions and perhaps a writer or two later, the final shooting script appears, complete with numbered scenes and a production company's name stamped on it. At this point the script has evolved into as near a perfect document as possible. Through countless hours of writing and rewriting, with input from other sources, it has acquired a kind of god-like grandeur that, at times, appears more than human. How could one person sit down and write such a marvel? Even if the credit rightfully remains solely with the original writer, he has had the advantage and disadvantage of countless ideas and revisions. Yet this is only the beginning.

Unlike a novel, poem, or short story, which are ends in themselves, a screenplay is an outline for something larger. In fact, producers and directors often scoff at screenplays that offer too vivid and literary descriptions or that seek to outline the action too specifically. The best screenplays are sparse on description and allow the characters and dialog to speak for themselves.

To complete its life cycle, however, the script has to be shot. And what is shot must be edited. And here is the rub. Some scripts that look brilliant on paper do not translate well to film. In fact, the more literary the script, the harder it may be to translate onto film. Depending on the producer and writer, some scripts are better refined than others. Studio films, because they have access to the top writers in Hollywood and the money to pay for them, often derive from painstakingly crafted scripts. They're high concept with complex plots, subplots, and clever, subtextual dialog. Yet they sometimes suffer from lack of daring or originality. A vintage cartoon shows a studio executive seated behind his massive desk and tossing a script back to the hapless writer slumped in his chair on the other side of the desk. The caption reads: "We can't do this. It's never been done before."

Independent screenplays, on the other hand, may suffer from less experienced writers, tighter completion schedules, and a minimum of budget, critique, and input. Yet films like *Pulp Fiction*; *The Cook, The Thief, His Wife and Her Lover*; *The Blair Witch Project*; *Sex, Lies and Videotape*; *El Mariachi*; *Slumdog Millionaire*, and countless others issue from parents with independent sensibilities. In the end, all screenplays end up as dailies on an editing machine somewhere. Yet, because a screenplay is not the end product, it mutates like a salmon as it swims upstream through the driving currents of production and postproduction. And as it mutates, those questionable genes that lay dormant in its structure begin to emerge. In some cases, they corrupt the body of the film. Despite all the time and attention that went into nurturing it, vaccinating it, feeding it organic pabulum, and taking it to the best schools, the script may go astray. Editors are often amazed how the problems that emerge on the Avid were never caught before entering the editing room. In a strange way, however, the problems may not have existed before then. They lay dormant, waiting to be visualized and turned into something tangible that can be seen, heard, and discussed.

But sometimes story problems of a more chronic nature rear their heads following production. Here, the editor or film doctor must resort to all the tools in his black bag to solve the issue and forward the story. One such case occurred during the editing of the indie film *Horseplayer*, starring Brad Dourif (see Case Study, below).

Case Study

The first feature film I edited by myself, *Horseplayer*, came from a cleverly conceived script by the film's director, a keen observer of human nature. It contained all the elements of a good indie film: unique, intriguing characters, edgy dialog, quirky plotlines, a strong existential theme, and a minimum of locations obtainable on a small budget. It had a thought-provoking theme about the power and selfishness of art and artists.

The story centers on a fellow, Bud, who likes to play the horses but, it seems, has a shady past. When the story opens he's working in a liquor store run by George Samsa (wonderfully portrayed by Vic Tayback), a large, fatherly boss with a quasi–Middle Eastern accent. Bud works hard trying to maintain his fragile stability, aided by the kindly boss who looks out for him, even bothering to remind him to check in with his parole officer. Along comes a young couple, Matthew and Randi, played by Michael Harris and Sammi Davis (the darling English actress who eventually became the director's wife). Matthew is an artist who paints wild, impassioned canvases, while his girlfriend, who he portrays to others as his sister, helps raise funds for his artistic endeavors. In the horseplayer Matthew discovers a prime subject for his art. He insinuates himself into his life, even to the point of giving him his "sister" and secretly stealing articles of his clothing. As their obsessive relationship builds, the girlfriend uses her association with Bud to bilk money from him, a couple of hundred dollars at first, then more (see Case Study, Chapter 12, Page 135). This money helps buy the paint, canvases, and brushes that the artist uses in his artistic study of this strange character. Bud would rather just be left alone, but this nefarious couple is relentless. As they continue to prey on him, they steal

(Continued)

Case Study (Continued)

not only his money but his soul. Eventually, the girlfriend pops the big question, "I need more money ... two thousand dollars." The horseplayer informs her that he doesn't have that kind of money, but not wanting to lose her affections, he promises her he can get it. He intends to borrow it from his employer.

In a crucial scene, the increasingly unstable horseplayer returns to the liquor store and asks his boss for the money. When George informs him that he doesn't have $2000, Bud doesn't believe him. He demands that he open the safe. At this juncture a critical plot point occurs. The two get into an argument, and, according to the script and the dailies, Bud lifts a figurine off the counter, threatens the unrelenting boss, and then clobbers him to death with it. Then he drags the body out to his car, tosses it in the trunk, and speeds off to the L.A. River, where he stows it among heaps of trash in one of the alcoves along the graffitied cement banks of this urban tributary. As the body flops into the refuse, we notice the hand of another of Bud's victims lying close by. It is a fairly intriguing and grisly scene but not appropriate to the story as it was developed.

As I was cutting the film, I plowed into this scene. Everything stopped. Up to this point I'd been involved in the tale, sympathizing with this hapless loser, Bud who was trying to get his life together while being preyed upon by a nasty, egomaniacal artist and his girlfriend. My other sympathies were with the liquor store owner, a decent enough guy who'd basically acted as a surrogate father to his troubled employee who'd been abused by his own father. A good little story. But now the dailies were asking me to kill off a character I liked, a character whose murder would instantly destroy any empathy I had for the perpetrator, Bud. After all, George had been kind enough to hire an ex-con, pay him a decent salary, look out for him, and befriend him. The one who deserved the horseplayer's vengeance was the evil artist. But what was one to do? This was the film, as shot. And, considering the low budget, there was no money for reshoots.

I called the producers and the director and discussed these issues with them. We all agreed that we'd taken a wrong turn and that somehow we needed to get the story back on track. But how? We had to cut out the murder. Once we cut out the murder, a major lift, we had to cut out the following scene where Bud drags the body to the car. And the scene after that where the body is dumped by the river also had to go. But if you cut out the murder scene entirely, you were left with some major gaps. First, what happened to Bud's promise that he'd try to get the money? Second, why wasn't the boss in any of the film's subsequent scenes? Third, why didn't Bud ever return to the liquor store?

This is the issue that one often encounters when it comes to making lifts. As much as some scenes might appear to slow the film down or smack the plot's trajectory in the wrong direction, they often contain bits of valuable information. Otherwise the writer probably wouldn't have included them. So, in the case of *Horseplayer*, what could we do to maintain the audience's sympathy for the protagonist, their distrust of the antagonist, and their connection to the story in general?

Where the Answer Lies

As is usually the case, the answer resided in the dailies. I watched the dailies over and over, searching for a solution. One finally made itself known. There was one take where the camera operator hadn't heard the director call "Cut!" and had waited to turn off the camera. By some wonderful fortune, it was the scene where Bud yells at his boss, brandishing the figurine and threatening to kill him with it. At "Cut" the actor broke character, lowered the figurine, relaxed his emotions, and turned away. That was all that was needed to recut the film. The initial scene would remain. It would still escalate in the same way, the two men shouting back and forth, one demanding the money and the other insisting that he didn't have it and ultimately firing the other from his job. Then, at that crucial moment, the moment when all seems lost, the moment when Bud raises the weapon and is about to bring the porcelain Indian crashing down upon his boss's bald skull, he realizes what he's doing. He realizes that he's relapsed into his old ways, that he's about to murder a man he truly likes, that he's been defeated by his own desires and lack of ability. He lowers the figurine and turns away as his boss, in a close-up, growls at him that he's a "punk, a dirty snot-nosed punk."

At that point, rather than losing all sympathy for him, the audience feels for the poor horseplayer who had tried to get his life together but had been hoodwinked by the artist and his girlfriend and whose impotent rage and attempt to impress the girl has lost him his job. Because of all this, he now endures the further verbal abuse of his boss. It's all there, without it being stated in words, but revealed in a series of cuts. The boss's last line was stolen from an earlier part of the scene where he curses Bud in a medium shot. The close-up was held in reserve until the very end of the scene where it could be most effective and, considering the change in angle and reading, it appeared to belong to that part of the scene.

The actual murder, of course, was lifted, as were two subsequent scenes of removing the body under the cloak of night and stowing it by the river. The scene that followed these—Bud pacing his apartment in desperation and confusion—fit perfectly and suddenly had a whole other meaning that the audience was at liberty to infer. We never expect to see the boss or the liquor store again because we saw Bud fired during the altercation, so that solved the issue of the boss's disappearance from the film. And, since the boss never gave Bud the $2000, a later scene where Bud tells Randi, "I couldn't get the money," remains unaltered. All the anger and frustration that has brewed in Bud's character is eventually unleashed, and the artist gets his comeuppance. When the artist's body is tossed in the rubble beside the L.A. River, it was simply a matter of enlarging the frame to remove George's body, who, through the magic of editing, has survived to sell more Jack Daniels.

This helps illustrate one of the more extreme, but hardly rare, applications of cinematic surgery: the use of lifts to enhance and clarify a story's meaning and character while keeping focused on the movie's spine. In the case of *Horseplayer*, the film gained the attention of a popular band, The Pixies, who supplied the songs accompanying the edgy score by Garry Schyman. *Horseplayer* became an Official Selection of the Sundance Film Festival and eventually received a domestic theatrical release, garnering many excellent reviews including from the *Los Angeles Times*. I doubt this would've happened if the murder scene hadn't been surgically removed in the editing room.

The Montage

In some cases the script includes a montage as part of its original outline. In other cases the montage enters the film in postproduction as a solution to matters neglected in the script. Either way, the montage is a story element that depends upon execution to make it work. As an editor's tool the montage can serve many purposes. In most cases it shortcuts what would amount to excessive screen time.

Editing's ability to expand or contract time becomes evident in the use of the montage. As *South Park* originator Trey Parker wrote in his lyrics to *Air America*'s montage sequence, "Anything that we want to go, from just a beginner to a pro, you need a montage." A montage is a way of condensing film time to show a progression that would take too long if pictured in detail.

Some montages, such as the exploits of Max Bialystock (Zero Mostel) in Mel Brook's classic *The Producers* as he bilks old ladies out of their money in order to finance his anticipated flop of a musical, amplify a particular aspect or process. In themselves the mini-scenes that compose these montages are devoid of the usual arc or development associated with a fully realized scene. They hover on one idea, reinforcing it in an intriguing or, in *The Producer*'s case, humorous way. Likewise, the news montage in *Ghostbusters*—a throwback to the spinning newspaper headline montages of earlier films—begins with a news reporter announcing the team's exploits and then transitions, via headlines that slide across the screen from *USA Today*, *New York Post*, *Time*, and so on, to shots of the Ghostbusters' vintage Cadillac racing to haunted locations and other images of the paranormal exterminators in action.

Other montages depict a progression of actions that would prove tedious to watch in their entirety but are informative and even compelling in small doses. *The Blind Side* used a progression of images set to Sean Tuohy's recitation of "The Charge of the Light Brigade" to recall Michael Oher's development from abandoned child to star athlete.

As with the sugar-coating on a bitter pill, stringing glimpses of nondramatic activities together with dissolves or straight cuts can help them go down easier. This type of montage is common in the getting-to-know-you sequence often found in love stories or romantic comedies. Mindful that the repeated encounters that contribute to intimacy are a necessary part of mating rituals, the writer feels compelled to sketch out multiple cases where the lovers can get to know each other. Unfortunately, quiet dinners and walks on the beach, which may be fascinating to those involved, prove less so to outsiders who view them. So rather than force the viewer to endure the generally conflict-free pleasantries of early courtship, the editor will accelerate the process through a series of brief images culled, at times, from larger scenes.

In the classic "Raindrops Keep Falling on My Head" montage from *Butch Cassidy and the Sundance Kid*, Butch Cassidy (Paul Newman) and Etta Place (Katherine Ross) gambol across the Wyoming countryside on a bicycle, pick apples, and enjoy each other's company in the absence of their mutual friend, Sundance (Robert Redford). In the same film, a montage of sepia photographs depicts Butch, Sundance, and Etta on a sojourn to New York before journeying by steamer to South America. The images' effectiveness prompted Vincent Canby of *The New York Times* to write, "The stills tell you so much about the curious and sad relationship of the three people that it's with real reluctance that you allow yourself to be absorbed again into (the film's) further slapstick adventures."

Other montages fill in important information or backstory by blending a series of incidents, often with a voiceover narration from one of the characters, as in the second Harry Potter film, *Harry Potter and the Chamber of Secrets*. Toward the middle of the film Harry Potter (Daniel Radcliffe) and Tom Marvolo Riddle (Christian Coulson) come upon the inert body of Ginny Weasley (Bonnie Wright) lying beside a pool of water in the Chamber of Secrets. In a flashback montage, 16-year-old Tom reveals answers to all the questions that were raised during the course of the film involving Ginny. While under Riddle's influence, we see her open the chamber, write messages in blood on the walls, and petrify Filch's cat, Mrs. Norris.

The elemental draw of the montage can be so compelling as to become a setpiece for the entire film. Consider the opening montage in *Apocalypse Now* choreographed to The Doors' song "The End." Or the riveting ending montage that accompanies the assassination of Robert Kennedy in *Bobby*. According to editor Richard Chew, it was one of the elements that initially attracted him to the script. Chew composed a gripping montage that follows the immediate aftermath of Sirhan Sirhan's fatal assault set to the powerfully eloquent speech delivered by Robert Kennedy on the occasion of Martin Luther King Jr.'s assassination.

Doctor's Note

In trying to overcome writer's block when crafting the script to *Bobby*, the writer/director Emilio Estevez checked into a hotel in the California coastal town of Pismo Beach. While there, he discovered that the woman at the reception desk had been at the Ambassador Hotel the night Kennedy was shot.

A Telling Story

Syd Field, in his classic book on screenplay writing, points out that audiences are willing to invest the first 10 minutes before judging a film. In screenplays it is important to grab the audience from the beginning, while establishing the story problem that must be solved within the last moments of the film. A major problem that arises in screenplays that don't work well comes from not knowing where to start the story and, once started, not having compelling enough scenes to hold the audience's attention. Movies and the scenes within them suffer from starting too early into the story or giving too much information up front.

Information

Expository dialog strives to explain rather than allow the characters' actions to show. Compare the opening scenes of an otherwise well-made film, *Taken*, with some of its later scenes. The early scenes are used to set up Bryan Mills (Liam Neeson), a former spy, and his problem: he's divorced from a wife (Famke Janssen) who went off and married a rich businessman (Xander Berkeley) because Bryan didn't spend enough time with her and her daughter (Maggie Grace). The difference between the scene where we learn that he's a retired spy and the scene where we learn that he's estranged from his wife and daughter points to the issues confronting the first 10 minutes of a film. The former information is related over a barbecue scene with his beer-drinking buddies. In it there exists basically no dramatic conflict, and the dialog blatantly explains who these people are. The film really begins to take off in the next scene where Liam goes to deliver a modest birthday present to his daughter at her extravagant birthday party. The nasty ex-wife tells him to leave the present on the table with the others, and the tension between them becomes immediately palpable.

Good writing leaves out information. It makes the audience crave for it, rather than dulling them by inundating them with facts. It straddles the line between clarity and confusion. In this way some films begin too soon. We see the writer at work, figuring out who his characters are, what their histories are, and where they are going. Sometimes it is best just to cut out those moments or, at least, severely trim them.

Narration, of course, is one of the most blatant forms of exposition. Because essential information is missing from the action in front of us, the filmmakers have chosen to explain it through narration. This works well, generally, in documentaries, where the demands of continuity prove less stringent and because interviews, not dialog, forward the story. In some cases, narration can work. Look at the opening of *American Beauty* or *Apocalypse Now.* Or the ending of *Up in the Air.* In other cases it demeans the audience's ability to glean what they need to know from the action. For a prime example of the dangers of exposition, look at *Angels and Demons,* the first half of which is weighed down with explanations, theories, and blatant messages.

As happens with films that rely on exposition, the emotion can dissipate, leaving the audience disengaged. A film's message resides in the audience experiencing the outcome of desire, whether the urge to solve a mystery, extract revenge, marry the right person, amass a great fortune, or rule the world. The audience experiences this through identification with the main character or protagonist. The struggles of the main character become their struggles, reflect on challenges in their lives, and, at the resolution, shed light on their own problems.

All these aspects reflect influences of the original story as written. In some cases the movies evolve from an original screenplay. In other cases the story can trace its lineage back to a novel or short story. But in any case, a perceptive editor can help solve the issues of heredity.

Check out a variety of film montages:

- *Princess Diaries* makeover montage
- *Dirty Dancing* falling in love while training montage
- *Ghostbusters* news montage
- *The Blind Side* college recruitment montage
- The Rocky series, especially *Rocky IV*, training montage
- *Harry Potter and the Chamber of Secrets* reveal-of-information montage

Chapter 14

Cardiac Unit

Pace and Rhythm: The Editor's Unique Tools

Like a patient hooked up to a cardiac monitor, a film can display an energetic and lively pace or it can flat-line. When that happens, the momentum dies and the rhythm falters. The film becomes a chore to watch. Through the use of shot selection, length, and juxtaposition, the editor pumps life back into the film. The power of rhythm and pace, that visual music that resonates on a deeply primal level, exerts such enormous influence that it is sometimes possible to overcome lapses in other areas, including story, through the creative and determined application of these qualities.

The dynamic 1980s film *Flashdance* entered life with a deluge of damning reviews, with *Variety* leading the way by calling it "virtually plotless, exceedingly thin on characterization, and sociologically laughable." Critic Roger Ebert even went so far as to suggest that its naturally talented star, Jennifer Beal, find "an agent with a natural talent for turning down scripts." Yet the movie overcame its negligible story by force of the editor's art. For its time, the film's pace was dynamic, the rhythm infectious, and the images compelling. Appearing only two years after the launch of a new cable channel known as MTV, *Flashdance* alerted audiences and critics to a fresh era in filmmaking. It defied conventional genres. If it was a love story, where was the plot? If it was a musical, why didn't the characters sing? Despite the fact that many reviewers criticized it for its banal and sparsely developed plot, all had to acknowledge the film's overwhelming success with audiences. By the end of the 1980s the film had become one of the most profitable motion pictures of the decade.

In this film, editing to the visual rhythms of dance wed with the exciting tempo of music contributed to an expansion of the postproduction art. *Flashdance* was nominated for the Academy Award in film editing and, though those awards sometimes ignore the year's best achievements, it became a barometer of films to come.

Doctor's Note

A lot has been written and discussed about the MTV style of editing. MTV editing has become another way to say fast-cut montage with music. But MTV, which is to say music videos, doesn't

(Continued)

The Healthy Edit. DOI: 10.1016/B978-0-240-81446-9.00014-7

Doctor's Note (Continued)

necessarily rely on fast cutting but on another editing concept that's been known to documentary filmmakers for decades: dynamic editing. As far back as Robert Flaherty's classic *Nanook of the North* or Buñuel's surrealist narrative *Un Chien Andalou*, the dynamic style of editing has applied. It melds disparate elements, linking them together through meaning rather than movement, through association rather than identification, through impression rather than narrative. Where continuity editing relies on matching repeated actions so they overlap from shot to shot, dynamic editing strings together a variety of images that are related by other terms, such as narration or musical lyrics. Jump cutting, now an accepted technique, harks far back to the French New Wave of the 1950s.

What some producers and film theorists refer to as MTV cutting is actually old editing techniques applied to a new commodity, the music video, as it appeared on MTV. Editing has always sought to achieve sparseness, to pare down to the essentials. In the sense that music videos are essentially montages set to music, this approach has entered into films from time to time, well before MTV, including the Beatles movie *Help!* or even the erotic sequence in the 1970s horror film *The Wicker Man*, in which a naked pagan dances out a spell on the other side of a wall from an investigating police officer. The music montage uses a variety of images, often in close-up, that transcend temporal and spatial considerations, and all set to music. The music video adopted a film convention and made it its own, not the other way around.

A note on close-ups: The predominance of close-ups in this type of editing isn't coincidental. It derives from the fact that close-ups, by nature of their image size, reveal more information in a short period of time. This phenomenon extends into the montage or music video sequence, where the cuts are often fast enough to require close-ups. Another aspect of the close-up is the intimacy and detail that it affords. As film moved away from the proscenium arch of the theater (such as in *the 1902 film Jack and the Beanstalk*) to active cutting, as in D.W. Griffith's *The Birth of a Nation*, tighter, more revealing angles became a necessity.

Case Study

Years ago, having already signed my contract but not having yet begun production on a Colin Firth feature, the producer called me into his office. The conversation went something like this: "You're not going to cut this thing like MTV, are you?" His tone and framing of the question assured me that I wasn't. So I replied, honestly, "No." "Good," he said, satisfied. Then I went ahead and cut it by what he probably would have considered MTV style, which is an energetic pace with short cuts that capitalized on the variety of angles the director had supplied. Some scenes even possessed jump cuts. When the day came for him to view the completed cut, the producer, in passing me on the way to the screening room, reminded me of his admonition, "No MTV, right?" I nodded. He sat down, the lights faded to black, the movie began, and he was treated to 100 minutes of fast-paced footage, consisting of over 2000 cuts, reinforcing a well-structured story and compelling characters. When the lights came up, he applauded. He turned to me and said, "See, it worked. You followed my advice." The point here is that the cuts worked, the story had a smooth flow to it, and the characters were engaging, partially because of the plethora of close-ups and variety of coverage to flesh them out. Because it worked, the producer was unaware of my use of MTV editing, as it were.

Visual Music

Since editing presides over a film's rhythm, it is often spoken about in musical terms. At the 1997 Academy Awards show, the presenters sought to illustrate the power of editing by equating it to dance, inviting Michael Flatley's Lord of the Dance troupe to stomp out the filmic rhythm to music. In fact, editing styles are often referred to with musical terms, such as *staccato* or *upbeat*. In an *L.A. Times* article, Director Arthur Penn, referring to his collaboration with editor Dede Allen on *Bonnie and Clyde*, commented, "What we essentially were doing was developing a rhythm for the film so that it had the complexity of music."

One of the finest compliments a composer can pay to an editor is that his cuts are easy to write music to, inferring that the film's pace and rhythm follow a definite and compelling pattern. The cuts flow with a music-like melody, and their tempo develops in a cohesive manner.

A wonderful tribute to the music of editorial rhythm occurs in the French film *Delicatessen*. Here, a series of associative cuts, growing shorter in duration and tighter in angle, build to a literal orgasmic climax. The action takes place in a bizarre tenement-like apartment building. In this scene, the main character, an unemployed clown (Dominique Pinon) applies a paint roller to the ceiling, then pauses and removes his suspenders. CUT TO:

- TIGHT 2-SHOT: A man and woman, kissing and necking, tip out of frame
- MS: The bedsprings give under their weight
- WS: The painter, tethered from the wall by his suspenders, paints the ceiling
- PAN of bedsprings shifting up and down, PAN to open shaft
- PULL BACK from vent in another apartment: The rhythmic sound of bedsprings meets up with a MS of a young woman playing a cello in her apartment, the bow drawing back and forth in rhythm to the creaking bedsprings
- CU: Bedsprings
- MWS: A woman swatting a dusty rug slung over the banister, in rhythm
- MW 2-SHOT: In another apartment a young man pumps up his bike tire, while an older woman watches television; the pump's sound joins the rhythm of the bedsprings
- CU: The bow crosses the cello strings, back and forth
- TIGHT PAN: The bedsprings
- MS: The woman beats the rug
- CU: The beating tool
- CU: A metronome moves in sync with the rhythm
- MCU: Hands pull and push on the pump's handle
- MWS: The painter thrusts the roller back and forth across the ceiling
- MS: A toymaker in another room drills holes in a toy noise box
- MS: The toymaker's partner strikes a tuning fork, moos to the tone, turns the box so it moos, huffs, and then repeats the actions in rhythm with the other tenants' actions
- CU: The bedsprings bounce wildly
- ALT. CU: The springs continue to bounce; at this point the pace of the cutting increases
- MS: The painter with his roller

- ALT. ANGLE: The roller thrusts head-on toward the camera
- MCU: The old lady quickly knits
- MCU: The young woman plays the cello
- MCU: The woman beats the rug
- MCU: The toymaker cranks down the drill press
- MCU: Hands continue to pump
- MCU: Bedsprings move faster and faster
- ECU: The metronome swings faster, the camera whipping back and forth with its movement
- MWS: The rug woman pounds faster
- MWS: The bicycle man pumps faster and faster
- CU: The bow sweeps back and forth across the cello's strings
- ECU: The beater smacks out the dust
- ZOOM IN AND OUT: The painter with the roller
- ECU: A bedspring
- MCU: Musician with bow
- ECU: Bedspring
- ECU: The man's climaxing face, eyes rolling into his head
- ECU: The bike tire pops
- MS: The cello string snaps
- MS: The painter falls with his roller
- ECU: Lover man's eyes closed, he grunts; Cut to black.

Through the use of cutting and sound, a strong rhythm permeates the scene. It builds to a thrilling and amusing crescendo, mirroring the impassioned lovers and their proximity to the other tenants in the apartment building.

Figure 14.1 Delicatessen, *1991. Copyright © Buena Vista Home Entertainment.*
(Photo credit: Buena Vista Home Entertainment/Photofest).

Doctor's Note

A word about *temp music* and its relationship to pace and rhythm. When placing temp music against a sequence that will be screened for others, such as a director, producer, or recruited audience, editors are sometimes amazed at how well their cuts will sync up with music that had not been written for it. This indicates the fluidity of the editing as well as the appropriateness of the music. On the other hand, editors also find that cuts of a questionable or difficult nature lose their sting and play better with the band-aid of good music. Experienced directors, who are aware of this, often request a viewing with the music turned off.

Sometimes, as in the case of an action scene, the temp music's rhythm is so compelling that when a picture cut hits offbeat, the awkwardness becomes immediately apparent. On occasion that shot may be trimmed or lengthened in order bring it back in line with the particular musical signature. Of course, most editors wouldn't dream of allowing sound or music to dictate their cuts, other than in music videos and dance sequences, yet there are few editors who haven't, at some time, made small trims in order to match a musical score. Obviously the temp soundtrack will later be replaced by the film's composer, but in this case the temp music has worked as a sort of metronome, reinforcing the editor's rhythm and alerting him when he deviates from it.

Pick Up the Pace

In the case of pace and rhythm, pace, the more straightforward of the pair, simply refers to rate of movement. Though the length of a cut contributes to the film's perceived pace, even greater significance lies in the information that the cut must convey. This movement is propelled by the on-camera action occurring within the frame, such as a yellow Ferrari whipping by at 100 miles an hour or the slow descent of a diver into an abyss. This, coupled with the rapid or slow succession of cuts, influences pace.

In terms of the action within the frame, a variety of factors come into play. Tighter shots tend to contain a limited amount of information which the audience can immediately grasp due to the close proximity of the image. For this reason cuts containing close-ups require less screen time. Wide shots, by their nature, generally contain more information within a frame and will play longer if the audience needs to absorb the action.

In the service of rhythm, however, a quick wide shot can also be effective, as when it serves simply to break the repetitive succession of tighter shots, as in a dialog scene. Here, jumping back for a moment allows the audience a breather from the cramped surroundings of the close and medium coverage. It also gives a chance to relocate the actors within the frame without introducing additional information that would require the shot to linger longer.

The Power of Pace

Nonlinear storytelling—not to be confused with the technical concept of nonlinear editing—has shadowed traditional narrative since the earliest days of filmmaking. In many cases, non-linear storytelling better reflects actual life since events rarely play out in a tidy, straightforward manner. Even within linear stories the incorporation of subplots helps break the artificial consistency of a single story line. Film's inclination to defy the Aristotelian conventions of time and place, as well as the basic three-act structure of a beginning, middle, and end, resides in its ability to warp time and space. Godard's comment that movies should have a beginning, middle, and end but not necessarily in that order reflects the nonlinear approach. The Brothers Quay's stop-motion animation film based on the brilliant novella by Bruno Schulz, *Street of Crocodiles*, achieves feeling and interest despite its seeming lack of story. A fascination with the shapes, sounds, and textures of crafted materials juxtaposed with animal flesh engenders a visceral eroticism and alienation despite the absence of a traditional character's desire.

Forms that rely heaviest on the editor's art, such as the documentary, often succeed by uniting conflicting images to generate dramatic interest. This, coupled with an energetic pace, can sustain a nonlinear structure over the course of a full-length feature. Think of it as a railroad handcar where the opposing forces of the seesaw motion drive the vehicle swiftly forward. Nonlinearity reflects the mind's rapid association of images that propel our actions—often beyond our conscious awareness. Films that splinter the narrative in various ways, including *City of God, Memento, Crash*, and *Sin City*, achieve vibrancy through well-paced editing. The negative opinion that some viewers hold of nonlinear films often derives from a lack of clarity and onward flow. These films become a burden, like a mind obsessing over a problem. David Lynch's rich, three-hour meditation on art and filmmaking, *Inland Empire*, found favor with some audiences but wore out many due to a leisurely pace, despite its compelling characters and surrealistic imagery.

Films like *Groundhog Day,* and, more recently *Harry Potter and the Prisoner of Azkaban, 50 First Dates*, and *Sliding Doors* require repetition in order to tell their stories. These also benefit from active pacing and the editor's ability to truncate action so as to overcome the potential tediousness of recurring situations.

 Case Study

A kid's film I once produced and edited followed a young video gamer into a fairyland forest. There he fought for his life by playing a game that had turned real. With each try he lost another life point and the game reset. In order to win the game and defeat the foe, he had to prevail at every level before he ran out of lives. Allowing him to replay through each level until he arrived at the final challenge required a pace that quickly reviewed, as if in glimpses, the previous levels and brought the audience up to the next realm of play without tiring them.

Anticipation

Part of what sustains the viewer's interest is his inability to know what will happen next. But he can always guess. Well-constructed films give just enough information so the audience can build, from their own experience and the experiences within the film, an expectation of the outcome. This anticipation in the face of the unknown maintains attention—especially if the anticipated consequence is a horrible one.

Shot length allows the editor to increase interest or heighten tension. When Tim Curry, in *The Rocky Horror Picture Show*, refers to "... ann-tii-cii-paa-tion ..." his amusing and prolonged pronunciation characterizes the essence of suspense. Extending a shot's length can, when judiciously applied, provide the needed tease that keeps an audience on the edge of their seats. The answer to their concern of what will happen next is postponed again and again until, in the hands of a skillful editor, the wait becomes excruciating. The trick lies in determining how long a shot can play and still maintain suspense before the wait becomes too lengthy and the audience lapses into boredom. Ultimately, it's all showmanship and whether through sleight-of-hand or a psychological striptease the audience's anticipation level should rise with each cut.

The pod rescue of the expulsed astronaut in *2001: A Space Odyssey* is an example of effective use of extended pacing to heighten tension while reinforcing a sense of reality. In watching the action one can imagine how the sudden introduction of too quick of a cut would shatter the scene's overall rhythm. While the astronaut, Dave, attempts to retrieve his dead comrade with the pod's robotic arm, the scene develops slowly and without words. Yet the tension is far from leisurely, for the audience has seen something that Dave is yet to discover: the termination of his comrades' life support systems by the recalcitrant computer, HAL. When Dave, having finally captured the man's body, orders HAL to open the pod-bay door so he may safely reenter the ship, the machine refuses. We are left to wonder what will happen next. How will Dave save himself and the expedition? Dave realizes that his only recourse resides in docking his pod against the mother ship and blowing open the emergency hatch so he may reenter the ship. This shift in tone and pacing effectively raises the tension as Dave realizes HAL's evil intent. This action contrasts with the scene's previously unhurried, yet suspenseful pace when Dave was still innocent of the machine's plans. The ensuing scene, inundated with flashing lights and intrusive, loud warning sounds, overcomes the silence of space to produce anxiety commensurate with the astronaut's life-or-death situation.

The rapid-fire cuts that charge through action films such as *Crank* show the effectiveness of short, quick images in raising an audience's pulse. In *Crank*'s case the audience's elevated heart rate reflects the on-screen character's need to avoid death by maintaining a rapid pulse. *Crank* was preceded years before by *Speed*, a fast-paced movie that established the premise of maintaining a particular velocity, in this case a bus traveling at 50 miles per hour, in order to avoid a predetermined demise. It supplied an excellent rationale to send the audience on a joyride of fast cutting. By today's standards, however, this wonderful, fast-paced film can appear dated in terms of action editing.

Doctor's Orders

Even in films that travel at lightning speed, it's important to vary the rhythm by occasionally slowing the pace, even if only slightly. This avoids wearing out the audience who would otherwise become inured to the rapid onslaught of images.

On the other hand, if the audience becomes comfortable with a particular pace or is able to anticipate the next shot or action, the perceived tempo will slow and their interest will wane. Watching a movie is a constant education in the new. As long as we're learning something, we're captivated and the time moves quickly.

Overstated

Another primary mistake occurs when an editor allows the information to loop back on itself. The pace slows because information is repeated. This redundancy is the opposite of the *ellipsis*, which catapults action forward through jump cuts, dissolves, and other shortcut devices.

Action films and documentaries, especially in their early stages, fall prey to this oversight. In these genres, the story is often told in images chosen from a wide variety of angles rather than through dialog. Because the story map is not as clearly drawn as in a dialog scene, the actions may linger longer than they need to. Or they may repeat. In the case of documentaries, a point of information might carelessly recur again and again. The editor must decide between reinforcing a point and its overstatement.

Tech Note

When cutting sequences that originated on film negative, including those where the negative is transferred to a digital format for cutting, editors should turn on *dupe detection*. Dupe detection places a colored bar above a shot, or section of a shot, signifying that it has been used previously. When repeating a shot that originated on camera negative, it's necessary to manufacture a duplicate negative of that shot if it will be used again in the movie. Of course, if the negative is transferred to a digital medium, such as a digital intermediate, it saves having to make another shot.

In the case of footage originating on video, dupe detection can help avoid redundancy. Unlike the days when all movies were cut on positive celluloid workprint made from the original negative where each shot could be used only once, today a virtual shot on an electronic system can be used ad infinitum.

Case Study

Editors become masters of timing. The timing of shots within a scene requires both intuition and experience. An editor I know used to boast playfully about his command of timing. This extended past the film to the realm of knowing just how long he could take for an extended lunch on Friday before the producer would be looking for him or when to check in with the director who had waited patiently to see his next pass. He always made it on time.

The Heart of the Matter

While today's young editors, having grown up with music videos, TV commercials, and video games, may possess a greater sense of pacing than their predecessors, they often pale when it comes to questions of story and character. For many of them, the adrenaline-infused sprint of an action sequence or the quick, varied shots of a dance number hold greater interest than the trials and tribulations of the human heart, which are the territory of the story. At times this reverence for fast pacing hides deficiencies in story or character development, patching up malnourished structure or performance. Particularly in comedies, musicals, and action films, maintaining a good pace encourages the audience to ignore lesser jokes, abandon logical concerns, and forgive embarrassing performances.

But adrenaline alone doesn't make a movie. Student editors today, with their greater command of pacing than the novices of the past, tend to miss out on the other half of the equation, which is rhythm. Rhythm directly relates to the development of story and character, since these are a matter of the heart.

Case Study

A student editor, working with supplied footage, cut highly energetic scenes composed of very short cuts. Eventually he became a director. At that point he fell prey to the director's affection for his material and, since he happened to edit his own scenes, allowed the pace to slow and the shots to linger longer than they needed to. To everyone's surprise, the film was a bore.

While *pacing* can be equated to tempo or the rate of movement, *rhythm* posits something harder to establish: a pattern of images that is consistent with the movie's content.

Rhythm Is Life

Because rhythm harks back to the most archaic, ecstatic rituals involving dance and music pounded out on ancient drums, it produces a strong influence on an audience. Mirroring the very basis of life itself—those diurnal cycles within the body controlled by fluctuations in serotonin levels, the pattern of the seasons, the ebb and flow of the sea, the systolic and diastolic beating of the heart, and ultimately the cycle of life and death—filmic rhythm dives beneath the surface of our rational minds, deep into the inner world of emotions.

While pacing can be fast, slow, or somewhere in between, rhythm is characterized by a pattern of strong and weak forces. This is accomplished by varying the choice of shots, the length of shots, and the placement of shots—again, the Editing Triangle. When the rhythm is off, it becomes obvious. Though most audiences could not delineate what's bothering them about a scene or a movie in those terms, the fact that it has somehow broken away from the natural order upsets their equilibrium. Consider this popular lampoon of a nursery rhyme "Roses are red/violets are blue/you may think this will rhyme/but it won't." How disconcerting. We're following a particular flow and then the flow is disrupted. Unless done for effect, this becomes an awkward way to tell a story.

But how does the editor come to terms with the enticing and all-encompassing concept of rhythm? How does he determine the scene's rhythm? How does he take its pulse to know what it requires?

Elements in a scene issue forth with greater or lesser energy. The selection of these shots and the order of their occurrence helps determine a scene's rhythm. In many cases the actors will supply the rhythm within a scene. Their emotional response to the story's action informs their readings and body language. Initially, this guides the editor in selection and length of shots. In dialog scenes, the line readings supply clues as to when and where to cut. In some cases, however, the actors' performances may be too rushed or too leisurely. At that point it becomes the editor's responsibility to put some air between the lines, supplying a much needed pause or, conversely, accelerate the performance by trimming out pauses, or physical business. Since all scenes contain *beats*, moments where the scene shifts gears, actors and directors work in terms of these beats. Editors should too. The beats help inform the rhythm of a scene. And rhythm, that very human yet elusive phenomenon, engenders emotion.

Influenced by character interactions that occur within the scene, the original emotions and direction of the scene evolve until a new effect is arrived at by the scene's conclusion. Like the overall story, the story within each scene begins with a particular purpose. As one character confronts another, circumstances change. The moments in a scene where a character's intent switches or transforms based on new experiences are the beats.

Doctor's Orders

Breaking a scene into beats provides a valuable tool for evaluating the plotting and to realize the scene's rhythm. This fluctuation of the actions within a scene molds overall rhythm. Find the beats.

The Graduate

The seduction scene in Mike Nichols's classic film *The Graduate* stands on its own as a superbly crafted sequence that plays like a self-contained movie. The scene opens with Benjamin Braddock (Dustin Hoffman) driving up to the opulent home of his father's partner with Mrs. Robinson (Anne Bancroft) in tow. The scene concludes with Benjamin returning to his vehicle while Mr. and Mrs. Robinson look on from their well-lit porch. Between the beginning and end of the scene, a series of significant beats propel the story forward and anticipate a decision that Ben will make two scenes later.

Here are the main beats:

- As a favor, unsuspecting Benjamin drives Mrs. Robinson home. It becomes the last time he is literally and figuratively in the driver's seat in this sequence.
- Mrs. Robinson convinces Ben to come inside her home. Ben resists but agrees, falling under her influence.
- Ben tries to leave. Mrs. Robinson offers Ben a drink. Ben declines, but she forces it into his hand, increasing her authority over him.
- Ben suspects he is being seduced, apologizes for saying so, and tries to leave.
- Mrs. Robinson stops him and offers to show him her daughter's portrait, which Ben innocently interprets as an opportunity to change the subject. Mrs. Robinson has succeeded in taking him to the next level of her control.
- In Elaine's bedroom Mrs. Robinson begins to undress, tossing her bracelet on the fresh covers, as if throwing down a gauntlet. The challenge is unmistakable.
- Ben tries again to leave. Mrs. Robinson convinces him to stay. His resolve weakens further. Her control over him increases. In his body language, he continues to step toward her as he insists on leaving.
- Almost free, Ben heads for the front door, but Mrs. Robinson insists he bring her purse upstairs. Her tone has changed from seductive to commanding. He obeys.

- Naked, Mrs. Robinson corners Ben in the room and closes the door. In flash cuts he glimpses her naked form. He knows it's wrong, but he can't help but look and be aroused.
- Mr. Robinson arrives home. Terrified, Ben tries to save himself by running downstairs to pretend that nothing has happened.
- Mr. Robinson greets Ben and offers him a whiskey. When Ben requests bourbon, Mr. Robinson reinforces his disregard for and authority over the young man by giving him the whiskey. Ben tries to remain calm. Mr. Robinson suggests Ben sow some wild oats.
- Mrs. Robinson appears. Ben jumps up. When she tells him, "Don't get up" he drops back into his seat like a trained dog. Her hold on him is complete.

Through the use of well-conceived photography, production design, and editing, this multifaceted scene evolves into a highly compelling experience. The camera's dominant and submissive angles, the shadowy downstairs contrasted with the well-lit upstairs, reinforce the feelings of control and subjugation. Sets and props, everything from an altar-like bar with its phallic drink dispensers and cigarette lighters to the virginal white room of the daughter Elaine, support the scene's action. Even Elaine's wall sports a large R for Robinson rather than the appropriate E. The audience is introduced to a controlling, disassociated couple of high-class alcoholics who will meet their psychological demise as a response to their transgressions.

Finding the Flow

Because rhythm is so compelling, it is imperative to find a particular flow that directs the cutting. Just as music guides the cuts in a music video, the interplay of dialog influences the rhythm of a narrative scene.

The answer to that is, in a sense, the revelation of one's style, the moment when the beginning editor transitions, as if through a rite of passage, from an apprentice to a master. Having accomplished an inner understanding of pace and rhythm, the editor discovers a sense of personal style. Even though rhythms vary from film to film, the editor brings with her a unique perspective.

One of the clearest guides to rhythm is an actor's performance. Well-trained actors create a discernable rhythm that the editor can follow as a guide in determining dialog length and character reactions. Added to this, some actors, including some of the best in the business, change their performance from take to take, so it is the editor's job to ascertain the best rhythm and support it.

 Case Study

In my experience, great talents like Jack Nicholson experiment with their performance, altering it from take to take. Nicholson consistently presents the editor with useable material because he has such a well-defined center from which he works. Yet, in selecting the most appropriate performance on the movie *Man Trouble*, it became vital to anchor the different acting approaches to the overall scene so as to achieve a smooth arc. When I was brought in to re-cut the final confrontation between Harry (Jack Nicholson), Redmond (Harry Dean Stanton), and Joan (Ellen Barkin), I was presented with a wide variety of performance choices from take to take. In crafting the correct rhythm it was necessary to evaluate the various energy levels and allow them to build in a way that was neither haphazard nor tediously consistent.

The length of a cut also affects the rhythm when shots of varying lengths are joined together. At times the repetition of identical shot lengths will reinforce a scene's rhythm as much as a pattern of longer and shorter cuts. In a documentary montage composed of static photos set to music, it often works to measure each to identical length. Again, it helps to think in terms of music. This is evident in the *Rule of Three* sequence (see Chapter 2), where a series of three shots reinforce a particular meaning. A writer, when listing qualities or instances, generally selects three items as opposed to two or four. Shakespeare took advantage of this pattern and forced his villains to break from it in their speech, making them appear vulgar or corrupt. The editor also takes advantage of this rhythm to communicate meaning.

The staccato bang bang bang of three shots measured out to equal length can produce an effective and precise visual rhythm. We see this in establishing shots that strive to give a wider sense of place than a single shot would supply. A wide shot of Iguaça Falls looking east, joined to a wide shot of the falls looking west, joined to a low angle shot of the falls can give a better sense of their vastness than a single wide shot. An explosion viewed from three angles looks much larger than an explosion that erupts in one angle.

Variety is one of the overriding features of good rhythm. It breaks the monotony of close-up, close-up, close-up, and initiates a pattern. As in music, rhythm also forms an agreeable melody. In other words, the pattern and length of shots contribute to a pleasing flow. If the flow is interrupted, a disturbance is introduced, as in horror films where a predictable pattern of shots is suddenly interrupted by an inconsistent move, such as a jump cut with a loud sound.

In David Lean's classic film *Lawrence of Arabia* the trek across the desert to Acaba is reinforced by the wide shots engendering the distance and hardship of the grueling journey. These are broken up with shots of the blazing sun, the sand, the individual riders on their camels, slowly worn down by the seemingly impossible attempt to approach Acaba from the desert rather than the sea so as to surprise the enemy. The sequence concludes with the false connection of the brilliant long focal shot of a ship moving across the desert sand.

At other times the rhythm reinforces jeopardy and excitement as in the lobby scene from *The Matrix*, where the viewer is showered with nearly as many images as there are pieces of shrapnel flying off the decimated walls and pillars. Even within this intensely dynamic action scene, the editor, Zach Staenberg, found moments to vary the pace to produce a compelling, mellifluous rhythm, exhibited in the extended cut to a slow-motion twirl by Trinity (Carrie-Anne Moss) or the leisurely bookends to the scene beginning with the amusing moment where Neo (Keanu Reeves) enters the metal detector. Here the guard asks if he is carrying anything metal, whereupon Neo exposes the arsenal beneath his cloak, igniting the firefight. The scene ends as placidly as it began with the two heroes, Neo and Trinity, stepping into the elevator and a final punctuation of the last tile tumbling from its place and onto the floor.

The Battleship Eisenstein

Eisenstein's theories of montage and the use of juxtaposition informed his cross-cutting and energetic tempo in films like *The Battleship Potemkin*. The prominence of his theories has been challenged, however, by some modern Russian filmmakers, particularly Andrei Tarkovsky. Tarkovsky resisted the theory of montage, giving precedence to the individual shot over the juxtaposition of multiple, uninflected ones. In films like

Stalker, indelible images are burned into the viewer's consciousness through their sustained appearance on screen. Where Eisenstein led the way with shots that flickered like embers on a breeze, illuminating the screen for mere seconds at a time, Tarkovsky's images can loiter for well over a minute, pawing at the earth but grounding us in their meaning. For some audiences this excessive lingering becomes intolerable. Others, however, find themselves immersed into a vastness of space and time that produces a sort of meditative state. In Tarkovsky's world as quoted in LaValley and Scherr's book *Eisenstein at 100: A Reconsideration* "editing has to do with stretches of time, and the degree of intensity with which these exist, as recorded by the camera. ...." Speaking of his fellow countryman and former teacher during lectures at the VGIK, or All-Union State Institute of Film in Russia, Tarkovsky concluded, "If (Eisenstein's) intuition let him down and he failed to put into edited pieces the time-pressure required by that particular assembly, then the rhythm, which he held to be directly dependent on editing, would show up the weakness of this theoretical premise.... Ignoring the need to fill the frames with the appropriate time-pressure, he tries to achieve the inner dynamic of the battle (in *Alexander Nevsky*) with an edited sequence of short—sometimes extremely short—shots." Tarkovsky believed that, in spite of the rapid cutting, the audience was "dogged by the feeling that what is happening on the screen is sluggish and unnatural. This is because no time-truth exists in the separate frames." In his stunning masterpiece *Stalker*, a sustained wide shot reinforces the sense of desolation that the hero and his charges experience while in the strange, metaphysical realm of The Zone. To Tarkovsky's credit he interrupts one particularly long but exquisite, extreme wide shot in this otherworldly realm with the very worldly ringing of a telephone which his isolated hero feels compelled to answer.

Scene-to-Scene Transitions

An important aspect of creating and maintaining rhythm involves supplying satisfying transitions. How the film story moves from scene to scene, place to place, character to character determines whether the overall rhythm will be smooth and logical or coarse and disjointed. Some of the flaws that occur at this stage involve confusion, disorientation, and fragmentation. Good transitions carry the audience along with them, clarifying where we are and giving a hint of where we're going. They pull us into the next scene.

Transitions may be as simple as the associative cut described in *Horseplayer*'s kissing scenes or as sophisticated as those in *Up in the Air* (see below). In a script, the transition may be accomplished simply by designating "CUT TO" or "DISSOLVE TO" at the end of a scene. That doesn't guarantee that the transition, when viewed in the context of the motion picture, will occur as seamlessly.

Transitions not only help maintain a smooth pace and rhythm but also a consistent tone and theme. Though transitions may be accomplished through the use of effects, such as wipes, fades, or dissolves, those might not be sufficient. Another approach may be required in order to accomplish the task. Whereas, in previous decades these tools were employed ceaselessly, today their influence has diminished. Scenes that would have been linked by dissolves in decades past now rely on straight cuts. Just as in medicine, leeches used to be considered a valuable adjunct to stemming a patient's fever and getting him on the right course; today simple rest and aspirin might do the trick. In some cases transitions become quite stylized, launching a motif that recurs throughout the film, such as the high-altitude city views with title cards that announced George Clooney's next destination in *Up in the Air*. The atmospheric angles reinforced the film's "up in the air" theme, and the airy titles—simple outlined fonts through which the background scene can be glimpsed—further enhanced the unattached theme. Even the peppy main titles set to quick-tempo music and containing similar views across America from above helped establish this motif.

Star Wars took advantage of another transition technique to reiterate its comic-book, matinee-like style. One futuristic scene metamorphosed into another by way of old-fashioned wipes. In *The Prize Winner of Defiance, Ohio*, the filmmakers employed another type of transition effect, the push, to slide one image after another past the screen. Before the Avid made it easy to mock up a variety of such effects, most editors relied on wipes or dissolves for transition effects. Such effects, which were once costly to manufacture and impossible to create in the editing room, have, with the arrival of digital editing, manifested at literally the touch of a button. With the advent of the digital intermediate (DI), these effects no longer require expensive optical printing processes in order to transfer them onto 35 mm film. Now, just as in the offline editing suite, they can be digitally created, along with other previously expensive items such as titles, and then recorded out to 35 mm film with no intervening step.

In the past, the film editor had to imagine the effect based on calculating which other frames would be employed to form the effect. Editors became used to what a three-, six-, or nine-foot dissolve would look like and designated its beginning and end position with a grease pencil line. As remains the case today, it was necessary to calculate the handle, the latent side of a dissolve or wipe, to ensure there was enough material to produce the effect. Editors today, accustomed to the ease of computerized editing and unaccustomed to or unaware of the need for handles, are sometimes confounded when they try to initiate an effect but are repeatedly foiled in their attempt. If the machine is friendly, it will prompt them with the notice that there is not enough footage available on the A or B side of the effect. When dissolving from Scene A to Scene B, only the first half of the A side will appear on the timeline. Conversely, only the second half of the B side will appear on the timeline. In a sense, the invisible A half and invisible B half will only appear when the dissolve is activated. As the A side fades out, the B side fades in to replace it. Therefore, a six-second dissolve requires six seconds of media on both the A and B side, not the three seconds that appear on each side of the timeline. If the editor has not allowed for this latent footage, the dissolve will come up short. In this regard, it remains important to ensure that an equal amount of footage exists on the latent side.

In building a dissolve, it helps to use the *match frame* command, to reveal the remaining footage in the Viewer or Source window. Also, by checking the latent B side of the latent A side or the A side of the latent B side, the editor can confirm that nothing unintended will appear in the dissolve, such as a flash frame or break in character. Where the outcome was less predictable in previous times, today nothing is committed to film until it has been worked out on the computer.

Tech Note

Today, editors can experiment with hundreds of different types of transition effects, loading them onto the timeline, viewing them, and undoing them with a quick tap of Command-Z on a Mac or Control-Z on a PC. The Avid presents a wide array of possible transitions, ranging from dissolves to hard-edged wipes, sawtooth wipes, clock wipes, and zigzag wipes on the Effects palette found under Tools. Likewise, offers a substantial menu of similar effects accessed in the Browser under the Effects tab. The Video Transitions folder opens to reveal various wipes and dissolves. Whichever way or whatever system the editor chooses, she will have at her fingertips a large and sophisticated variety of transition effects. In Avid some effects can even be promoted to 3D effects by clicking on the 3D button on the bottom right of the Effects Editor.

Overdose

One serious affliction that occurs when editors are first introduced to this pharmacy of effects is the tendency to overdose on them. At first they may appear to be a cure-all for awkward transitions or malingering stories. Because they are easy, showy, and visually striking, they find their way into many more rough cuts than they should. In some cases they appear silly or out of place, and at worst they slow the pace.

Movie trailers often resort to fades, wipes, and dissolves in order to jump action and story in a dynamic way so it may appear permissible. But trailers incorporate them for a different reason. Often fast paced in order to create excitement and communicate a lot of information in a small period of time, usually around two minutes, the trailer may use quick fades to black or white in order to entice the viewer toward more. As soon as the snippet of a scene appears on screen, it is already fading from view, pulling the viewer deeper and deeper into its web, wanting more.

Blacking Out

In practice, particularly in the case of feature films, fades cause more harm than good. Just as in a medically induced coma, nothing happens with a fade. No image, no sound. The film just lays there, immobile. It becomes a perfect opportunity for the audience's mind to wander or to remember that popcorn they meant to buy when they walked in. Except when there is really no other way to tell the story, fades should be avoided, other than at the beginning and the end of the film, just as they appear, in a sense, at the beginning and end of life. Film doctors often earn their stature by such simple procedures as removing a collection of fades that another editor had left in or that the director had insisted upon. It's amazing how the pace increases when you avoid blackouts and stick with the movie.

Doctor's Orders

The only fades should be at the beginning and the end of the film: fade in and fade out. Otherwise, avoid them.

Ban Banners

Along the same lines, steer clear of banners. Banners are the title cards that appear in a rough cut to designate missing footage, such as "Shot missing" or "Scene missing." With electronic editing systems banners have become more prevalent and detailed, since editors using the Title tool can easily generate descriptive banners. Instead of "Shot missing," a banner might designate "Medium shot of Ted holding an eggbeater." In that instant a visual medium is turned into a verbal medium and the rhythm is broken. Remember, rhythm can be as important as story and character, and by peppering a cut with banners, it upsets a major aspect of the film. Of course, in the silent era, title cards were used when necessary, but most people find that the break in rhythm is one of the most disconcerting aspects of silent films. Today we don't have to resort to that. Except as shorthand notes for the editor's personal reference or as a guide for a reshoot crew, rough cuts filled with banners should not be shown to directors or producers. It is hard enough for most people to view a rough cut, let alone interrupting the flow constantly with banners that begin to look like excuses for not having the correct shot. But what is the solution? Find a shot that comes close to the original intent or cut the scene around it until you can actually have the footage you need to make it work.

A corollary to this occurs in the special-effects film. In this case many shots will not be immediately available to the editor due to the time required to produce sophisticated special effects. Wireframes, green-screens, and partial renders are often available, however, and can fill the gap where the completed effect will eventually reside. These too are preferable to text banners. A wireframe of a spaceship wins out over a card that says, "Place spaceship here."

Narration

Likewise with narration. Narration is a way to convey a great deal of information in a shorter period of time than it would take to portray the same information in a scene or where portraying it would be tedious. In this way it acts as a bridge to carry the audience from one narrative location to another. When trying to determine whether to use narration, first edit the scene without the narration, imbuing it with as much information as possible. Then take a look and see if there is any vital information still missing. If there is, consider adding some voiceover or ADR. If not, consider leaving out the narration.

Shot Size

Lastly, if we are not going to rely on dissolves or other effects to generate scene-to-scene transitions, how do we accomplish this crucial task? Sound and images are basically what we have to work with. Using these, we can craft almost all transitions. The easiest and most common way to maintain rhythm and clarity is to make sure that the shot that opens the next scene is different enough from the one that ended the preceding scene. Except in the case of associative cuts, such as the kiss in *Horseplayer*, supplying contrast immediately clues the audience into the change that has occurred. If the previous scene ended on a wide shot of the African plain, why not begin the next scene with an extreme close-up of a strawberry plucked from a serving bowl? This was the case in the indie film *Lost in Africa*. After revealing the vast expanse of Africa, the sight of a strawberry catches our attention. It is not a fruit that one usually associates with Africa. Further, it is bright red and in close-up, which is also a contrast to the last scene. We're clearly somewhere else. But where are we? This transitional shot has prepared us to enter the next scene. The next shot reveals the answer—we're in a safari picnic, set up on tables in a civilized manner with fresh fruit. This will prefigure the brutal change of events that is about to befall our characters as they are attacked and taken hostage by a band of poachers, determined to hold them ransom for the return of one of their own. In cutting the scene, we had a lot of more obvious shots we could have opened the scene with, but beginning on the strawberry proved most successful. Therefore, vary the shots. If a scene ends in a wide shot, start the next one with a close-up, and vice versa. Another sensory aspect that the editor has at his disposal is sound. Where the previous scene ends with a subdued tone, maybe a kiss, a gentle breeze, or a sigh, start the next scene with a car horn, an explosion, or a slap. Interestingly, in well-written stories, the scenes often tend to alternate in a way that allows for contrasting sounds and images. Being aware of this will help an editor cure difficult scenes or sequences, as well.

In some cases, sound supplies the best transition. Placing a prominent sound, such as source music, a scream, or a car horn, can pull the audience immediately into a new scene, particularly when this contrasts with the ambiance of the previous scene. Anything that catches the audience's attention, whether a sound or action, can distract them from a previous shot and can help bridge a difficult transition. It's like a magician's sleight-of-hand trick where a motion he makes with one hand distracts the viewer from the object he's obscuring with the other hand. From our hunter-gatherer beginnings, humans are hardwired to follow movement over stillness, sounds over silence.

The Pre-lap

Another way that sound helps bridge a difficult cut is through the use of overlaps, or more concisely, *pre-laps*. In *The Graduate*, following the intensity of the attempted seduction by Mrs. Robinson, Ben approaches his car while Mr. and Mrs. Robinson linger in the doorway. To fill the silence between them and transition to the next scene, the editor, Sam O'Steen, placed Ben's father's voice, "Ladies and gentlemen, your attention please, uh, for this afternoon's feature attraction ..." pre-lapping the cut to the brightly lit daytime scene of the father at the family pool, where Ben will later be revealed in his scuba suit. The early entrance of dialog coupled with the cut from night to day, wide shot to close-up, creates a smooth transition.

Another case is the montage. Montages have the effect of transporting the viewer beyond the immediate scene. Through a series of divergent shots, montages may recap what has transpired before, or they might reinforce a current point, as in a documentary. When the montage ends, departing from it can be as awkward as awakening a sleeper from a dream. In many cases a dissolve or even a straight cut will suffice, but in other cases introducing incoming audio ahead of the next scene's video can aid in a smooth return to the story's present reality.

Case Study

In editing a feature documentary on still photographers, I occasionally found it valuable to go away to a short montage of a photographer's stills. In one case this appeared during a meeting with the editor of the photographer's book. Leaving the montage and rejoining the book editor was helped by hearing the editor's voice briefly pre-lap the cut to his face as he spoke.

Other helpful uses of dialog pre-laps occur when transitioning from an exterior establishing shot to an interior where the dialog scene takes place. By hearing the dialog begin before the cut to the speakers, the audience anticipates the transition and is therefore ready for the abrupt change of scene. This move also reinforces the fact that the speaker is in the same environment as we have established in the preceding shot.

The Intercut

The key to effective rhythm resides in the process of *intercutting*. The efficient use of intercutting helps provide the audience's emotional response to the action on screen. It also moves the action along in a compelling way. It is the editor's most valuable tool.

Intercutting supplies a much needed variation in pattern and therefore audience response. Just as juxtaposition of images creates meaning within a scene, the juxtaposition of scenes creates meaning within the movie. Like shot-to-shot juxtaposition, the intercutting of scenes blends best when a long scene is truncated and the remaining action placed following another scene.

By intercutting scenes (see this chapter's Case Studies) the movie's rhythm and pacing improve drastically. The challenge presented to one who decides to break a scene into various parts and intersperse those parts with other scenes is to create the transitions that make it feel as if that's the way it was intended all along.

Case Study

During my stint as head of postproduction for LIVE Entertainment, before it became Artisan and eventually absorbed into Lionsgate, I was in charge of overseeing a film entitled *Suicide Kings* that was edited by Chris Peppe. The opening of the film introduces a group of preppy friends as they plot to retrieve the kidnapped sister of one of the boys. To accomplish this they've decided to kidnap the former don, Carlo Bartolucci turned Charlie Barret (Christopher Walken), of a New York mafia family, convinced that through his influence the Godfather can procure the safe return of the young woman. What they don't realize is that they're about to invite the devil into their midst, for this New York don is craftier and more powerful than they are.

The story's opening could have unfolded in a straightforward manner. We see the boys on the rooftop clandestinely plotting out the kidnapping, using a couple of old chairs and an inflatable dummy to represent the kidnap victim and the car. They argue over how best to sedate their victim and who will be the one to inject him with Haldol. Once they've figured out the plot and who will carry out the actions, we're ready to see their best-laid plans effected.

At that point the action shifts to the private club where the boys will meet Charlie Barret and convince him to join them for a night on the town. The father of one of the boys is a member of the club, and they easily insinuate themselves into the booth usually reserved for the don. When Charlie Barret appears and graciously allows them to remain at the table, they invite him to join them. Over beers, they fulfill the plans they had conceived earlier.

Proceeding in this manner would have produced a very linear and plodding rhythm. As it turns out, the two scenes are intercut with each other, each reinforcing information learned in the other. In this way the linearity is broken up, producing a varied and more engaging rhythm allowing the juxtaposition of actions to supply greater tension and anticipation.

Case Study

A few years after *Suicide Kings* I had the opportunity to edit a romantic comedy starring the popular singer Michael Bublé: *Totally Blonde*. It was a very amusing film, but it suffered from two scenes that were overly long. They weighed down the film's otherwise lively and cheery pace. The scenes comprise the tales of two couples out on a date. One is the sincere and romantic character Van Martin, portrayed by Michael Bublé. As the owner of an upscale nightclub, the smitten Van has closed it for the night in order to present an impressive private dinnershow to Meg Peters (Krista Allen). When his intended date stands him up for a night out with the volleyball star Brad Wilson (Brody Hutzler) from her former high school, Van settles for an evening with her best friend, Liv Watson (Maeve Quinlan), who has come looking for her. He ends up dining with the girlfriend and, over an intoxicated game of Truth or Dare? kisses her and falls for her, and the pair end up making out in his swimming pool.

Next we see Meg, who has gone off for a bizarre night on the town. Brad takes her to get fast food at Super King, where he delights in torturing "the Super King peon" who's taking his order by mimicking static on the speaker. After that they head to lover's lane, where, instead of making out, they arm themselves with walkie talkies and sneak around the parked cars at Brad's request. Eventually they find their way back to her apartment.

Where in the script these two different dates occurred sequentially, in the final edited film they occur concurrently. As amusing as these two different date scenes were, they became interminably long when viewed sequentially. Even the best dialog and action usually becomes exhausting after about three minutes. By intercutting the two couples so their dates appear to occur concurrently, they became much more intriguing and, because the audience was engaged, fun and funny. Since this was not the intention of the script, the transitions had not been built into the scenes. Instead I had to determine where to break each scene, where to enter the other scene, and then where to interrupt that scene in order to jump back to the previous scene, back and forth, until both scenes resolved themselves.

To accomplish this, it required first cutting each sequence individually as written. After that, I viewed the cut scenes over and over again until the natural breaks became clear. The scenes' beats became obvious, and sections could be severed from each other. Then, through the use of the character's physical actions, the scenes could be linked so they seemed to have more of an association with each other than existed when alone. Where previously they were only linked by a larger, overall plot thrust and knowledge of the relationships of these characters to one another, intercutting the scenes placed them next to each other in a way that illuminated the vastly divergent dating styles. It was like saying, "Here, compare these apples with these oranges; now compare these oranges with these apples." It became a dialectic, each cutback reinforcing the premise that these couples were very different and perhaps not meant for each other.

In dividing them off, the trick was to discover a place in the dialog that evoked a punch line or cliffhanger, something to entice the audience to return to the story they had just left. In the Van-Liv date, this moment occurs when Van offers Liv something to drink and she admits that she likes alcohol but it makes her horny. CUT TO: the Meg-Brad date where the jock, eager to torture the effeminate Super King clerk, insists on the toy watch that's supposed to come with his meal, calls him a peon, and drives off. CUT TO: the shot glass that Liv has just

(Continued)

Case Study (Continued)

emptied—even after the warning of her vulnerability to vodka—makes an audible smack as she deposits it back on the table. The abrupt sound and movement yank us into the scene and back into their world.

Keep in mind that previously the scene would have continued much longer, extending from Van's offer for dinner and drinks to their drinking and clapping down the glasses and getting to know each other over a game of Truth or Dare? without the intervening action at the Super King burger restaurant. This story now develops into a game of Truth or Dare? that finally evolves into a passionate kiss on the lips—a good place to cut, with the anticipation of further sexual engagement. So we rejoin the other couple, Meg and Brad, driving up to an outlook with a view of the city at night and the parked cars of other lovers. In the end the two dates, which we have tracked as they continue to develop in parallel yet different ways, culminate with a question: Are these couples right for each other, or should they be with other people?

By assigning transitions to each scene, the overall sequence plays as if this were the way it was originally intended. Propelled by the parallel action, the movie glides along with its amusing and enticing evening out. It has established a workable and engaging rhythm that will carry on throughout the movie. Had the proper transitions not been created in these scenes or if the transitions were not able to be found, the sequence might have exposed its craftwork and interrupted the delightful pace. As a side note, had the transitions not presented themselves or had they appeared terribly awkward, it might have been a clue to the editor that such a strategy wasn't working and perhaps the scenes were not meant to be treated in this fashion, although this is rarely the case. Usually, intercutting is the right move, superior to protracted scene telling.

℞

Intercut, and then intercut some more!

Chapter 15

Bedside Manner

Politics of the Editing Room

Wherever human beings work together politics come into play. Even in rarefied environments such as Zen monasteries, ashrams, and other institutions dedicated to peace, harmony, and enlightenment, heavy politics abound. Look at Jonestown or the commune of Bhagwan Shree Rajneesh, the womanizing, Rolls Royce–collecting guru. For an ascetic or monk the discovery of politics may be particularly disturbing, since the life he has chosen is supposedly free of such worldly issues.

But in the film business, politics comes as no surprise. Working in an editing room can be like living on a submarine, a long journey in close quarters. It helps to be able to get along with others, and sometimes that includes dealing with politics.

Bedside Manner

In the medical profession, the behavior that a physician assumes with his patient is called bedside manner. An editor, as well, develops a bedside manner. This allows him to navigate the sometimes tumultuous waters of the editing room. As any good writer or psychologist knows, humans do things for all sorts of reasons, some good and some bad. So politics becomes a factor. Ulterior motives come into play in all lines of work, and sometimes it is hard to sift through the verbiage to find the truth. Clever politicos will frame their requests or statements as if in the other person's best interest: "I know how proud you are of the cut, so I've arranged for you to screen it for the suits."

In some situations defending the cut that he and the director have arrived at becomes the primary focus of an editor's job. While editors at times enjoy the privileged position of working alone and undisturbed, this peace, like most things in life, is mutable. Deadlines arrive, emergencies arise, tempers flare, opinions fly. In general the editor's allegiance is to the director. As key participants in the filmmaking process the editor and director share a bond of mutual trust and creative spirit. In most cases the director brought the editor onto the film and expects the editor to fulfill his vision in the best way possible. This includes defending him

The Healthy Edit. DOI: 10.1016/B978-0-240-81446-9.00015-9

167

against the onslaught of producers, studio executives, and distributors who, for better or worse, harbor their own opinions and motives about the film. Conflict, the essence of drama, is great on film but not in the editing room.

No Surprises

Feature film producers often call the editing room to inquire about the director's footage or to try to influence his cut. If the producer wants to review material, it is a good idea to make sure that the director is aware of this. It is, after all, the director's cut. And directors don't like to be surprised.

 Case Study

As an assistant editor, one of the best lessons I learned the hard way was when a producer asked me to make a picture change, assuring me that he'd already okayed it with the director, who was out of town. I was pleased to be singled out and entrusted with the task. I assumed that the director and main editor were aware of this. They weren't. When the director saw the altered scene, he was furious. The producer was wrong to ask for the change at this stage of the process, and I was wrong to proceed without independent confirmation from the director. To make matters worse, the producer refused to admit it, so I became the sacrificial lamb. "The chameleon at work," the producer's assistant told me proudly, as if I was supposed to appreciate that. Only later when tempers cooled did the director take me aside and acknowledge that he knew that the producer, who was too afraid of him to ask directly, had insisted on the change. And that next time I should let him know beforehand.

Screening the Rough Cut

If you let someone know ahead of time about what is going to happen, they are prepared and have time to adjust their expectations. Editors have an ongoing dilemma of when to show the cut. Even though most producers insist that they know how to view a rough cut, they don't. The editor's diplomatic skill in diverting this request until he is confident that he can present the best possible cut becomes tantamount to survival in the editing room. And, most importantly, it benefits the film. As much as most editors want to be flexible and cooperative, showing a cut before its time can be devastating to the director as well as to the editor. If the cut will take another day or so to complete, it is important to remain firm and try to defuse the request. Of course, experienced producers generally understand this and the more experienced editors generally arrive at a working cut in a shorter period of time.

Keep in mind that in some cases a scene just doesn't work. As mentioned previously, you may wrestle with it over and over, but ultimately you discover there are flaws in the scene. At that point it is sometimes a good idea to minimize the expectation by discussing the problem scene ahead of time. After all, the editor usually knows whether his cut is working or not. Something informs him, either excitement at how the cut's impact doesn't diminish on multiple viewings, or a discomfort each time it does. As the old adage goes, "If something's not right, it's wrong," and you'd better get it fixed before you screen it.

The Best Policy

In its simplest, most elemental form, politics is nothing more than understanding the other person's needs and trying, as best one can, to respond to them. This posits that participants in the marathon process of feature filmmaking communicate with one another. Why not ask and clarify what the director is looking for rather than try to guess? Honesty helps. As Mark Twain observed, "If you tell the truth, you don't have to remember anything."

Like everyone, directors have moments of insecurity, some more than others. They depend on the editor to protect them by providing the best possible cut. Developing confidence as an editor and film doctor is one of the best sidekicks you can have. But confidence cannot be faked. One can try and, even for a while, get away with it. Ultimately, it undoes you. If you are not sure of something, say so. If you have a question, ask. Admitting that you don't know is a form of confidence.

All Ears

Another aspect of bedside manner is listening. Don't we all prefer doctors who listen to us rather than those who impatiently scurry to get on to the next patient or interrupt us as if unconcerned about our wellbeing? The best doctors are those who listen, who weigh what is being said, who develop a rapport with their patients. Some producers and directors are people of few words, sometimes withholding either out of their own insecurity, a loss for what to say, or a need to maintain power in the relationship. Most are ignited by their ideas and the joy of the process and will gladly chat about issues that arise.

Putting aside the obvious value of conversation, of give and take, what is the best approach for each of these types of personalities? The simple, across-the-board answer is to listen. We learn by listening. We also put the other person at ease and bring him or her to our side.

One of the chief complaints patients have regarding their doctors is that the doctor fails to listen to their concerns. Wise doctors know that this is not only essential in creating trust but also to understanding the patient's issues. Many interactions occur on a less than rational level. Malcolm Gladwell, in his book *Blink*, tells of the medical researcher Wendy Levinson who evaluated the interactions between doctors who had been sued for malpractice by their patients and those who hadn't. According to Gladwell, "The surgeons who had never been sued spent more than three minutes longer with each patient than those who had been sued did.... They were more likely to engage in active listening, saying such things as 'Go on, tell me more about that,' and they were more likely to laugh and be funny during the visit. Interestingly, there was no difference in the amount or quality of information they gave their patients...."

The same holds true in filmmaking. Something as simple as listening separates a well-functioning editing room from one that is at odds with itself and others. Often editors complain that directors don't know what they want or aren't able to articulate it. Yet, if one takes the time to really listen, the information is probably there—or at least much of it. This, beyond any clever manipulations, diplomacy, or subterfuge, can make the biggest difference. Even if something isn't stated directly, a good listener can perceive through tone, context, even body language what is needed.

Listening can apply to getting the job as well. In a job interview the director wants to know that you have seen some of his work, wants to know you are enthusiastic about his project or the script, and wants to know that you are capable of pulling it off. Beyond that, most directors mainly want to share their vision with you. After all, that's probably what drove them to venture into this project in the first place. If you listen and can sincerely see what the director sees, you're in a good position. Unless they ask, the person isn't waiting to hear your critical review of the script or theories on filmmaking. Your reply will come in the form of a cut. This is not to say you should remain mute or withdraw—far from it. What it does say is that this person has worked very hard developing his project, getting funding for it, and preparing to film it, and now he is going to hand his baby over to you, a person he may not even know. He wants to feel that you're patient, that you listen, and that you're flexible, and, occasionally, he wants you to mirror what he's telling you so he's sure you got it.

Case Study

Day after day the director reminded the editor, "I really want to see that shot of the horse in the establishing shot." The editor didn't think it was an important shot, so he ignored the request. Eventually the director got the assistant to cut it in. The editor discovered this and was annoyed because that's his job. But the director reminded him, "I kept asking you to put in the horse shot." Things went downhill from there. In this case, it meant a call to the film doctor.

Case Study

It's important to ask questions, though always asking questions, especially as a shortcut to discovering something you could find out on your own, can be detrimental. As a novice assistant editor I was constantly called upon to perform tasks I had no idea how to accomplish. Rather than weigh down the editor with questions, I figured it out on my own. This meant that I truly learned what to do. Today it's even easier to get answers, particularly to technical questions, through the Internet or by contacting technical support. Making friends with other editors or assistants, as well as people at the labs and rental houses, also helps. When you get stuck, there will be someone you can turn to. If it's a really big favor, a lunch might be in order. As easy as it is to get answers from the Internet, the volume of technical issues has increased, particularly with the development of new technologies such as digital high definition and 3D.

Staying Seated

Stay in your seat. This means don't give up control. It's especially important today, when many directors have a cursory or better knowledge of software such as Avid or Final Cut Pro. Even though Moviolas were incredibly simple machines, it was nearly impossible to avoid ripping, scratching, or breaking the film if one hadn't developed the physical agility to run the equipment. Today, though more crowded with options, software-driven nonlinear editing systems are physically easier to operate. So, when an editor goes for a coffee or bathroom break, the impatient director may be inclined to jump in and continue the cutting. Some are even bolder and will ask the editor to move aside and let them have a go at it. Having developed the skills and confidence to occupy the editing chair, the editor needs to maintain control of the editorial helm of the film. This is not a power trip. This is, as all decisions should be, for the good of the film. Even though the editor may be easygoing, affable, and flexible, it does the film a disservice if he abandons his position on the film. Abdicating the editing chair allows for haphazard treatment of the producer's most valuable asset.

On the other hand, as with much of filmmaking, there are no hard-and-fast rules. Editors and directors who have worked together for years sometimes bend this rule, due to a deep connection and shorthand that can forward the project. But for the most part, editing the movie is not the director's job. If a director is editing his own film in order to further exert his control or to overcome an inability to explain what he wants, he should reconsider. Sometimes films that are edited by directors would have been better off if the director hadn't sat in the editing chair. Even good films would probably be a little peppier, a little smarter, and a little shorter if the director had allowed himself that restraint.

Dailies and Rough Cuts

Studio executives often don't know how to look at dailies. If the dailies are presented in the order they were shot in, as opposed to script sequence, the situation grows even worse. The best political move has little to do with politics—organize the dailies in lined script order, as discussed in Chapter 7, so the viewer has the sense of watching a story rather than a collection of disjointed takes.

Case Study

I've done several stints as head of postproduction and was always amazed at how little most production executives know about viewing dailies. They generally enjoyed watching the actors and commenting on their performances, adding quips about their negotiations with the actor's agent or remarking at how tired the actor looked on a particular day. They admired the attractive pictures that the DP shot or groaned at a shot that was out of focus. What they had trouble watching for is sufficient coverage and whether the dailies supply enough shots with decent performances to put a movie together. Tune out the minutiae and keep your focus.

The Answer Is Yes

As an editor you have to learn to take yes for an answer. Too often we keep talking after the decision has been made in our favor. Continuing the pitch after you've achieved the goal makes a producer wonder if he has made the right decision. After all, if this guy feels the need to continue to justify his actions, maybe there is something wrong.

As a side note, remember that editing is all about timing, which includes patience. Sometimes you have to wait for "Yes." Even if you diagnose a problem and have a sense of how to fix it, this may not be the best time to broach it. In some cases you may have to wait until after a screening of the first cut to voice your idea.

The Poor Craftsman

The adage "It's the poor craftsman who blames his tools" remains as true today as in medieval times. Editing, by its nature, is both a creative and technical medium. It requires deep aesthetic understanding combined with refined technical skills. Occasionally the equipment creates problems. Equipment failures can be frustrating and even embarrassing. This can be particularly disturbing when you are in the middle of a screening or on the way to one. It is important to keep in mind, however, that it is the equipment and not the editor that has failed. All equipment fails from time to time. Avoid getting flustered. Most people understand technical difficulties. Briefly explain what has happened, and then, if you have the expertise, fix it. If not, make sure you know someone who can. Having a technically adept assistant is a major asset. It takes the onus off the editor, proves the value of having assistants, and solves the problem quickly.

But there's another side to technical issues. Inexperienced or incompetent editors, unwilling to admit their own shortcomings, blame the equipment. An assistant, who worked on only a couple films but had caught the director's eye, was promoted to full editor on the director's next film. At first, things went smoothly, but then the editor hit snags for which he was ill-prepared. He became unnerved. The rental house that had supplied the editing system began to get daily calls regarding the equipment. In fact, the machine was in fine working order, but the assistant-turned-editor was uncomfortable working at an editor's level. Unwilling to admit this, he blamed the equipment. The experience became unpleasant for him and the director, and it became his last stint as an editor.

Case Study

Some years ago, I had the opportunity to spend time with one of cinema's greatest film editors, the late Ralph Winters. He'd cut such classics as *The Thomas Crown Affair*, *The Pink Panther*, *The Great Race*, and *Ben-Hur*. It was from him that I learned to cut dialog (and have passed that information on in this book). I also learned a few things about the politics of the editing room. He once told a story that was reproduced in *Editing*, a magazine originated by the Eagle Eye Film Company, and that I quote here: "I had a situation where I had a producer on one side of me and a director on the other; they hated each other.... And every time we sat down in the projection room to run something, they'd argue. And I was in the middle, becoming very unnerved. I didn't want to choose sides. I thought the director was a better moviemaker, but the other guy was pretty good, too; he'd produced a lot of films. So one day a close-up came on the screen, and the producer leaned over to me and said, 'No, no, that's on there too long.' And the director overheard him, and he spoke to me and said, 'It's too short. Lengthen it.' I went back to the cutting room and looked at that close-up. It didn't need trimming, and it certainly didn't need adding. I didn't touch it. The next time we ran it, I poked the producer and said, 'Better!' Turned to the director, 'Better?' They both said it was better."

What's the Big Deal?

Another aspect to consider as a creative person is that often the company you're working for does not share the same concern about making art. Their interest is in making money. Lots of it. Granted there are some executives who feel truly devoted to the artistry of the medium, but often that is because they were in a creative aspect of filmmaking at some point earlier in their careers. The rest really are mainly concerned with money and power. So don't be disappointed when you can't appeal to them in terms of artistry. If you try to appeal to them, it may have to be in terms that reassure them of the fiscal benefit of your request or suggestion.

A corollary of this refers to any contract you make. Many producers and executives are ethical people, priding themselves on dealing fairly with people, anxious to give as much or more to those who work for them as they receive in return. Others are eager to ensure that they take as much as possible and compensate as little as possible. They may hold carrots, speaking of future work, larger projects, and bonuses, but generally the intention is to get as much as they can without paying for it or, rather, paying very little. An artistic person's strong suit generally isn't business. If truth be told, most would work for free because they love what they do. But everyone must find a livelihood and a means of supporting themselves.

In this regard, considering an independent production company your friend because they're outside the system may be an illusion. The Latin warning caveat emptor, "Let the buyer beware," which puts some of the responsibility on the buyer for purchases of inferior or fraudulent products, can easily be reversed to caveat venditor, "Let the seller beware." If you are taking a nonunion job, you should have an agent or an attorney look over any deal memo before you sign it. You need someone on your team, someone who is willing to go to bat and be the bad guy. Despite what the producer or legal affairs guy might tell you, the contract may mean something completely different. One word on a contract can make the difference between whether you get a screen credit on a film, receive the points or bonuses owed to you for your hard work, or make the producer richer with what is rightfully yours.

 Warnings

Don't work for a flat. A flat deal means you will receive one flat sum for the project. No less, no more. Initially, it may seem like a reasonable wage, but what if the film goes into reshoots or takes longer to complete than anticipated? Your time is tied up, and you are paying to help the producer finish his film. A guaranteed flat is slightly different in that it guarantees a certain amount of money, no matter if the film is completed or if it's completed ahead of schedule. Still, a flat is a flat and best avoided.

What about deferred salaries? Maybe the producer can't pay you up front, but he's sure the film will be a big hit, and even if it's not, he's sure to be able to sell it to cable, video, or the Internet. At some point in the distant future, he'll pay you the money you've agreed he owes you. Most people who agree to defer their salaries never see a dime.

 Doctor's Note

In navigating one's career in film editing, it's important to realize that even the most popular editors don't necessarily work all the time. I've known Academy Award winners who, while most likely to work consistently, still worry at times that they'll never work again. Editing, and most jobs in the motion picture business, are precarious. They don't come with the same guarantees that

(Continued)

> **Doctor's Note** (Continued)
>
> corporate work promises. Though the work is variable, it's usually better paid per hour or per week, partially because it is understood that the worker's savings may need to bridge her from one job to another. Also, these workers have the satisfaction of participating in the artistic branch of the business. They are the ones who actually make the movies. Without them, the business would not exist. The ones who enjoy consistent employment year after year are usually those who work for the corporation, which is the studio, or in services such as laboratories or post houses. But even those change. Studios used to employ the majority of workers in Hollywood. When the studio system broke down in the 1970s, independents proliferated. Today, with the rise of new technologies and distribution systems, the trajectory of jobs is again changing. The apprentice who was hired to code the film dailies has gone the way of the proverbial buggy whip salesman. The companies that sell and repair splicers have all but disappeared. As some had predicted years ago, the film business is the paradigm for jobs of the future. Workers who once believed they could commit to a job for life and be assured of consistent work and a healthy retirement find themselves laid off, cut back, hired part-time, or doing piece work—events that are familiar to most film workers.

The Strength of Weak Ties

In light of employment trends, it helps to consider a concept that sociologists have coined "the strength of weak ties." This refers to the phenomenon that job offers and help come from the most tangential areas. As important as it remains to make and sustain connections, to stay in touch with people you've worked with before, the universe seems to have constructed a scheme that is partly out of our control. One pursues a particular job with a close friend or with a director one has worked with before. Sometimes it works—and some of the top directors have a fierce loyalty to their team, which includes the editor, director of photography, and production designer—but sometimes not. Yet, out of nowhere, an acquaintance, a chance encounter, a weak connection presents a need and, rather than requiring months of courtship, demands immediate fulfillment and you're the one. In this regard, it's good to always be prepared. Have your resume in order, your website up to date, and your clothes pressed.

Committing to a Project

Several times I've been brought in on films that were produced or directed by nonfilmmakers. That is, they had never studied filmmaking, never made a film before, and, in one case, rarely went to the movies. There are some people who describe themselves as nonfilmmakers but are driven by a passion so strong that it needs to be expressed. Such was the case with the team who made the stunning Academy Award–winning documentary about dolphin slaughter in Japan, *The Cove*. Part of what elevated their passion to something tangible and engaging was the employment of an experienced editor, Geoffrey Richman, who'd edited Michael Moore's *Sicko*. He was able to help them construct the story and put all the pieces together.

Case Study

One can rarely predict the fate of the films one works on. Big-budget studio films can flop and low-budget indies can make history. Of course, the converse is also true. Ironically, I was the editor on a low-budget film for New Line, *Poison Ivy (The New Seduction)*, for which the expectations were rather low. I agreed to do it mainly for the enjoyment of working with a director I liked, Kurt Voss. We never tested the film. We expected it to go directly to video. Yet it became a cult classic and made a small fortune. Ten years after the film came out, *Maxim* magazine was calling it "Everybody's favorite guilty pleasure." Ten years after that, I was still being contacted to give interviews regarding it. Who knew?

Doctor's Note

The focus of this book is on the health of the film and, specifically, the edit, but a few words should be said about the health of the man or woman who puts the film together. The hours can be long, the tensions high, and the work exhausting. It helps to maintain a good attitude and a healthy regimen. Too many times I've seen excellent editors undone by the stumbling blocks of the trade. Alcoholism, obesity, and hypertension are some of the ills facing editors. Other editors, realizing that their bodies are what they depend on to sustain them through the hard labor of editing a feature film, make a point to eat well, get exercise when they can—even if it amounts to occasional breaks to walk around the block—and avoid smoking and excessive drinking. With the advent of electronic editing, new options have opened up for editors. Even though nonlinear editing systems have required editors to cut faster and make many more decisions per hour, they have also brought new mobility to the editor. Many editors can work at home or at offices near home, cutting down on commuting and other issues that effect health and productivity. The editing room used to require hundreds of pounds of equipment and thousands of feet of film in a fixed location, but that has changed. When the edit codes for an entire feature film can be carried on something as light and small as a flash drive and entire sequences can be streamed over the Internet, the portability of the art has truly changed for the better.

Film Doctoring

The position of film doctor is a privileged one. Where editors are usually recruited by the director, in the case of film doctoring, the editor may have been brought in by the studio or the producers. Rather than doing the director's bidding, the editor is following his own instincts, supported by a bond company, a producer, or the studio. As Jon Poll, who has film doctored many comedies, points out, the editor is usually coming in with free reins. The film is in trouble, and he's there to fix it.

Here the politics can be tricky. Directors have mixed reactions to this sort of addition. Some welcome it, confident that new eyes will help the project. Others resent it at first, though in most cases they realize that something wasn't working. They're actually relieved down the line when they see vast improvements.

Editors, as well, have varying responses. Some are unwilling to admit their shortcomings and react defensively. Others view the doctor's visit as a chance to improve the film on which they're credited.

Jon Poll points out that when he comes on a picture as a film doctor, he brings with him one rule: You can't fire the editor. He feels he's not there to replace anybody. He's there to make the movie better. This approach benefits everyone. Often one finds that an editor is happy to work alongside the film doctor because he gets to experiment with cuts that previously he might have been afraid to try. In some cases it becomes a learning experience.

COMPLETION BOND

A completion bond is a form of insurance that guarantees the film's completion, even if the director fails to deliver or the film goes over budget. Studios, due to their deep pockets, don't usually rely on bond companies. Independent productions with any sizable budget usually include a completion bond in their budgets.

Of course, on some films the editor has already been dismissed. The movie is in trouble, and, rightly or wrongly, the desperate producers pointed the gun at the editor. Now the film has lain dormant, floundering for several weeks or months. The budget barely supports extending the schedule, let alone keeping on twice the editorial staff. In these cases the film doctor may be the last person standing.

Here are some favorite movie lies that might ring true.

- "Honestly, I just found out about it."
- "I couldn't bring you in on this one because the producer had someone else in mind."
- "I couldn't bring you in on this one because the director had someone else in mind."
- "The check's in the mail."
- "We'll make it up to you on the next one."
- "They'll never notice it."
- "It'll only take a minute."

Chapter 16

Triage

Emergency Procedures

When asked to help with the editing of a motion picture where work has already been under way for many months, film doctors often find a producer or post supervisor who, at his wit's end, is anxious for someone who can alleviate the pain. Yet many of these filmmakers feel that, having suffered as much as they have, they can no longer afford the time or expense that had previously been allotted. But this is the moment when it is most warranted. If the film becomes releasable in the hands of the new editor and garners a decent return, then the producers will be more than compensated for the cost of the intervention. In any case, the skittish producer or director may ask for a trial period, such as two weeks.

Case Study

On several occasions I have had producers announce that they are bringing me in for two weeks "just to polish" the cut. They assure me not to expect any more employment than that. So I know I had better have something really good to show by the end of that time. After two weeks they generally see such a significant difference in their movie that they extend the editing phase. This experience is not unique; it happens to any good film doctor. A new or more insightful approach can make a film look as if it were a completely different movie.

Two Weeks

What can an editor do in two weeks? And what if, as is sometimes the case on low-budget indie films, the budget cannot support an extended editing period? How can the editor make the best of an exceedingly short assignment and still benefit the production? Think of this as the triage period. These are the emergency moments when a life hangs in the balance. Of course, as we need to remind ourselves when things get too intense, filmmaking is not generally a life-or-death profession.

The Healthy Edit. DOI: 10.1016/B978-0-240-81446-9.00016-0

Any good doctor knows that prescribing medicine before carefully diagnosing an ailment can lead to disaster. The same applies to film editing. It takes a certain amount of patience and understanding to properly diagnose an ailing scene, sequence, or film. Since we're all used to watching movies, the viewer initially may respond by unconsciously filling in the gaps for himself. If it seems that the good guy is too exposed as he runs from a barrage of automatic weapon fire, escaping without a scratch, the viewer may tell himself, "It's hard to hit a moving target" or some other justification. But movies are not intellectual exercises. Movies move. The editor must become the audience—an extremely discriminating audience—and supply the answers by way of the edit..

In triage situations, such as the ER, a series of basic procedures are enacted. Vitals are taken, the patient is stabilized, any bleeding is stopped, and breathing is restored. For the editor, these first moments can hold the greatest promise. The initial screening when he is asked to offer an opinion is the purest. It is the best chance to perceive the problems. Your first instincts are usually correct. The editor asks herself, "At what point did I become confused?" "Why does the character do that there? Wouldn't he do it earlier?" And so on. Like an ER doctor, the editor has a set of examinations to perform and operations to follow.

In discussing his reediting of *Red Dawn*, Richard Pearson mentioned how it first became necessary "to *stabilize* the film." The director wanted someone who had nothing to do with the script, someone who could come at it with no preconceptions. Even though the previous cuts were quite good, there were structural and character issues that first had to be resolved. When taking on a new patient, Pearson first watches the entire film, mindful of his initial impressions. Then he looks at all the deleted scenes, manufactures some new moments, and sometimes requests additional photography. "I think of that as aligning the spine of the patient. There are pieces that need to be aligned to make sure you have proper story and character traction, that everything is tracking," he explains. Once the patient is stabilized, the editor can delve into more specific or detailed work.

Symptoms

As in medical triage, start by looking for symptoms such as confusion, slow gait, lack of interest, lack of affect. In many triage cases it is advisable to begin at the beginning ... and at the ending. Concentrate on the opening and closing scenes. Most likely, the film got off on the wrong foot, and this misstep in pace, rhythm, character, or structure has rippled through the entire work. In some cases the ending has little bearing on the beginning. Or maybe it's not in tune with the expectations set up by the particular genre.

The tracking of the plot, the characters' emotional journeys, and their arcs are typical areas where issues arise. Is the story obtuse, meandering, or confusing? Is the structure predictable and excessively linear? Are the characters' personalities reflected in the choice of shots? If time and cost are the primary issues, an inventive and insightful editor can help diminish damage and enhance the health of a cut by attending to these immediate story considerations.

A primary culprit here is the lack of focus on the main character. Films that begin with a variety of characters where each is given fairly equal treatment lose interest because the audience has no one in particular with whom to connect. If there are multiple stories afoot, such as in *Babel, Crash,* or *Traffic,* those stories and their characters need to be broken out into separate chapters. But usually there's one main character and his antagonist who need to be clearly represented. If this is established early on and the audience is clear whom they're supposed to be watching, it will help clarify much of the later material.

Doctor's Note

Shortcutting the post process is never a good idea. The triage methods discussed here are useful for not only desperate films that have consumed much of their time and budget but also as a starting point for troubled films that offer reasonable editing schedules.

Fully realizing a damaged ending may take more time than is allotted, but a couple of quick fixes can help alleviate some of the suffering. One of the more common dilemmas occurs in multiple or wrong endings. By revisiting the story's opening, the editor discovers the original story conflict that needed resolution by the film's end. If the ending does not bear a relationship to the issues raised in the beginning, there is probably something wrong. Also, if at an earlier point the protagonist's problem or need has been overcome, then everything that happens after that point is probably superfluous and can be cut. Or else the resolution of the problem needs to be delayed.

Looking in the opposite direction, one discovers unfocused or sloppy openings. Remember, the first image that appears on the screen sets the tone for the whole movie. Beginning with a less than riveting shot or series of shots can damage what follows. Think thematically. Locate shots that reinforce the film's overall meaning and visual concept. Never be arbitrary.

Pacing is a major issue that can be helped in a matter of weeks but usually takes much longer to fully realize throughout the entire film. Trimming here and there will accelerate a stalled pace and contribute to overall interest. A word of caution: Unless the time allows, a shot-by-shot recut for pacing of the opening scenes can sometimes hinder the overall film's perceived momentum. The contrast of a well-conceived, energetically paced opening that after several scenes slams into the preexisting condition of a tired and plodding middle only exacerbates the problem.

Audio Issues

As with humans, the film may initially respond to technical intervention. Video and audio issues can damage otherwise workable scenes. Don't underestimate the effect that poor sound has on the overall picture. Humans are sensitive to sound and react to inappropriate or inaccurate sound effects, as well as sounds that are too prominent or too faint. Who likes to be yanked out of a pleasant dream by a sonic boom or a hand shaking one's shoulder? Bad sound has this effect. Listen for overmodulated or excessively low sound, dropouts, and misplaced audio. Carefully checking the audio meters as well as evaluating the subjective hearing experience through high-quality monitors will help fix this problem. In dialog a common error occurs when the beginning or end of a word is cut off or the beginning of a new sentence is left hanging with nothing to accompany it.

In terms of dialog it is crucial to hear it. Though this may seem obvious, it is not always the case. Ensuring clarity often means something as basic as adjusting the volume. If the original sound was recorded too low, the volume may be deficient even with the audio mix tool maxed out at 12. In this case it is possible to push it further by altering the scale to allow more headroom (see Tech Note, below). Most nonlinear editing systems give multiple options for adjusting volume, including a sound mixer, keyframing, and, on FCP, an in-track volume bar that can be raised and lowered.

If music plays behind the dialog, it may require lowering the music to allow the dialog to come through. The inclination to push the dialog up in order to overpower the music tends to multiply the signal and produce a loud, even noisy mix. When effects are added as well, sounds that were originally clean and audible by themselves become distorted.

> **MOS**
>
> A Hollywood term with a German sounding phrase, MOS, like many film terms, was originally coined as an on-set joke. When emigrant director Erich von Stroheim announced with his Austrian accent that he was going to shoot the next take "Mit out sound" (without sound) the set culture picked up the German word "mit," meaning "with," and repeated it. Eventually "Mit out sound" evolved into the abbreviated form known today.

Also, the sudden absence of sound, particularly where an MOS shot is left without filling in the ambience, can be disconcerting to an audience. Though not always apparent on a conscious level, these flaws and inconsistencies create an unconscious disturbance in an audience.

In the past, editors did not usually mix the audio themselves. Even for a temp dub the film required the skills of sound editors or, at minimum, rerecording engineers working with 35 mm single- or full-coat sound film on multiple rolls corresponding to each reel of the picture. Today, both Avid and FCP offer up to a hundred individual audio tracks (though not all can be monitored at once), along with sophisticated audio tools that allow equalization, filters, compression, and so on. Avid, who partnered with Digidesign, the makers of Pro Tools, the state-of-the-art sound editing system, links to some of the most powerful audio tools in the industry. FCP Studio is bundled with an extensive mixing and sound creation program known as Soundtrack Pro.

As the editor builds his picture cut he can assemble multiple effects and music tracks, and modify them through an audio mixer or by the use of keyframes. In this way the temp dub is carried along with the picture cut and updated on each subsequent version, available to be laid off at any time.

Tech Note

The analog VU meter uses an averaging system in order to give a sound rating in decibels (dB). Modular meters and digital audio meters give discreet readings. With digital meters the average and useable sound level occurs around −12 dB rather than 0 dB of the analog system. Music is usually mixed below that level, around −18. It is important to note that the more forgiving analog audio signal distorts when subjected to overmodulation. Digital audio, however, vanishes at excessive volumes. This is known as *clipping*.

Tech Note

Sometimes audio tracks have been recorded or inputted at an excessively low volume, making it impossible to adequately raise them through the sole use of the audio mix tool. It this case it is possible to create a higher dynamic range by raising the headroom. In FCP under Modify go to Audio and then to Apply Normalization Gain. By setting this below 0 (−6 often works) it will add room to further raise the sound level. Avid has a useful audio and video mixdown feature that allows you to combine tracks into one. This works well for complex effects involving multiple tracks as well as the ability to consolidate audio tracks. This is particularly useful in the case of a sound-designed effect, which requires multiple tracks to create but plays as a single unit. This mixdown track becomes a separate track on the timeline with all the various volumes wrapped into one and appearing as a normal setting on the Mix tool. This allows the gain to again be raised if necessary. Also, in FCP, dragging a multiple track audio sequence into the timeline renders it as a single track that can be reopened into its constituent parts by double-clicking on it.

Filters and equalization tools also allow an opportunity to clean up tracks that may be hampered by noise such as a fluorescent hum that, occurring around 60 Hz, can be notched out. The sound packages also give the opportunity to enhance the reality by *futzing* a voice through a telephone or loudspeaker.

Not only do sound volume and clarity make a significant impact in the life of a film but also placement. Anything out of sync is going to call attention to itself and distract the audience. But careless placement also plays a significant role. In this case the culprit might be a music cue that ends a couple shots too early. Or a temp cue that is merely chopped off or faded rather than music edited so its natural ending occurs at an appropriate point in the film. When all else fails, however, the simple inclusion of a loud sound, such as an explosion, a door slam, or a gunshot can cover the awkward end to a music cue. The introduction of this new audio information takes sudden precedence over the music. By the time the new sound has culminated, the audience has forgotten about the previous music.

Case Study

To illustrate the highly subjective influence that sound has psychologically, consider the response to a scene where the music ran out a few shots before the end. Since there was dialog running over the music, the viewer believed he was actually paying attention to what was said rather than to the underlying score. When the music made a natural fade, the viewer felt that was the end of the scene. He was put off when the dialog continued. He felt that all the important information had been imparted and the scene was over. In fact, there remained a final, revelatory sentence that hung in the silence. The editor recut the music so it ended at the true conclusion of the scene. Without revealing this to the viewer, he again played the scene, and this time the viewer insisted that the dialog now ended earlier and at its appropriate point. In fact, no shots or dialog had been changed.

Video Ills

Similarly, video presents an inherent set of issues to be considered. If the color and density continuously shift within a scene, the viewer may unconsciously get the impression that the scene is ending and a new one is beginning. Footage that is not properly rendered or is incompatible creates jumps or hesitations that pull the viewer out of the story. Anything that does not directly pertain to the story and characters or overall style becomes a distraction that invites the audience to remove themselves from the film. In that way, including banners or other nonessential on-screen notations in a rough cut interrupts the viewer's involvement in the film. Where the editor feels the need to make notes, Final Cut Pro's marker system and Avid's locator system allow an easy, unobtrusive way to hide reminders throughout the timeline.

Alterations in color and density also harm the perception of a cut. No matter how smooth the editing may be, when a shot that is too green and bright is placed directly next to a shot that is too red and dark, the seamless feel of the movie is interrupted. Taking advantage of the color correction tools on most professional nonlinear editing systems helps alleviate this problem.

Case Study

Simple technical corrections can produce a significant effect for the audience, who initially is the producer. Years ago, before cutting electronically, I was one of the editors on a film where the previous editor had spliced the entire movie using two-perf splices. These tape splices jumped each time they went through the projector, as well as producing a thin line on the top and bottom of the screen. Though probably unconscious to the audience, the overall effect was of a jumpy, ill-timed movie. To solve the problem we removed each splice and replaced it with a stronger, less obtrusive four-perf splice. This alone improved the perceived quality of the film, since it appeared to flow better. All this occurred before making any changes in the actual picture.

Tech Note

Over the years the question of the perfect tape splice has been debated. Since each 35 mm film frame is four perforations (abbreviated: *perf*) in length, the placement of the tape on the film determines how much or little of the splice the audience will see when it's projected onto a 40-foot screen, where any irregularities, including bubbles and dust, grow into gigantic monsters. The debate hinged on whether two-perf, four-perf, or eight-perf splices were the least intrusive. To this editor, the eight-perf splice proved best.

The eight-perf splice with its strength, along with the fact that it needed to be placed on only one side of the film, the celluloid side, and that it covered the entire the A side and the B side of the cut, made it perfect for exhibiting a rough cut. Its only disadvantages were that it captured microscopic bubbles that had to be removed, and if the film found its way back to the editing bench, it was harder to break open the splices for further trims. On the other end of the spectrum appeared the Inviso splice, which placed tape on both sides of the film but outside the 1.85 aspect ratio, making it virtually invisible. Unfortunately, it would often fail after the initial

---

screening, exposing the adhesive and making the film catch as it unspooled. The standard two-perf splice was even worse since it produced a tape line on the top and bottom of the screen when projected. The other effective splice, which didn't require back-splicing on the film's opposite side, was the four-perf. Though it could be seen, the fact that two perfs extended into the A side and two perfs into the B side of the splice meant that a faint line appeared briefly in the middle of the frame. This was much less distracting than the animation of a line jumping from the top to the bottom of the frame.

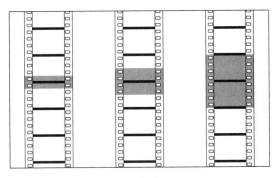

Figure 16.1 *Various types of splices.*

The actions described in this chapter will quickly help stem the bleeding and put a film on the path to good health. Generally, however, it takes longer to proceed from what would be a quick polish to a full restructuring and renewal. With the speed of nonlinear editing, however, it is more likely today to accomplish a reasonable facelift in a short period of time. What might not necessarily occur are the deeper discoveries and realizations that materialize when one lives with a film and its director for an extended period of time. These are the kind of realizations that separate truly profound work from everyday productions.

℞

Try this checklist when time is of the essence:

- What are the structural issues?
- Is it clear who the main character is? Does his or her objective drive each scene?
- What technical issues are diminishing the film's presentation?
- Is the opening strong enough?
- Does the ending relate to the problem that was set up in the beginning?
- Does the film go on too long? Does it continue past the actual ending?

Chapter 17

Post-mortem

From Final Cut to Exhibition

Since this is the last chapter, it is appropriate to say a few words about endings. The question often arises "Which is more important, the beginning or the ending of a film?" Some believe that the beginning holds the most significance, since at that moment the filmmaker has an opportunity to grab the audience, to get them involved with the characters and conflict that will follow. Others, however, believe that the ending is the more important aspect of a film because what happens there will remain with the audience after they leave the theater.

At the beginning of a film an audience is primed and attentive—that is, assuming they haven't been worn out by the avalanche of television-style advertising that has infiltrated the motion picture theaters these days. At the start of the film a viewer watches and listens closely to understand the rules and values of this new world he has entered. In this regard, audiences will usually tolerate slow or even confusing openings. They assume that if they hang in there, all will eventually be revealed. By the time they reach the end, however, they expect to understand what the story is about, to feel empathy for the characters and to experience a satisfying resolution. Maybe even a revelation, an epiphany. Not all movies have happy endings, but good movies have satisfying resolutions. It will have a direct connection to issues raised during the beginning of the film, as they relate to genre.

In the case study of the Christmas movie *Prancer* in Chapter 3, we examined the first half of the ending which was altered in the final editing process. Following the farewell between the girl, Jessie, and Prancer, the reindeer disappears into the woods. But that is not the final ending. One more beat has to occur before the film ends. Originally, this was left equivocal. Jessie and her father (Sam Elliott) wander out to the edge of the forest and discover the reindeer's hoof prints in the snow, leading to the edge of a cliff. "He couldn't have jumped and lived," says Jessie. "Maybe he flew," replies the

---

EPIPHANY

The ah-ha effect that well-crafted stories bring to their audience. The epiphany comes from a realization of a deeper meaning within the context of the story. This term was brought into the world of storytelling by the novelist James Joyce (*Ulysses, A Portrait of the Artist as a Young Man*).

The Healthy Edit. DOI: 10.1016/B978-0-240-81446-9.00017-2

father. In that moment we realize that the once skeptical and detached father has gravitated to his daughter's side while the innocent believer, Jessie, has gained some skepticism. But the answer as to what really happened to Prancer was left inconclusive. In other genres this may be appropriate, but not in a Christmas movie where the audience has come to anticipate something magical, an epiphany, a reaffirmation of the season. To promote this concept I agreed to return to the editing room late at night to review the scene with the director and producer before the film was to be locked. It was finally decided to go with a more revealing and, I felt, satisfying ending. As Jessie gazes up into the sky a glow passes over her face and she sees a tiny spark of light arching through the firmament. It joins a team of other reindeer drawing a sleigh across the full moon. Through editing and the use of simple visual effects it was possible to alter the film's outcome. This enchanting ending, tempered by the darker, more serious aspects that the director brought to the film, added a crucial extra beat, fulfilling the expectations of the audience. With the use of shot selection, juxtaposition, sound, and visual effects, the movie's equivocal conclusion became a magical ending consistent with the film's genre. This ending fulfilled the anticipation that had been set up during the course of the film.

Audiences expect that the couple hours they devote to watching a movie will be worthwhile. They hope not to be disappointed. Motion pictures, like all stories, are a way of bringing order to our lives. In our daily struggles and triumphs, few of us experience the tidy, concise, and well-structured progression of events that a movie presents. A successful ending supplies the audience with answers and a sense of coherency that our lives often lack. In the following examples of *Made in Heaven* and *Fatal Attraction*, we see how knowing when to end, as well as finding the proper ending can make all the difference in a film's success.

Made in Heaven

Made in Heaven, directed by Alan Rudolph and starring Tim Hutton, Kelly McGillis, and Debra Winger (along with a slew of cameos ranging from Neil Young and Tom Petty to the cartoonist Gary Larson), took well over a year and a half to complete. Part of the reason it took so long resided in the difficulty of discovering the correct ending for the picture. It was really quite a simple story: boy meets girl, boy loses girl, boy finds girl again and marries her. The twist was that they met in heaven, and, since the girl was a new soul—she was made in heaven—it was her turn to travel to earth for the first time. Mike Shea (Tim Hutton) convinces Emmett (Debra Winger)—the writers were careful not to call her God—to send him back to earth, as Elmo Barnett, to find Ally Chandler (Kelly McGillis), his true love. The deal is, if he finds her within 30 years, they will be together forever. If not, they will never see each other again and Elmo will be returned to heaven.

As the film develops Elmo and Ally cross paths, live separate lives, fall in and out of love with the wrong people, and eventually both end up in New York City. Elmo, on his 30th birthday, has just celebrated a record deal. On his way down Fifth Avenue, he encounters Ally, who has just discovered that the guy she loved has married someone else. As Ally and Elmo's eyes meet, a car sideswipes Elmo.

In the first version, as Elmo's body sprawls on the pavement, his soul is sucked back up to heaven, where Emmett informs him that he'll be okay because she found him in time. But some studio executives did not feel this was enough, so they paid to shoot additional scenes where Elmo is placed in an ambulance and transported to the hospital in critical condition. At the hospital doctors fight to save his life. Finally he regains consciousness and is moved to a private room. Ally, having seen the accident, arrives to visit him. As Elmo and Ally speak, they recognize their love for each other and the music rises.

In the final version, these additional scenes were cut out. So was the original ending with the car hitting Elmo and his subsequent sojourn to heaven. What became clear was that a deal was a deal. Once they found each other, the movie was over; extending the movie past that point with the false jeopardy of an accident was a waste of time and a frustration to the audience.

Affairs of the Heart

Fatal Attraction, a film about a middle-aged family man, Dan Gallagher (Michael Douglas), who has an extramarital affair that comes back to haunt him in the guise of Glenn Close, originally suffered from an inappropriate ending. The film was entitled *Affairs of the Heart*, and in its original incarnation, which was never released in theaters, homicide detectives appear at Dan Gallagher's home to arrest him for the murder of Alex Forrest (Glenn Close). After the police escort Dan away, his wife runs into the house to call the family lawyer. As she waits on the line, her eyes wander to a cassette tape tucked inside the address book. On the tape she sees the words "Play me." She pops the tape in the cassette player and is treated to the suicidal confession of the woman whom her husband was said to have murdered. She jumps up and calls to her daughter, "Come on, honey, we're going to go get Daddy." A nice, neat ending.

Originally, this ending must have seemed like the perfect conclusion to the story: Even though Dan Gallagher is initially arrested for murder, it turns out that everything is going to be okay because the woman who has been stalking him and threatening his family has eliminated herself from the picture and generously left a tape announcing her intentions. On the surface this conclusion appears to have tied up all the story's loose ends. On paper it worked well enough to sell the script. But, according to John Wiseman, former VP of Post Production for Paramount Pictures, it did not play well with test audiences. Every time the studio previewed it, the film failed. The ending proved a perfect example of telling, not showing. The audience needed to see the solution, not just hear about it.

Ultimately, the filmmakers ended up rewriting, reshooting, and reediting a new ending, one that embodied the visual power of cinema rather than relying on the written and spoken word. They created an ending that fulfilled the expectations set up by the story and by the genre. The new ending brought the characters into direct conflict with each other. They went mano a mano. There was no easy way out. The forces of good and evil battled to the death. And the film became a huge hit.

Reediting

Stories aren't just written; they're rewritten. Films aren't edited; they're reedited. That is one of the aspects that makes storytelling different from life. Unlike life, where revision amounts to not making the same mistake a second time, storytelling offers the opportunity to rework decisions, actions, dialog, and their consequences until you get it right. On the other hand, as Joseph Campbell pointed out, when people look back over the course of their lives, there seems to be a kind of order, coherency, and, hopefully, refinement. In this way stories mirror life. They are life with all the dull and tangential parts cut out. That is the job of the editor: to take these life stories—tales of loss and victory, isolation and love, injustice and righteousness, despair and hope—and craft them into lean, coherent, effective movies.

When you begin the rough cut, you sketch in the story and dialog through the careful selection of shots. At first you keep your critical faculties at bay. You don't want to hamper the creative process by trying to make the perfect cut from the start. You keep it loose. Ernest Hemingway used to say, "The first draft of anything is shit." Your first cut may be that way too. But before you show it to anyone, you'll fix it.

With experience you learn to follow your initial impulses, not to rein in your ideas too tightly. You know when it is bad, when a cut isn't working, but you keep moving. When you finish, you put it aside for a couple hours, or maybe a couple days. Then you go back to it. Upon review you see clearly what works and what doesn't. What seemed well honed at the end of a long day of cutting will expose a deluge of flaws in the light of the next morning, or days later. You make changes. You apply that critical eye and ear that you'd held at bay during the first assembly. You consider the steps that make for a healthy edit and apply them. The cut improves. Before you finally show it to the director, you have refined the cut many, many times.

Doctor's Note

When editors used to cut on film, the mantra was to "cut it long" because it was easier and less noticeable to trim later than to have to tape film back together if someone changed his mind. Imagine a hairdresser or a seamstress who begins by cutting off too much.

Based on the director's response, he will give notes, sometimes minimal, sometimes extensive, regarding what he feels the cut needs to make it better. At that point the editor and director work together to polish the film. In recutting the film, editor and director come up with fresh ideas, substitute new shots for previous ones, move scenes around, and imagine new approaches to telling the story. In some cases the ending might replace the beginning. Or a favorite character might disappear because his involvement didn't connect with the overall story. At this stage all the adjustments that had been postponed, such as trimming out an entrance and starting with the actors midway into the scene, will occur. This will help improve the film's pace and rhythm. After the editor has made every possible refinement that he and the director can conceive of, the film is ready to head into the final stage of the process.

The Free-for-All

This movie that the editor has nourished, cared for, and coddled from when it was only a few takes old is now ready to go out into the world. With the completion of the director's cut, the editing room doors open, and all the other major players (the stars, the producers, the studio executives, the distributors, etc.) march in with their opinions. Not only that, but people whom the editor and director have never met and will never see again have opinions as well. They have opinions about *your* film. And, in a sense, that is as it should be, because movies are made for audiences.

So, editor and director endure the recruited screenings where friends and family or the general public are invited to watch their film and to say what they think. If the screening goes well, the test audiences will laugh at the funny parts, cry at the poignant moments, and cheer at the end. But not always. There's always someone who says, "It stinks," even if it's *Gone With the Wind*.

The audience surveys involving the general public are sometimes referred to as *the cards*. "We're doing the cards this weekend," producers will say. The cards are the questionnaires that the test audience fills out at the end of the film. They ask questions like "Would you recommend this film to a friend?" or "Were you satisfied with the ending?" After those results are tallied and evaluated by a research group, they are reported to the producer and director. There are score boxes ranging from excellent to poor. The goal is to have 90% or more favorable rating in the first two boxes.

Some filmmakers dislike this part of the process. It can be painful. It can be humiliating. And, most disturbingly, it can be wrong. But often it's not, and the job of the filmmakers is to cull out the pertinent opinions from the irrelevant ones. Asking recruited audiences to tell you how to fix the film would be wrong. That's not their job. Their job is to respond by filling out the survey at the end of the screening and to respond during a focus group discussion.

Audience responses span the gamut from elated to devastated. After the first screening of *Affairs of the Heart*, some audience members actually hissed at the screen. When it later returned to the screen, cloaked in a new name and with a new ending, *Fatal Attraction* made motion picture history as one of the biggest hits of that decade.

One of the most valuable aspects of screening rough cuts for an uninitiated audience comes from the clarity achieved. After having seen various versions over and over again, it becomes difficult for the editor and director to maintain objectivity. As Richard Pearson explains "You're filling in blanks that the audience doesn't. . . . You may think things are tracking when they're not." An audience may think that a particular look means something that it doesn't. In *Red Dawn*, for example, a character gets shot in the leg. Because of the physical reaction and the gun used, the test audience believed he'd been mortally wounded, when, story-wise, he was just supposed to be hit in the leg and survive. Sorting through the intended message and the audience's perception of it remains an important aspect of editing and film doctoring. Along with this, there are other places where an audience's response can be revealing, such as in understanding the stakes, correctly perceiving the physical blocking, and modifying the tendency to overdo the intercutting.

The End Is Near

At some point along the way, maybe a year or more after filming began—following many changes and screenings, sometimes in distant cities to unrelated audiences—no more objections arise at least no significant ones. Almost overnight all the intense scrutiny, prescriptions, and predictions come to an end. The picture is given a clean bill of health. It is *locked*.

Now is the time to begin handing the movie over to the crews who will take it to the final stage of completion. It is sort of like when an excellent general practitioner refers his patient to other specialists. On a film these include the sound editors, the effects crew, and the composer. Some of these specialists, such as the visual-effects crew, will have been on the film since the beginning.

Doctor's Note

With the addition of digital 3D the playing field has expanded even further. Tim Burton's *Alice in Wonderland*, though shot in traditional 2D, was digitally enhanced during postproduction to allow projection in 3D. The predominance of digital postproduction has raised new questions about who actually contributes to the creation of a film. In an article about the cinematography of *Avatar*, *Variety* pointed out that 70% of the film "was created digitally without (the cinematographer's) contribution."

Others, such as the composer, may be seeing the movie for the first time. But one of the first questions they ask is "Is the picture locked?" From here on, it will be more expensive and time-consuming to make changes.

Case Study

In the final stages, when asked if the picture is locked, the answer is usually "Yes, it's locked" even though the editor knows—and others do too—that creative endeavors are rarely that easily abandoned. There may still be changes. A case in point is *Moving Violations*. During the final sound mix—only days before the film was set to open on screens across America—the director, Neal Israel, got an idea. Not just for a trim or two but to shoot an entirely new scene. The studio liked him, and they liked the idea, so they allowed him to leave the rerecording stage, gather a small crew, and shoot the scene. After it was shot, there wasn't enough time to transfer the negative to a workprint (today that would entail transferring it to digital media), so I was required—very carefully—to view the negative over a light box and note the corresponding action on a clear strip of celluloid film. This cued film was then cut and projected so we had something to mix to while the negative went to the negative cutter to be integrated into the final movie. Amazingly, the scene sounded fine, and the film made its release date. Rather than locked, I prefer the term "latched."

The Specialists

Once the picture is locked, timecoded copies are screened with the sound editors and composer. In these *spotting sessions* the editor and director discuss the placement of sound effects and music with the sound editor and the composer. The timecode is used as a reference to note the in and out points.

In the composer's case he may have already seen a version of the film with a temp dub. Some composers refuse to listen to temp music, and understandably so, fearing that they will be unduly influenced. Others use it as a guideline. According to composer Mark Adler (whose credits include *Food, Inc.*, *Bottle Shock*, and *The Rat Pack*), "The temp track should be a safety net and not a springboard. ... If the temp becomes the jumping off point—the springboard—there's a very real danger that the score will lack originality, freshness, and a unique sound and feel which is specific to the film." Either way, the spotting session is an opportunity to discuss where music cues will begin and end, as well as the emotional tone of the composition.

In music spotting, a distinction is made between *source* and *score*. Source music emanates from objects in the scene, such as radios, iPods, stereos, and so on. Sometimes the composer is responsible for producing this, while at other times the source may come from a prerecorded song. Occasionally, these songs are determined by forces other than the director or editor. In such cases the studio or its music supervisor may have arranged for tunes as part of a marketing plan, as well as with hopes of enhancing the appeal of the film's soundtrack.

Case Study

Years ago, on a film for 20th Century Fox, the editing crew was handed a recording by an unknown group and told that it had to be included in the movie, probably as source music. Since no one was very pleased with the song, it was placed in the car radio so it could be turned off soon after the scene began. The song was by a group called The Red Hot Chili Peppers, who eventually became very popular.

It is incredible what a great score can do for a film. Music has the ability to lift a good film to an even higher level, as in the rousing, orchestral scores of *Pirates of the Caribbean* and *Gladiator*. Think of the classic adventure scores of *Indiana Jones* or *Star Wars*, and you'll know the influence that a composer such as John Williams has on a film. Alfred Hitchcock often used Bernard Herrmann to compose suspenseful scores for his films. And Tim Burton's magical, otherworldly movies come alive with Danny Elfman's music. Carter Burwell's edgy score for *Twilight* added depth and direction to the film. And what about the eerie music that pervades other horror films? Music helps bring tension, majesty, romance, and catharsis to a scene. Yet, as seen in films like *Bullitt*, sometimes it is best to let a scene play without music. In that case the sound effects supply the "music."

Sound editors are responsible for dialog, *ADR*, hard effects, *Foley*, ambiences, and sound design. Using programs such as Pro Tools or Logic, the sound editor enhances the synced and edited production track that the editor assembled. The dialog will be relayed with extensions, ambiences that can be crossfaded from one character's dialog to another's, in order to provide smooth transitions from cut to cut. The dialog is then predubbed to set the optimal levels and *EQ* (equalization). The levels alter the gain (volume) and the EQ alters the frequency range.

In some cases the quality of the recorded dialog is so poor that it needs to be replaced. *ADR*, also known as automated dialog replacement, requires the actor to rerecord his lines in a soundproof booth. Since the sound will be clearer and cleaner than can be achieved on most sets, the editor must add a secondary track of ambience or *roomtone* that matches the scene's environment in order to create a natural sound.

> **ROOMTONE**
>
> The set's neutral ambience, usually recorded at the beginning or end of the shoot, is known as *roomtone*. It supplies the necessary audio fill for spots where the background sound would otherwise drop out, such as in MOS or ADR situations.

Case Study

ADR serves other purposes as well. In *Mannequin 2* with Kristy Swanson, the director and I used ADR to replace several actors' voices with the voices of other actors. In the story, the villain was

(Continued)

Case Study (Continued)

protected by three muscle-bound thugs who were supposed to have voices like California's former governor. Though they looked the part, their voices and accents weren't strong enough or consistent enough to be convincing. So we hired several actors from a *loop group* who could replace their dialog. It worked great, and the audience believed these were their real voices.

Another use for ADR is to supply information that was left out of the original script. Often the editor temps in these lines in response to questions raised during the test screenings. A new line of dialog is placed over the actor's back or at other points where the audience won't see the actor's lips.

Just as dialog is replaced, so are certain sound effects. For the most part there are few effects in the final movie that were recorded on the set. Except when the sound mixer is astute enough to record *wild sound* (nonsync sound) of unique ambiences or effects, most of the sounds are gathered and cut into the soundtrack during postproduction. The sounds of footsteps and other moves are rerecorded on a Foley stage. The Foley stage has pits with different surfaces, such as sand, leaves, steel, concrete, and so on. A Foley walker watches a projected scene from the film and mimics the actor's movements exactly. The sounds he creates are recorded and then

Figure 17.1 *One of Hollywood's top Foley artists, Gary Hecker, in action. (Photo courtesy of Gary Hecker.)*

cut into sync with the picture. Today Foley has reached beyond its original purpose to supply background effects for looped dialog. Through Foley most of a scene's effects, including wind and explosions, can be generated live. Some Foley artists will supply vocal sounds, such as efforts, grunts, and even a horse's breathing.

In the final mix all the various tracks are blended together and equalized. Potentially hundreds of tracks are woven down into a small subset of stereo tracks. Finally, the stereo tracks will be encoded onto a soundtrack negative that, like the film negative, will be printed onto a roll of film stock to be projected in theaters. In Figure 17.2 three soundtracks have been printed onto the filmstrip. The analog Dolby SR track, which looks like two parallel waveforms, lies to one side of the picture area. But where's the digital surround track? Since the filmstrip is already crowded, Dolby cleverly placed the digital track between the sprocket holes. If you look closely you will see how the sprocket area on one side looks much grayer

Figure 17.2 *35 mm release print. Though not immediately apparent, this film strip contains three soundtracks. The track with the waveform is Dolby SR. The gray area between the upper sprocket holes is Dolby Digital. And the stripes on the outer edges of the film support SDDS. In some cases a fourth format, DTS, is encoded next to the Dolby SR waveform. It appears as white dashes.*

than the one on the other side. The gray area is made up of thousands of tiny black and white dots that produce the digital signal. If you look even closer, you'll see the Dolby logo in the middle of all those tiny dots! The outer edges of the film, bordered with light green stripes, holds the digital information for Sony Dynamic Digital Sound (SDDS). When played back, digital surround sound gives the audience a heightened experience of being in the scene. Rain falls all around, bullets whiz past, wind shakes the leaves, and so on.

After the Hard Labor: Delivery

The time has come to deliver the film. For independent filmmakers that may mean completing a digital or 35 mm print that can be shopped around at film markets such as the American Film Market and Cannes. Or they may enter the movie in one of the hundreds of film festivals, such as Sundance, Toronto, or Tribeca. In either case the movie must look and sound as good as possible, since it will be judged on its presentation. That is the editor's responsibility.

For films that are produced by studios or that already have a distribution deal, the editor and postproduction supervisor are responsible for fulfilling the *delivery requirements* that have been previously negotiated with the distribution company. The delivery lists can be daunting, and it is important to be aware of what is being asked for. Delivery lists can run up to 20 pages or more, giving exact specifications for the motion picture that is being turned over to the distributor. These items include the original cut negative or digital master; dailies; trims; IP (interpositive), IN (internegative) or DI (digital intermediate); soundtrack negative; Dolby masters; M&Es (music and effects tracks); lined script; composer's cue sheets; composer's music masters; fully timed answer print; check print; video masters; audio master tapes; and corresponding elements for the trailer.

But how do all these elements fit together in the end? Accompanying this chapter is a breakdown of the workflow. Keep in mind that the work that was once united on the editing system is broken down into audio and video elements that were split off to the different departments. Now they must be delivered. In the case of the picture, the editor and her assistant will print out a negative cut list to be given to the negative cutter. This can also be used to produce a DI (digital intermediate). As well as listing every shot and its length, the negative cut list also lists the beginning and ending key numbers for every shot in the movie.

Doctor's Note

The DI has made unprecedented inroads in the postproduction arena. In 2003 only 15% of films were using the digital intermediate or DI process. At the time the process was expensive—over $100,000 for a feature film—and its quality suspect. Some studios had tried it and reverted to the traditional IP/IN process, preferring the filmic look, the lower cost—around a tenth the price at $10,000—and ease of use. By 2010, however, according to *Variety* over 90% of films were using the DI process.

While many films still require the services of negative cutters, this position is slowly being replaced by machines that read the cut lists and select the shots from high-definition video masters to build directly onto a digital intermediate. Of course, with the rapid advance of digital technology, someday celluloid release prints will disappear. They will be replaced by digital media that will be transmitted, via satellite or fiber optic lines, and projected onto theater screens. Welcome to Digital Cinema.

Following is a breakdown of the workflow with which every filmmaker should be familiar. It incorporates current procedures, though, as noted, digital innovations are beginning to alter some of these steps.

Original camera negative

Transferred to digital video

Inputted into the editing machine

Editor cuts the movie in nonlinear digital realm

Editor outputs a negative cut list, or edit decision list, along with timecoded video

Sound editors build tracks for final mix, and composer creates score for final mix

Negative cutter conforms negative to film editor's template or digital master is conformed directly from an EDL

Figure 17.3 *The Production Slate.*

Cut negative is timed (corrected for color and density) at the film lab to produce an answer print

Timed color negative is printed to an interpositive (IP) or digital intermediate (DI)

Internegative (IN) is struck from the IP or DI

Check print is made from the IN

The final sound mix is transferred to a soundtrack negative

Multiple release prints are produced from the IN combined with soundtrack negative

Using high-speed printers, hundreds, sometimes thousands, of release prints of approximately 12,000 feet in length are produced by the film lab. These are distributed in sets of five or six 2000-foot reels to theaters throughout the United States and the world.

Figure 17.4 *Scissors.*

The End Backward

Movies are best cut in reverse. That doesn't mean the editor should start at the end and work backward. It implies something more subtle than that. It suggests that movement enfolds into itself. Strangely, that which will play best in forward motion will reveal itself when played backward. This may sound counterintuitive and even a bit bizarre, yet it works. Let's back up a moment to try to understand this phenomenon.

Flow, that hard to define but impossible to miss quality, is essential to editing. And flow, a deeper movement operating beneath the surface of story and character, is what editing is all about. Interestingly, the concept of flow is demonstrated in the physics of an ink drop experiment. In visits with the late theoretical physicist and colleague of Einstein, David Bohm, I had the privilege of discussing with him his theories of order. His straightforward approach and deep understanding brought clarity to the issue of flow, connectivity, and order. These elements also play a significant role in the art and craft of film editing.

One of Dr. Bohm's discoveries that particularly resonated with me derives from an experiment he performed using an ink drop suspended in glycerin. The glycerin was held between two cylinders. As the inner cylinder rotated, the ink drop dispersed into the glycerin, eventually disappearing. When Dr. Bohm reversed the rotation of the inner cylinder, however, a strange event occurred. The drop reunited with all its elements, reappearing before one's eyes.

The experiment was repeated, this time adding an additional drop after the first disappeared. This drop also disappeared after additional turns of the cylinder. Yet, when the process was reversed, the drops reappeared in the order in which they were dispersed. It was similar to running a movie in reverse.

The Healthy Edit: Creative Editing Techniques for Perfecting Your Movie

This striking yet simple experiment reveals a deeper order that exists in movement and, perhaps, in the universe as a whole. Dr. Bohm spoke in terms of implicate and explicate order. In this experiment the ink drop, the explicate order, enfolds into the implicate order. Just as with a hologram, the whole image is enfolded into the one. While the explicate order is knowable and describable, the implicate order is beyond description.

This experiment illuminates a profound and rarely discussed editing technique. In film editing we perform a version of this experiment every time we cut a scene. On a practical physical level we are encoding information into film or video through a variety of cuts. But in a deeper sense, we are creating flow by enfolding multiple elements into a larger whole.

While enfolded within the movie are separate, describable elements—a shot's length, an actor's close-up, the sound of a car horn—the larger, overall order from which these separate elements arise cannot be stated. This is the value of experience, creativity, and spontaneity. In film editing, it is impossible to discover the implicate order while working piecemeal or step by step. Yet an experienced editor, one who has thorough command of the technology as well as an intuitive understanding of the process, must trust in the implicate order.

Something occurred to early film editors when running their films in high-speed rewind on Moviolas, Steenbecks and KEMs. Though the movie made no particular sense in this direction, the images revealed a kind of flow, enfolding into each other. Where the cut wasn't working, one noticed a break in the flow. For some, it became a way of checking their work.

More importantly, when making an edit it is possible to determine the perfect frame to cut on by stepping backward into the cut. This means roughly determining the end point of the cut and then playing the clip backward until one feels the exact frame to begin on. Determining that, the editor then plays forward to find the end. The end becomes the beginning, the beginning the end. Using the J-K-L keys on electronic systems, today's editors can discover the exact right frame. In this sense, the film is assembled in reverse!

We know that film, in its mask-like quality of illusion, provides stories and entertainment for people throughout the world. But in its enfolding of images and content, it can reveal a connection to something deeper, a reflection of human experience.

It all began with an idea that progressed to a screenplay that was visualized by a director and was finally put together by an editor. The editor and the director are often the only members of the creative team who see the film through to its completion, beginning with production and progressing to a release print projected onto a theater screen. Along the way, every aspect of filmic medicine has come into play. Whether fighting for the life of a struggling film that requires another's intervention or maintaining the health of a robust and innovative film to which he is aligned, the editor possesses the key to the kingdom. It is an amazing process. Especially when done well.

Rx
Enjoy the process, since the end result may be a long way off. Stay healthy.

Glossary

3/2 PULLDOWN
A process of reconciling the difference between film rate and video rate. When film that runs at 24 fps is transferred to interlaced video running at 30 fps, it becomes necessary to compensate for the additional six frames. This is accomplished by inserting an extra field to every other frame. With the increasing popularity of 24 fps progressive video, this requirement is disappearing.

3D
Any stereoscopic projection system that produces a three-dimensional effect for the audience. Utilizing the manner in which humans perceive depth through the comparison between information perceived by two eyes, 3D processes equip cameras with double lenses, slightly offset to mimic the different angle from which two eyes perceive objects. This double image was originally recreated by running two interlocked projectors with the same images simultaneously and later by printing the two offset images onto a single filmstrip. Special lenses, originally red and blue but later employing polarized light, isolated the separate images for each eye.

A

ACADEMY LEADER
A span of film preceding the first frame of picture in order to allow synchronization of sound during editing and release printing. The leader has a picture start mark, a countdown with audible pop for sync at the two-second or three-foot mark. This is followed by three fect of black to allow for a smooth changeover during projection. Though the sweep leader has been used interchangeably with film and video, it was originally intended for use with television as a countdown in seconds. The theatrical film leader displays its countdown in feet. Both run for the same length.

ADR
Automated dialog replacement. A process previously known as looping designed to substitute good dialog for bad or poorly recorded dialog. When an actor's reading falls below the director's expectations or the ambient sound in a scene has rendered the dialog difficult to understand, the actor rerecords his or her lines in a soundproof booth. These are later cut into the sequence to replace the previous sound.

ALPHA
A transparent video channel. When alpha is turned on, images behind it are revealed. A common example is titles. The text is composited with an alpha channel so that background images can be seen behind the title.

ANAMORPHIC
A widescreen process that involves squeezing the image through the taking lens of the camera, then unsqueezing it at the projection stage. This allows a greater amount of information to be optically compressed into the film frame and then displayed across a wider screen area. The process was originally developed in France by Dr. Henri Chrétien, then purchased and renamed CinemaScope by 20th Century Fox. Following its introduction many other widescreen processes appeared, including Technirama, Vistascope,

Superscope, VistaVision (where the film moved through the camera sideways) and Techniscope (using half-sized frames that were stretched into full frames in the lab).

ASPECT RATIO

The height-to-width proportion of the picture frame. The newest aspect ratio, 16×9, was derived by incorporating the theatrical standard widescreen of 1:1.85 with the television scan. The previous TV standard was 4×3 or 1:1.33 based on the frame size of the 16 mm frame used in early television news coverage, as well as the requirements of the electronic scan. Anamorphic 35 mm is 1:2.35.

AVID MEDIA COMPOSER

Avid's standard digital nonlinear editing system for motion pictures and television.

AVID UNITY

A network of drives allowing multiple editors at multiple stations to work on the same project.

B

B-ROLL

Originally referred to the tape deck used to play the supporting material that reinforced information from on-camera interviews. This deck was labeled B, while the primary deck containing the interviews was A.

C

CAPTURE

To input digital media into a nonlinear editing system.

CGI

Computer-Generated Images. This general term refers to a plethora of visual effects, from compositing to animation, that are created by use of a computer. Originally used to describe the realm of 2D compositing, CGI has advanced into the area of 3D compositing. Films like *Avatar* or *The Lord of the Rings* rely heavily on this.

CHANGEOVER MARK

Indicators that are placed at the end of a film reel to signal to the theater's projectionist that the current reel is ending and the next reel should begin. They appear on screen as dots or circles in the case of release prints or slash marks in the case of a workprint, both occurring in the upper right-hand corner. These marks are placed 12 feet and one-and-a-half feet from the end of the reel signal projector start and changeover, respectively. At the appearance of the first mark the projectionist turns on the second projector and then, at the second mark, he throws the douser that covers the beam on the first projector while exposing the beam on the second projector. With the advent of multiplex cinemas, this became unwieldy, so the entire movie is now spooled onto a gigantic platter, eliminating the need for a changeover. In single-screen theaters, however, the use of the changeover remains.

CIRCLED TAKES

The director's preferred takes within a scene. In the case of film, these are the ones that will be printed.

CODEC

An abbreviation for coder/decoder or compressor/decompressor. In order to minimize the consumption of hard drive space on the computer where the media and rendered effects reside, it's necessary to utilize a compression scheme. By compressing the media into smaller packets, the codec allows the editing system to perform more efficiently. Initially, when memory was at a premium, it was necessary to create sophisticated codecs to shrink complex information into a small enough space to avoid overtaxing the system's speed and memory. Now as hard drives expand from gigabytes to terabytes and eventually to pedibytes, more memory becomes available, but cameras grow in capacity as well, moving from standard definition to high definition. This in turn requires greater memory consumption, so well-designed codecs remain an important issue. Some current codecs include Avid's DNxHD, Panasonic's DVCPRO HD, and Apple's Intermediate Codec.

COLOR CORRECTION

Also known as *grading* or *timing* in the film realm, color correction is the act of enhancing the color, contrast, and density of a video image. Most NLE systems contain color correction effects. In Final Cut Pro this option is located under the Effects tab in the Browser window and can be dragged onto a clip in the Viewer. In Avid two color correction filters, Color Effect and Color Correction, reside in the Effects palette and are launched from the Effects Editor and the pulldown window under Toolset, respectively. In both systems the initial correction can be saved and applied to similar shots throughout the sequence. Almost every shot requires some manner of color correction. This is influenced by the conditions under which the scene was shot, the color and density of the surrounding shots, or the need for any special effect such as desaturation or high contrast.

COMPLETION BOND

A form of insurance that guarantees the film's completion, even if the director fails to deliver or the film goes over budget. Studios, due to their deep pockets, don't usually rely on bond companies. Independent productions with any sizable budget generally include a completion bond in their budgets.

COMPONENT VIDEO

A type of video signal that has been divided into two or more separate signals for high-quality transmission. Generally, the signals are carried by S-Video cables or by red, green, and blue RCA plugs designated as YPbPr for luma and chroma, or by discreet, uncompressed color signals as RGB. It can carry everything from 480i to 1080p.

COMPOSITE PRINT

The film print with a soundtrack printed along its edge. The first version of this married print is known as the first trial answer print. When ready for exhibition in theaters, it will be a final release print.

COMPOSITE VIDEO

An analog video signal that combines three different signals for brightness, hue, and color saturation, also known as YUV. The signals are generally carried by a yellow RCA jack. LaserDiscs utilized a true composite signal.

COMPOSITING

The combination of multiple images within a frame. Previously this was accomplished by incorporating mattes in an optical printer. Today most compositing occurs in a computerized environment.

CUT

The physical or, in current use, virtual separation of one section of media from another. Geographically, the place where one shot is joined to another one is at the *cut*. Electronic nonlinear editing has introduced many new terms to the editing vernacular. What is often referred to as a sequence also used to be known as a *cut*.

D

DAILIES
Also known as *rushes*, dailies are the scenes and takes from the previous day's shooting. If shot on film, these are usually transferred onto a digital format, such as digital tape or a hard drive, and then captured into the nonlinear editing system.

DA VINCI
A high-quality color correction system, now owned by Blackmagic Design.

DI
Digital Intermediate. This format replaces the film interpositive as a way of producing duplicate negatives to be used during release printing of the motion picture. The advantages of the DI lie in the fact that the original negative or high-definition master can be scanned into a computer's hard drive and manipulated to correct color, introduce effects, remove scratches, and so on, then recorded back out to create a new 35 mm negative. Unlike the film interpositive, the DI does not introduce another generation of grain that would degrade the image.

DIGITIZE
A term that is being edged out by the term "capture," where media, generally from videotape, is imported into the nonlinear editing system. Since the dailies were originally transferred to analog tape, they then had to be converted into digital format—digitized—in order to play on the computer. Now that most video tape is digital, there is no need to digitize it. With the arrival of digital cards such as the P2, XD, and SD, "capture" has evolved to "transfer."

DOWNCONVERT
Copying high-resolution media to a lower resolution format in order to increase processing speed and decrease memory usage.

DRAG AND DROP
A nonlinear editing feature, found on systems like Final Cut Pro, for moving clips from bins into the time and from one position on the Timeline to another. The editor clicks on the desired clip, then drags it across from the Browser into the Viewer window or downward into the Timeline. If the clip contains in and out points, the selected portion will be edited into the Timeline.

E

EDITDROID
George Lucas's system that used laserdiscs to store media. While requiring that the dailies be burned to two redundant laserdiscs, EditDroid offered a graphical interface with a timeline, source, and record monitors, much like current nonlinear editing systems. Though it received fairly limited use, it became the true pioneer of the timeline–based systems in use today. One of EditDroid's disadvantages lay in its use of laserdiscs that had to be burned professionally, usually at a remote laboratory.

EDL
Edit Decision List. A log generated during the offline editing session, reflecting the in and out points and duration of each cut, as well as indicating the original source material. The EDL is used to recompile the editor's cut using original footage in an online session.

ELLIPSIS

The omission of a linear element in action, story, or dialog that, while normally included, does not affect comprehension when removed. The ellipsis aids pacing by leaving out elements that aren't absolutely necessary. A jump cut is an example of an ellipsis.

F

FINAL CUT PRO

Apple's nonlinear editing system. It comes bundled as Final Cut Studio, a complete postproduction software system including systems for compression, sound editing and mixing, color correction, and DVD authoring.

FIREWIRE

Apple's brand name technology for high-speed data transfer between computers and peripherals such as hard drives at rates up to 800 Mbps. Also known as IEEE 1394, iLink, and Lynx.

FLEX FILE

A text file created during the telecine process to link the film's key numbers with the timecode of the video media on which the dailies have been transferred. This information is loaded into the offline editing system. It also contains scene, take, camera roll, and audio roll information. When this information is inputted into the Avid, it allows for the telecine tape to be batch digitized with complete location information.

FOP/FFOP

First frame of picture.

FPS

Frames per second.

FULLY FILLED

Refers to delivery of effects tracks where the entire motion picture is 100% filled with sound so no dead spaces exist. The sound can consist of ambience, Foley, or hard effects. This requirement relates to the delivery of M&E (music and effects) tracks.

G

GOP

Group of pictures. The manner in which images are preserved on DVDs in order to encode a large amount of detailed information in a small space. Using this MPEG compression scheme, an actual full picture occurs at set intervals, with the interstitial frames consisting of only the variations from the full frame. The collection of information from the full frame to the last recorded variation is known as the GOP.

GREENSCREEN

A solid green background upon which actors or foreground objects are photographed, enabling a background scene to be composited in postproduction. In order for the greenscreen to work effectively, it must be evenly illuminated and the foreground objects should be lit so as to differentiate them from the background.

Glossary

H

HD

High Definition or high def. High definition, which by nature is digital, divides into various resolutions ranging from 720 to 1080, various frame rates from 24 to 60, and a choice between interlaced and progressive.

HDMI

High Definition Multimedia Interface. An audio/video interface capable of transmitting uncompressed video and up to eight channels of uncompressed audio. It provides the next generation up from component video for use with high-definition monitors.

HEAD BED

The string of interviews or talking heads in a documentary. Through digital nonlinear editing, the construction of these tracks has become much easier.

I

INSERT

A close-up of a significant object within the context of a larger scene.

INTERCUT

Alternating shots or scenes within a sequence.

J

JUMP CUT

A discontinuous cut that leaps forward in time, thereby producing gaps in the normal sequence of actions. Some of the first notable jump cuts used for artistic purposes occurred in films of the French New Wave, such as those of Godard and Truffaut.

K

KEM

Keller Elektronik Mechanik. The German-made flatbed editing machines capable of displaying multiple picture and sound heads in formats ranging from 35 mm Academy to CinemaScope and VistaVision. The KEM 8-plate Universal, introduced in 1960, became the standard Hollywood editing machine for several decades before being replaced by computerized nonlinear editing systems such as the Avid.

KEY CODE

A latent barcode that corresponds to the film's key numbers. These appear when the exposed camera negative is developed. The codes are read by an electronic reader connected to the telecine machine.

KEY NUMBERS

Edge numbers that Eastman Kodak, Fuji, or other film manufacturers embed into the edge of motion picture film negative. Upon developing, these numbers appear. They consist of two letters designating the type of film stock and a series of numbers occurring at one-foot intervals on 35 mm and half-foot intervals on 16 mm. In order to make conforming of the original negative to the editor's cut sequence possible, the codes are transferred into the nonlinear editing system. In this way the NLE system can reference each

202

frame of media. As the editor makes his cuts, every decision is recorded by the editing machine in terms of codes, in order to be used at a later time to compile the editing list.

L

LASERDISC
The first optical disc storage medium using helium-neon lasers to read the composite video information. The LaserDisc was about the size of a vinyl record and was the precursor to the CD, DVD, and Blu-ray discs. Early computer-based editing systems, such as EditFlex and EditDroid, used the LaserDisc to store the video and audio information.

LATENT EDGE NUMBERS
The film negative's edge numbers that print through to the positive workprint.

LETTERBOX
The black mattes that appear on the top and bottom of a widescreen image that has been transferred to video and played on a screen that is not compatible with that aspect ratio, such as when a 2.25 aspect ratio film is transferred with the full aspect ratio (rather than being blown up to fill the frame) and played back on a 4×3 television monitor.

M

M&E
Music and effects tracks produced during the rerecording stage and supplied to a distributor for use in foreign distribution. Since this mix lacks dialog it allows foreign distributors to supply dubbed dialog in their native languages.

MATCHBACK
For film dailies that are transferred to video and then conformed back to film after they are edited. By tracking timecode and key numbers, the NLE system can create a negative cut list for matching the video decisions back to the original film negative. When setting up a project on an NLE system, the editor must designate the film matchback option before proceeding with the editing process.

MATTE
A film or video silhouette that, when combined with other images, allows a portion of an image to be transmitted while holding back the rest of it. Mattes provide the elements for compositing multiple images.

MOS
Mit Out Sound. A Hollywood term with a German-sounding phrase, MOS, like many film terms, was originally coined as an on-set joke. When immigrant director Erich von Stroheim announced with his Austrian accent that he was going to shoot the next take "Mit out sound," the set culture picked it up and repeated the German word "mit," meaning "with" until it became the abbreviated form known today.

MOTION CAPTURE
Abbreviated as mo-cap, this process employs iridescent markers placed across the body or face. As the subject moves before the lights, the markers glow, pinpointing every movement. These spots are captured and stored into the computer, creating a moving skeleton on which skin, clothing, fur, and other textures can be placed.

MOVIOLA

The world's first editing machine. Its inventor, a Dutch-born electrical engineer, Iwan Serrurier, dubbed his home movie player the Moviola, a take-off on the home music player of the time, the Victrola. The Moviola became the standard editing machine for over 60 years.

MPEG

Moving Picture Experts Group's acronym for a compression standard used for encoding digital audio and video information.

N

NEGATIVE CUT LIST

The list that is generated by an NLE system and consists of in and out codes representing every cut in the movie. This list, along with timecoded video, allows the negative cutter to accurately conform the film negative to the NLE sequence. Once the negative is conformed, it can be printed onto positive stock or transferred to a digital medium such as a DI.

NONLINEAR EDITING

Also known as NLE. The computerized editing systems that allow instantaneous random access to any frame of media. During the editing process clips can be arranged and rearranged, inserted, or deleted at any point in the sequence, eliminating the need to rebuild the cut starting at a change point, as was the case with linear tape-to-tape systems. NLE systems accomplish this task by accessing established media through mutable addresses. These addresses are easily stored as text files for project backup or to create EDLs or negative cut lists.

NTSC

The video standard organization in the United States known as the National Television System Committee. The analog composite video standard is 525 vertical lines per frame at 30 frames per second (or 60 half frames, interlaced). In Europe the PAL standard allows for 625 lines at 25 frames per second. Digital High Definition is making these standards obsolete.

O

OCN

Original camera negative.

OPTICAL PRINTER

The standard tool for creating motion picture effects before the introduction of digital manipulation. The optical printer was basically a projector joined to a camera, allowing for the introduction of effects when rephotographing a film image. Its uses ranged from creating dissolves and wipes to compositing mattes and titles, employing a process known as bi-packing.

P

P2 CARD

A high-density digital storage medium designed for use with Panasonic's high-definition cameras.

PAPER CUT

Constructing a cut by viewing raw footage and noting the timecodes. This timecode list is then brought into the editing session as a guide to build the sequence.

PARALLEL CUTTING

The juxtaposition of images to give the sense of different activities occurring in different environments at the same time. Also known as cross-cutting. The early film director D.W. Griffith was responsible for the development of parallel cutting which first appeared in Edwin S. Porter's *The Great Train Robbery*.

PERSISTENCE OF VISION

A phenomenon where the mind briefly recalls the previous film or video frame, blending the images in order to create the illusion of movement. Some believe it results from a brief afterimage on the retina. In recent years, however, skeptics have questioned the theory's validity in general.

PICKUP

An additional shot that covers a portion of a previous take, using the same setup. This also refers to additional coverage gathered after the initial production.

PICTURE FILL

Sometimes referred to as sound fill; it has been replaced by the *slug* in NLE editing. When the audio resided on sound film, recycled film was used to slug out areas of the soundtrack where no audio occurred, such as MOS sections, in order to maintain sync. The fill usually came from old or faulty release prints that the lab had withdrawn from circulation.

PICTURE SAFE

The area of a video image that will actually be seen on a standard television monitor. While the entire image may appear on the computer monitor, a certain amount of cutoff can occur when transferred to television monitors. NLE systems offer a setting that will display a grid designating the safe area.

PLATE

The action background that joins with foreground characters or objects, either in the CG realm—such as the digitally created dinosaurs performing in front of live action sets in *Jurassic Park*—or as backgrounds for rear-screen projection.

POV

Point of View. An angle that portrays the scene through a character's eyes. It may be a roving handheld shot, as when a character enters an ostensibly empty room and searches for another occupant. Or it might be a static angle, such as when a character peers through a telescope.

PREMIER PRO

Adobe's digital nonlinear editing system. Like Apple's system it can be purchased in a bundled Creative Suite including tools for digital imaging, animation, and audio production

PROGRESSIVE

An advance from the original interlaced video format that required the image to be constructed from two frames, each displaying half of the image—one with the odd-numbered lines and the other with the even-numbered lines. Progressive video displays each frame in its entirety.

Q

QUICKTIME
Apple's proprietary codec for encoding and playing back audio and full motion video of various formats. Designated in a file extension as .mov, it is capable of running on Mac and Windows operating systems.

R

RADIO CUT
An audio portrayal of what comprises the documentary, generally built from interviews and the temporary narration.

RANK CINTEL
One of the most popular types of electronic telecine transfer machines.

REEL
Stored on metal or plastic reels, the completed cut was divided into various parts, such as Reel 1, Reel 2, and so on. A reel become synonymous with a portion of edited movie. A film reel is either 1000 feet long or, in the case of an A-B reel for theaters, 2000 feet long. On average a film runs 10 to 12 1000-foot reels long.

ROLL
The uncut material, such as in a daily roll, a Moviola roll, or a KEM roll. These range in size from several feet for a Moviola roll to 1000 feet for a daily roll or KEM roll.

ROOMTONE
The set's neutral ambience, usually recorded at the beginning or end of the shoot. Roomtone supplies the necessary audio fill for places where the sound would otherwise drop out, such as in MOS or ADR situations. In practice, editors sometimes prefer to cull ambience from pauses between dialog lines, rather than use prerecorded roomtone, since the ambience is often truer. For instance, clothing movement or a passing plane may occur in one area but remain absent during the standard recording of roomtone.

ROTOSCOPE
The frame-by-frame creation of a matte. Rotoscope is often used to produce a matte where one was not originally intended, such as replacing a label on a bottle. In *Mac and Me*, for instance, the apple juice cans used to be Coca-Cola. Rather than let the ubiquitous brand proliferate the film, it was decided to alter it occasionally by rotoscoping in a different label. Despite this valiant attempt, some reviewers still criticized the film's use of product placement.

S

SCRIPTSYNC
Avid's text-based editing feature. After importing a text file of the shooting script, the editor can link each character's lines to the corresponding media. By clicking on a particular line of text, the editor can play back the associated dialog take.

SD
Standard definition or standard def. Its standards vary depending on regions throughout the world, generally from 525 to 625 vertical lines of resolution. The main standards include NTSC, PAL, and SECAM.

SEQUENCE

A series of scenes, such as in a chase sequence where multiple actions take place over a variety of locations. With the advent of nonlinear editing, sequence has also come to refer to the entire series of shots comprising a scene or entire movie. The sequence is represented by video and audio tracks, usually designated as V1, V2, and so on, or A1, A2, and so on, along the timeline.

SETPIECE

Scenes that an audience will remember for the heightened level of production value and increased stakes. They are carefully conceived beforehand so as to unfold according to a prescribed formula. The Quidditch scene in *Harry Potter and the Sorcerer's Stone* or the lobby shoot-out in *Matrix* are examples of memorable setpieces.

SHOCK CUT

A staccato tempo to the editing that often results in the cut occurring sooner than the viewer would expect. Originally attributed to editor Dede Allen.

SLATE

The clapper sticks used to identify the scene, take, roll number, shooting date as well as the director's and cinematographer's names. Scenes are usually designated as 45A-1 and called as "Scene 45 Apple, Take 1." As amusing as it is to imagine other alphabetic nomenclature, such as Aardvark, Banana, Creampuff, Dingo, and so on, the standard scheme of Apple, Baker, Charlie, and so on provides a ready-made arrangement and understanding as well as a consistency that doesn't distract the actors' attention when announced and can be deciphered by an editor.

STEALING A SHOT

The use of a scene or portion of a scene in a way that is different from what was intended by the director.

STEENBECK

A flatbed editing console produced by Wilhelm Steenbeck of Hamburg, Germany, and using multiple picture and sound modules. The 16 mm and 35 mm sound and picture film was held in place by pivoting shoes and moved in sync through a system of sprocketed rollers. Where Avid and FCP can be operated using a three-button J-K-L (forward, stop, reverse) scheme similar to the KEM, the Lightworks nonlinear editing system adopted a version of Steenbeck's slide controller. A *New York Times* article from 1970 declared that the Steenbeck made "the standard Moviola film-editing machine seem as outdated as a pinhole camera."

STOCK FOOTAGE

Material shot by a third party not associated with the film's production. It is licensed, usually based on time and usage (such as worldwide in perpetuity). Stock footage is generally located through stock footage libraries, though sometimes individual cinematographers will own the rights to unique footage, such as Paul and Gracie Atkins's well known coverage of underwater lava flows.

T

TELECINE

The process of transferring film images to a video medium such as digital tape or a hard drive. The telecine uses an electronic beam to scan each film frame and turn it into video information.

TIMECODE

Also known as SMPTE Time Code or Linear Time Code. An electronic code consisting of hour, minute, seconds, and frames that corresponds to each frame of video or audio. In audio the shift of various tones represents the time signature, while in video it is accessed as a numeric graphic. Timecode functions in drop frame or non drop frame modes.

TITLE SAFE

The area on a television monitor where titles will fit without being cut off. NLE systems offer a setting that will display a grid designating the safe area. When composing a title on an NLE system, it is important to display the title safe reference in order to avoid losing a portion of the title when the sequence is later played back on a TV monitor.

TOD

Time of Day. A form of timecode where the numeric increments are based on clock time rather than a pre-set time.

TRT

Total Running Time. The length of your movie.

TWO-POP

One frame of 1000 Hz tone that occurs on a motion picture leader at three feet or two seconds before the first frame of picture. In television the countdown leader is depicted as a clocklike sweep that increments by seconds, whereas on feature film the leader's countdown numbers flash by at every foot. Either way, the two-pop on the soundtrack corresponds with a mark on the picture, confirming that they are in sync.

U

UNDERCRANK

The process of accelerating on-screen action by slowing the film's movement through the camera. In the early days of film, cameras required manual cranking rather than electric motors to drive the moving parts. By undercranking the motor, the film travelled through the camera at less than standard speed, so the action appeared to be moving faster when projected at normal speed. Today, using high definition cameras, under-cranking can be achieved electronically, with no moving parts.

V

VEGAS PRO

Sony's digital nonlinear editing system.

W

WILD SOUND

Sound that is not recorded in sync with the picture. Wild sounds, such as ambience, roomtone, and voiceover, may be synced later with the cut in the editing room.

Index

A

Abbot and Costello Meet Frankenstein, 58
A Bout de Souffle (Breathless), 47
absurdity, in comedy, 68
accidents, in editing, 25–27
action
    cutting on, 12
    emphasizing in adventure films, 77–78
    matching, 12
    and pace, 151
    trims in, 113
action adventure films
    conflicts in, 137
    crank effects, 75–77
    emphasizing action, 77–78
    guideposts, 73–75
    heroes in, 72, 72
    overview, 71–72
actors *See* characters; dialog
Adler, Mark, 190
ADR (automated dialog replacement), 191–192
adventure films *See* action adventure films
Affairs of the Heart, 187, 189
agendas behind documentaries, 87–88
Air America, 144
Alice in Wonderland, 190
Allen, Dede, 48–49
alternative treatments *See* nontraditional treatments
ambiences, 191
American Pie, 68
American Pie 2, 68
analog VU meter, 180
anamorphic process, 40–41, 40f

anatomy, applied to film editing, 4–5
ancillary words, removing from dialog, 134
Anderson, Lindsay, 48
Angels and Demons, 82, 146
angles, varying, 14
animals, bringing personality to, 23
anticipation, caused by pace and rhythm, 152–153
Apatow, Judd, 71
Apocalypse Now, 145
Apple editing system, 38
Apply Normalization Gain setting, Final Cut Pro, 181
apprenticeship, 53
approach, editorial
    filling gaps, 20–22
    further diagnosis, 24
    overview, 18
    what audience learns from scene, 24
    what scene is about, 19
    who scene is about, 22–23
    wrestling with material, 24–25
Aron, Arthur, 79
arousal, and horror, 79
associative cuts, 135–136, 162–163
attraction, and horror, 79
audience
    expectations, 186
    exposition, reaction to, 146
    films, reaction to, 1, 2, 188–189
    opening shots, reaction to, 185
    overlaps and expectations of, 126–127
    what is learned from scenes by, 24
audio *See* sound
audio tracks, for documentaries, 85
Austin Powers films, 70–71

auteur editors, 88–89, 91–92
automated dialog replacement (ADR), 191–192
Avatar, 58, 71–72, 127, 190
Avid editing system
    versus Apple system, 37–38
    audio editing in, 180, 181
    digitized media, 36
    frame icons, 101
    frame view bins, 97f
    lifts, 109
    locators, 102–103
    as producer's friend, 46
    select sequences, 103
    simple edits in, 39
    story order, 100–101
    terminology, 37–38
    transitions, 160–161
    trimming in, 110
Avid Express, 38
Avid Media Composer, 36f, 38

B

backing up projects, 38
backstory, filling in with montage, 144–145
backwards, viewing film, 195–196
banners, 161–162
Battleship Potemkin, The, 113
beats, 155–156
Because I Said So, 122–123
bedside manner, applied to film editing, 7, 167–168 *See also* politics
Bilcock, Jill, 139
bins, 37–38, 100–101, 109
Birdcage, The, 69, 70, 123, 123f, 124
Birth of a Nation, The, 62–63

black and white film, 48
Blair Witch Project, The, 88
Blazing Saddles, 68
Blind Side, The, 144
Blink, 169
blocks, documentary editing as
    playing with, 85–88
blowing up frames, to create insert
    shot, 59
bluescreen compositing, 64–65
Bobby, 145
bodily functions, in comedy, 68
Bohm, David, 195, 196
Bonfire of the Vanities, The, 4, 92
Bonnie and Clyde, 48–49, 149
Borat, 88
Brando, Marlon, 132
Brecht, Bertolt, 47–48
B-roll, 84
Buber, Martin, 84
Buff, Conrad
    dailies, 104
    genres, 58
    King Arthur, 105–106
    script, importance of while editing,
        101–102
    Training Day, 134
Bullitt, 191
Burns, Ken, 88
Burton, Tim, 190
Butch Cassidy and the Sundance Kid, 144

C

cameras, real-time compositing in,
    64–65
Campbell, Joseph, 187–188
Canby, Vincent, 144
Canvas Edit Overlay, Final Cut Pro, 39
cardiology, applied to film editing, 4
    See also pace; rhythm
cards, the, 189
Carrie, 80–81
Casablanca, 21
celluloid film *See* film

CGI (computer-generated images), 64
Chaplin, Charlie, 127–128
character-based comedies, 70
characters *See also* dialog; rhythm
    in action adventure films, 77
    close-up shots, 93–94
    determining who scene is about,
        22–23
    entering scenes, treatment of, 54
    in family films, 84
    main, lack of focus on, 178–179
    multiple dialog takes for, 128–129
    over-the-shoulder shots, 94
    problems with, 5
    2-shots, 94
chase scenes, 73
checkerboarding cuts, 125, 126
Chew, Richard, 101, 131, 145
Cinefex magazine, 65
"cinema irrité", 114–115
cinéma vérite, 87
CinemaScope, 41, 92–93
circled takes, 98
cliché, in student films, 48
clipping, 180
clips
    defined, 37–38
    meaning of in editing systems, 109
    staggering in documentaries, 86, 86f
close-ups (CU)
    abbreviation for, 108
    coverage with, 93, 93f
    and dialog substitution, 132–133
    in MTV editing, 147
    pace, 151
closing scenes, analyzing for
    problems, 178, 179
CMX editing system, 35, 111
Coburn, Arthur, 75
Colavita effect, 12
color
    digital intermediate, 45
    to establish emotional or
        environmental tone, 44, 45f

film doctoring, 182–183
color coding, in Final Cut Pro, 102
color timing, 43–44
colored pages, 100
comedy
    basic structure of, 68, 69
    incidents that make us laugh, 68
    overview, 67–68
    performance in, 69–70
    romantic comedy, 71
    sight gags, 70–71
    "surf the laughter" technique, 70
    timing in, 69
committing to project, 174–175
completion bonds, 176
composers, 190
compositing, 64–65
computer-generated images (CGI), 64
confidence, of editor, 169
conflicts, in drama, 137
continuity
    allowing errors in, 50–52
    paying attention to, 14–15
    Prancer example, 21–22
continuity editing, 11–12, 147
contracts, job, 173
contrast, in transitions, 162–163
control of editing process,
    maintaining, 170–171
Convent, The, 79
conventions, genre-related, 57–58
Cove, The, 174–175
coverage
    achieving appropriate
        close-ups, 93
        establishing shots, 92
        insert shots, 94–95
        master shots, 92
        medium shots, 93
        over-the-shoulder shots, 94
        overview, 91–92
        reverse angles, 94
        2-shots, 94
        wide shots, 92–93

in comedy, 69
defined, 9–10
gaps
  examining, 104
  example of, 105–106
  filling, 104
  overview, 103, 104
  shot list, 106–108
organizing dailies
  finding order, 97–100
  overview, 96–97
  selects, 102–103
  story order, 100–102
synchronizing, 95–96
cowboys, 93
craftsmanship, 171–172
Crank, 75, 153
crank effects, 75–77
cross-genre, 58–59
"crossing the line", 13–14
CU *See* close-ups
cutaways, 133–134
cuts *See also* cutting
  defined, 3
  introducing characters by, 54
  motivated, 14
  in nonlinear editing, 40
  varying, 14
  when working with film, 39–40
cutting
  on action, 12
  dialog, 125, 126
  letting camera settle before, 12
  before (or after) people and/or
    objects enter frame, 14
  in reverse, 195–196

D

Daddy Long Legs, 44, 45f
dailies
  coverage, 91
  delivery of, 95
  fixing screenplay problems, 142–143
  importance of to editor, 19

organizing
  finding order, 97–100
  overview, 96–97
  selects, 102–103
  story order, 100–102
politics, 171
de Palma, Brian, 80–81
deferred salaries, 173–174
Delicatessen, 149–151, 150f
delivering film, 193–195
delivery requirements, 193
depth, in film, 29–30
detail, attention to, 52
DI (digital intermediate), 41, 45,
  193–194
diagnosing films, in film doctoring,
  178
dialog *See also* rhythm
  cutaways, 133–134
  excessive, editing, 135–136
  exposition, 127
  film doctoring, 179, 180
  improvisation, 134
  new technique for, 128–129
  overlaps, 125–127
  overview, 121, 122
  performance in, 131
  pre-laps, 163–164
  shaping performance, 137
  "show don't tell" technique, 127–128
  sound editor role in fixing,
    191–192
  substitution, 132–133
  subtext, 122–128
  superfluous words, 134
  tracking beats, 131–132
  trims in, 112
digital 3D, 190
digital audio meters, 180
digital dailies, 95, 96f
digital intermediate (DI), 41, 45,
  193–194
digital surround sound, 193
digital terminology, 109

digitized film, 36
Dinner for Schmucks, 69
diplomacy *See* politics
directors
  editing by, 114–115, 118–119,
    170–171
  influence of on comedy, 70
  listening to, 169–170
  politics regarding, 167–169
  screening rough cut with, 168,
    188–189
  shot lists, 106–108
director's cut, 188
dirty dupes, 118
disorientation, in action adventure
  films, 73–74
dissolves, 61–62, 160–161
documentaries
  overview, 84–85
  playing with blocks, editing as,
    85–88
  tips for, 88–89
Dolby, 66
Dolby SR tracks, 193, 193f
Double Roller mode, Avid editing
  system, 110
double-system recordings, 95
Dracula, 81
drag and drop, 39–40, 85
Drag Me to Hell, 80–81
drama, conflicts in, 137
drop frame timecode, 87
dupe detection, 154
dynamic editing, 11–12, 147
dynamic range, 181

E

Eagle Eye Film Company, 34
Eastman Kodak, 44
Ebert, Robert, 147
ECU (extreme close-ups), 93–94, 108
edge numbers, 95–97
edit decision list (EDL), 35
EditDroid editing system, 35–36

Editflex editing system, 35, 111
Editing magazine, 172
editing process *See also* success
    strategies
  continuity editing, 11–12
  dynamic editing, 11–12
  frame, importance of, 40–43
  importance of to movie-making,
    45–46
  Kuleshov effect, 10–11
  making cut, 9–11
  overview, 39–40
  pace, 9
  postproduction procedures, 43–45
  profession, 17–18
  rhythm, 9
  rules of
    cuts motivated by cut before, 14
    cutting before (or after) people
      and/or objects enter frame, 14
    cutting on action, 12
    eyelines, maintaining, 14
    letting camera settle before
      cutting, 12
    matching action, 12
    180° rule, 13–14
    physical continuity, 14–15
    varying cuts, 14
    visual bridges, creating, 12–13
editing triangle, 10, 10f, 72, 113, 155
editors *See also* film doctoring;
    politics
  accidents, 25–27
  approaching scenes
    filling gaps, 19–22
    further diagnosis, 24
    overview, 18–19
    what audience learns from
      scene, 24
    what scene is about, 19–20
    who scene is about, 22–23
    wrestling with material, 24–25
  careers in film business, 173, 174
  as doctor, 3

  health of, 175
  influence of on comedy, 70
  as masters of timing, 154
  opportunities for related to
    documentaries, 88–89
  politics regarding, 172
  profession, 17–18
  in reediting process, 188
EDL (edit decision list), 35
Effects palette, Avid editing system,
    160–161
Effects tab, Final Cut Pro, 160–161
eight-perf splices, 182
Eisenstein, Sergei, 106–107, 113,
    158–159
electronic systems, early, 35–38
Elizondo, Hector, 69–70
ellipsis, 153
embarrassment, in comedy, 68
emphasizing action, in action
    adventure, 77–78
endings, movie
  Affairs of the Heart, 187
  analyzing for problems, 178, 179
  Made in Heaven, 186–187
  overview, 185–186
enlarging image, to create insert shot,
    59
epiphanies, 84, 185
equalization, audio, 181
equipment, and craftsmanship,
    171–172
establishing shots (ESTAB), 92, 108
Estevez, Emilio, 145
Evan Almighty, 68
excessive dialog, editing, 135–136
Exit Through the Gift Shop, 88
expectations
  audience, 186
  genre-related, 59–60
explicate order, 196
explosions, 77
exposition
  in action adventure films, 72

  excessive, 127
  "show don't tell" technique,
    127–128
  and story of film, 145–146
exterior action, anticipating, 54–55
extract function, Avid editing system,
    109
extreme close-ups (ECU), 93–94, 108
extreme wide shots (EWS), 92–93,
    108
eyelines, maintaining, 14
eyes of animals, bringing personality
    to, 23

F
fades, 161
Fame, 92
family films, 83–84
Family Man, 83–84
fantasy
  compositing, 64–65
  computer-generated images, 64
  motion capture, 65–66
  overview, 61
  visual effects, 61–64
Fatal Attraction, 2, 187, 189
Field, Syd, 145
filling gaps, 104
film
  benefits of, 29–31
  dailies, 95–96
  dialog substitution, 133
  dupe detection, 154
  matchback, 37
  splices, 182, 183f
  terminology, 37, 109
Film & Video magazine, 103
film business, careers in, 173, 174
film doctoring *See also* editors;
    success strategies
  audio issues, 179–181
  example of, 116
  general discussion, 2–3
  overview, 177

politics, 175–176

problem symptoms, looking for, 178 179

two week trial periods, 177–178

video issues, 182–183

film museum in Lone Pine, California, 60–61

film time, 113–115, 144

filters, audio, 181

Final Cut Pro

    audio editing in, 180, 181

    bin folders, 97f

    clips, 109

    color coding in, 102

    drag and drop editing of documentaries, 85

    frame icons, 101

    lifts, 109

    marker system, 102

    select sequences, 103

    simple edits in, 39–40

    story order, 100–101

    terminology, 37–38

    transitions, 160–161

    trimming in, 110–111, 111f

final mix, 193, 193f

financial considerations, 172–174

Fish Called Wanda, A, 68

Flaherty, Robert, 87

flash frames, 95

Flashdance, 147–149

flat deals, 173

flatbed editing machines, 33–35

flow

    finding, 157–158

    seeing while watching film in reverse, 195, 196

Foley stage, 192–193, 192f

Foley walkers, 192–193

formulas, filmmaking, 58, 83

Forster, Marc, 73–74

four-perf format, 41

four-perf splices, 182–183

frame icon, Avid, 101

frames

    defined, 37–38

    importance of to editing process, 40–43

Francis-Bruce, Richard, 77–78

French New Wave, 47–48

fullcoats, 95

Fuqua, Antoine, 105, 134

futzing, 181

G

gaps

    examining, 104

    example of, 105–106

    filling, 19–22, 104

    overview, 103, 104

    shot list, 106–108

Geneva drive, 31–32

genre editing styles

    action adventure

        crank effects, 75–77

        emphasizing action, 77–78

        guideposts, 73–75

        heroes in, 72

        overview, 71–72

    comedy

        basic structure of, 68, 69

        incidents that make us laugh, 68

        overview, 67–68

        performance in, 69–70

        sight gags, 70–71

        "surf the laughter" technique, 70

        timing in, 69

    conventions, 57–58

    cross-genre, 58–59

    documentaries

        overview, 84–85

        playing with blocks, editing as, 85–88

        tips for, 88–89

    expectations, 59–60

    family films, 83–84

    horror, 79–81

    overview, 57

ritual objects, 59

romantic comedy, 71

science fiction and fantasy

    compositing, 64–65

    computer-generated images, 64

    motion capture, 65–66

    overview, 61

    visual effects, 61–64

    thrillers and mystery, 82–83

    Westerns, 60–61

geography, in action adventure films, 73–74

Get Poster Frame function, Final Cut Pro, 101

Ghostbusters, 144

Gladwell, Malcolm, 169

gloves, 38

Godard, Jean-Luc, 47, 151–152

Goldmember, 70–71

"goodies", looking for in scene, 52–53 *See also* selects

Gordon, Demian "Dman", 65–66

Graduate, The, 156–157, 163

Great Dictator, The, 128

Great Train Robbery, The, 62

Green, Bruce, 58, 68–70, 128

greenscreen compositing, 64–65

Griffith, D.W., 62–63, 76, 76f

growth process, film as

    inherited traits, 140–143

    overview, 139

    Romeo and Juliet example, 139–140

guaranteed flat deals, 173

guidepost shots, in action adventure, 73–75

H

half-reelers, 76–77

Hamlet, 92

handles, 160

Hangover, The, 68

Harry Potter and the Chamber of Secrets, 144–145

*Harry Potter and the Prisoner of
    Azkaban*, 63f
head beds, 84–86
headroom, 181
health, of editors, 175
Heaven's Gate, 34–35
Hecker, Gary, 192f
Hemingway, Ernest, 188
heredity, applied to film editing, 4
    See also screenplay problems
heroes
    in action adventure, 72
    stages of initiation, 61
    in thrillers and mysteries, 82–83
high definition video, 30
High Noon, 3
Hitchcock, Alfred, 14, 81, 83
horror, 79–81
Horseplayer, 135, 141–143
Hotel Chevalier, 112
"How to build a better action hero"
    article, 72
hyperbole, in comedy, 68

I

I Am Sam, 131
If. . ., 48
implicate order, 196
improvisation, 134, 137
in-camera effects, 61–62, 64
Inception, 18, 103
independent production companies,
    173
independent screenplays, 141
information
    filling in with montage,
        144–145
    leaving out, in screenplay, 146
Inglourious Basterds, 113–114, 114f
inherited traits, in screenplays,
    140–143 *See also* screenplay
    problems
Inland Empire, 152
inner struggle, in dramas, 137

innovation *See* nontraditional
    treatments
insert edits, 39–40
insert option, Avid editing system,
    109, 110
insert shots, 59, 94–95, 94f, 109
insert stages, 94–95
instruments, editing
    early electronic systems, 35–38
    editing process
        frame, importance of, 40–43
        importance of to movie-making,
            45–46
        overview, 39–40
        postproduction procedures, 43–45
    film, 29–31
    flatbed editing machines, 33–35
    linear editing systems, 29–31
    low-cost systems, 38
    medical principles applied to film
        editing, 6
    Moviola, 31–33
    nonlinear editing systems, 29–31, 35
intercutting, 164–166
interior action, anticipating exterior
    action, 54–55
interlaced video format, 30, 30f
interviews, listening during, 169–170
Invention of Lying, The, 122
Iron Man 2, 74–75
Israel, Neal, 52, 53, 68, 190

J

Jack and the Beanstalk, 148
James Bond franchise, 82–83
Jarmusch, Jim, 58
Jerry Maguire, 122
job contracts, 173
job interviews, listening during,
    169–170
jump cuts
    in action adventure films, 77
    defined, 12, 48
    in horror films, 80–81

popularity of, 48–49
jump scares, in horror films, 80–81

K

Karath, Kym, 25–27
Kasdan, Lawrence, 60
KEM (Keller-Elektronik-Mechanik)
    flatbed editing machines,
    33–35, 34f
KEM rolls, 34
Ken Burns Effect, 88
keycodes, 35
King Arthur, 105–106, 105f
Knight, Arthur, 62–63
Koyaanisqatsi (Life Out of Balance), 89
Kramer, Wayne, 75
Kubrick, Stanley, 64
Kuleshov effect, 10–11, 23

L

labyrinth, filmmaking process as, 2
Landau, Jon, 65
laserdiscs, 35–36
latched films, 190
laughter
    incidents inspiring, 68, 69
    as measuring device of comedy, 67
lavaliers, 132
Lawrence of Arabia, 158
*Le Voyage dans la Lune (A Trip to the
    Moon)*, 63–64
Lean, David, 127, 158
length of shots, 113–114, 152–153
Let Me In, 88
Levinson, Wendy, 169
Life Out of Balance (Koyaanisqatsi), 89
lifts
    comedy example, 116
    defined, 109
    filling gaps, 104–105
    Horseplayer example, 142, 143
    overview, 109
    process, 115–119
Lightworks editing system, 37

linear editing systems
   dialog substitution, 133
   flatbed editing machines, 33 35
   Moviola, 31–33
   overlaps, 125, 126
   overview, 29–31
lined scripts, 98–101, 99f
listening, in politics, 169–170
Liveliest Art, The, 62–63
locators, Avid editing system, 102–103
locking picture, 189–193
logs, for documentaries, 89
Lombardo, Lou, 75
Lone Pine, California film museum, 60–61
long shots, 92
Lorentz, Pare, 88
Los Angeles Times, 72
Lost Horizon, 2
Lost in Africa, 162–163
low-budget horror films, 80
low-cost editing systems, 38
Lucas, George, 35–36
Luhrmann, Baz, 139–140
Lynch, David, 152

M
Mac and Me, 26, 51, 54
Made in Heaven, 44, 186–187
main characters, lack of focus on, 178–179
Mamet, David, 106
Man Trouble, 157
Mannequin Two: On the Move, 23, 23f, 54, 191
mark in icon, Avid editing system, 39
mark out icon, Avid editing system, 39
marker system, Final Cut Pro, 102
Markiewicz, Pete, 33
marriage, editing as, 118
Marshall, Garry, 58, 69–70
master shots (MAS), 92, 108

match cut, 49–50
match frame command, 160–161
matchback, **37–38**
matching action, 12
Matrix, The, 158
matte photography, 62
Maxim magazine, 175
McLuhan, Marshall, 1
medical principles applied to film editing
   anatomy, 4–5
   bedside manner, 7
   cardiology, 4
   editor as doctor, 3
   film doctor metaphor, 2–3
   heredity, 4
   instruments, 6
   overview, 1, 2
   psychiatry, 5
   surgery, 5–6
medium close-ups (MCU), 108
medium shots (MS or MED SHOT), 93, 93f, 108
medium wide shots, 92–93
Meet the Parents, 70
Méliès, George, 61–64
melody, and rhythm, 158
metacommunication, 122
Michelangelo, 5
microphones, 132
Miss Potter, 18
Modern Times, 68, 127–128
modular meters, 180
monaural sound, 66
monsters, in horror films, 79
montage
   Eisenstein's theories of, 158–159
   general discussion, 143–145
   Kuleshov effect, 10–11
   in music videos, 147
   as transition, 163–164
Montage editing system, 35
Moore, Michael, 88
MOS, 180

motion capture, 65–66
motion control, 128
motion effects, 75–77
Motor Trend magazine, 74
movie trailers, 161
Moving Violations, 52, 68, 190
Moviola
   general discussion, 31–33
   handmade films, 45–46
   and KEMs in same editing room, 34–35
   overlaps on, 125
   trimming on, 110
MS (medium shots), 93, 93f, 108
MTV editing, 147, 148
multiple dialog takes, 128–129
Munich, 45–46
Murnau, F.W, 81
music *See also* sound
   behind dialog, 180
   pace and rhythm as visual, 151
   score, 191
   source, 190–191
   spotting sessions, 190–191
   temp, 151
music cues, 190
music videos, 147
mystery, 82–83
myth-making, film as, 58–59 *See also* genre editing styles

N
naïveté, of editor, 3
Nanook of the North, 87
narration, 146, 162
narrative editing, 62–63
National Geographic documentaries, 84, 87–88
nature, conflict of man against, 137
Neely, Hugh, 76–77
negative cut list, 35, 193–194
negative cutters, 115
neutral shots, 13–14, 107
New Wave *See* French New Wave

New York Times, The, 144
New Yorker, The, 5, 6f
Nicholson, Jack, 157
No Country for Old Men, 137
Nolan, Christopher, 103
nondramatic activities, montages for, 144
non-drop frame timecode, 87
nonfilmmakers, working with, 174–175
nonlinear editing (NLE) systems *See also specific systems by name*
 crank effects, 75–77
 cuts, 3
 dialog cutting, 121
 dialog substitution, 133
 documentaries, 85, 85–86
 early systems, 35–38
 general discussion, 29–31
 low-cost systems, 38
 multiple dialog takes, 128–129
 overlaps, 126
 reversing action, 136
 rise of, 35
 saving lifts, 118
 trimming in, 110–111
nonlinear storytelling, 151–152
nontraditional treatments
 continuity errors, 50–52
 looking for "goodies" in scene, 52–53
 match cut, 49–50
 off-camera characters, 53–55
 overview, 47–49
North by Northwest, 83
Nosferatu, 81
notes, taking during first reading of script, 117

O

Observer Effect, 88
OCN (original camera negative), 95
O'Connor, Dennis, 20
off-camera characters, 53–55

offline editing, 35
On Directing Film, 106
180° rule, 13–14, 94
1.85:1 aspect ratio, 40–43
One-Eyed Jacks, 61, 132
1639 aspect ratio, 40–41
online editing, 35
opening scenes
 analyzing for problems, 178, 179
 audience reaction to, 185
optical printer, 64
organizing dailies
 finding order, 97–100
 overview, 96–97
 selects, 102–103
 story order, 100–102
original camera negative (OCN), 95
O'Steen, Sam, 163
outtakes *See* lifts
overcranked footage, 75–77
overdosing, transitions, 161
overlaps, 121, 122, 125–127, 163–164
overstatement, of pace, 153–154
over-the-shoulder shots (OV/SH), 93, 94, 94f, 108
overwrite edits, 39–40
overwrite option, Avid editing system, 109, 110

P

pace
 anticipation, 152–153
 cutaways, 134
 fixing problems with, 179
 general discussion, 4, 9
 MTV editing, 147, 148
 overstatement, 153–154
 overview, 147–149
 power of, 151–152
 temp music, 151
 and trimming, 113
 use of, 151
 visual music, 149–151

paper cuts, 84–85
Parker, Trey, 144
paste insert option, Final Cut Pro, 109
paste option, Final Cut Pro, 109
Pathé, 44
pay off, in comedy, 68, 69, 70
Pearson, Richard
 dailies, 101
 film doctoring, 178
 guidepost shots, 73–75
 screening rough cut, 189
 script, importance of while editing, 101
 spending time on set, 3
 trimming process, 112
 visual effects, 64
Peckinpah, Sam, 75
Penn, Arthur, 149
perceived time, 113
perfectly cut films, 50
performance *See also* dialog
 in comedy, 69–70
 importance of, 5
 and rhythm, 157–158
performance capture, 65
persistence of vision, 31–32
personality, bringing to animals, 23
physical continuity *See* continuity
Pickford, Mary, 44
pickups, 104–105
Pinter, Harold, 81
pirating, 63
placement, sound, 181–182
plates, 64, 65
playhead, Avid editing system, 39
playing with blocks, editing documentaries as, 85–88
plots, 20–22
Plow That Broke the Plains, The, 88
point of view (POV), 106
Poison Ivy: The New Seduction, 77–78, 175
politics
 bedside manner, 167–168

committing to project, 174–175
communication, 169
craftsmanship, 171–172
dailies and rough cuts, 171
film doctoring, 175–176
financial considerations, 172–174
general discussion, 7
listening, 169–170
maintaining control of editing
    process, 170–171
overview, 167
producers and directors, 168
screening rough cut, 168
strength of weak ties, 174
taking yes for an answer, 171
Poll, Jon
    comedy, film doctoring, 78
    film doctors, 175, 176
    genre, 58
    performance issues, 70
    "surf the laughter" technique, 70
    timing in comedy, 69
Porter, Edwin S., 62–63
postproduction procedures, by editor,
    43–45
POV (point of view), 106
Prancer, 19f, 20–22, 84, 185–186
prefiguring action, 54–55
pre-laps, 163–164
Pride and Prejudice, 18
Princess Bride, The, 53–54
Prize Winner of Defiance, Ohio, The,
    160
problem symptoms, looking for,
    178–179
producers, politics regarding, 168,
    172
Producers, The, 144
profession, film editing, 17–18
progressive scan, 30
protagonists *See* characters; heroes
psychiatry, applied to film editing, 5
    See also dialog
psychological time, 113

Pudovkin, Vsevolod, 10, 106
punch line, in comedy, 68, 69, 70
pushes, 160
puzzle, filmmaking process as, 2, 5,
    20, 104

Q
Quantum of Solace, 73–74, 74f
questionnaires, audience, 189
questions, asking in order to solve
    issues, 170

R
radio cuts, 84–85
Raimi, Sam, 80
reaction shots, 70, 133–134
reality, in documentaries, 87
real-time compositing, 64–65
recurring situations, and pace, 152,
    153, 154
Red Dawn, 178, 189
reediting, 187–189
reels, 32
reinforcing ideas, through montage,
    144
Reitman, Jason, 50–51
repetition, and pace, 152, 153, 154
reports, comparing to script
    supervisor's notes, 99–100
revealing information, in thrillers and
    mysteries, 82
reverse angles, 94
reversing action, 136
rewind, viewing film in, 195–196
rhythm
    anticipation, 152–153
    cutaways, 134
    Eisenstein's theories, 158–159
    finding flow, 157–158
    general discussion, 4, 9, 154, 155
    The Graduate example, 156–157
    influence of, 155–156
    intercutting, 164–166
    MTV editing, 147, 148

overview, 147–149
scene-to-scene transitions
    banners, 161–162
    fades, 161
    narration, 162
    overdosing, 161
    overview, 159–161
    pre-laps, 163–164
    shot size, 162–163
    temp music, 151
    varying by slowing pace, 153
    visual music, 149–151
Richman, Geoffrey, 174–175
ripple delete function, Final Cut Pro,
    109
Ripple function, Final Cut Pro,
    110–111
ritual objects, genre-related, 59
Roach, Jay, 58
Rock, The, 72, 77–78
Rocky Horror Picture Show, The,
    59, 152–153
Roll function, Final Cut Pro,
    110–111
rolls, 32
romantic comedy, 71
Romeo and Juliet, 139–140
roomtone, 191–192
Rope, 4, 14, 83
Rosenberg, Frank P., 61
rough cuts
    banners in, 161–162
    politics, 171
    reediting, 188
    screening, 168, 188–189
Rule of Three sequence, 158
rules of film editing
    breaking, 49
    cutting before (or after) objects
        enter frame, 14
    cutting on action, 12
    eyelines, maintaining, 14
    letting camera settle before
        cutting, 12

rules of film editing (*Continued*)
    matching action, 12
    motivated cuts, 14
    180° rule, 13–14
    physical continuity, 14–15
    varying cuts, 14
    visual bridges, creating, 12–13
Runaway Bride, 69–70
Running Scared, 75
running times, 87
Rush Hour, 58
rushes, 91 *See also* dailies
Russian Ark, 4, 83
Ryan's Daughter, 127

S
salaries, deferred, 173–174
Scary Movie franchise, 58
scene bins or folders, 100–101
scene order, 96–98
scenes *See also* rhythm
    approaching
        filling gaps, 19–22
        further diagnosis, 24
        overview, 18
        what audience learns from
            scene, 24
        what scene is about, 19–20
        who scene is about, 22–23
        wrestling with material, 24–25
    defined, 9–10
    flawed, and politics, 168
    importance of when overlapping,
        125–127
    intercutting, 164–166
    looking for "goodies" in, 52–53
    scrapping, 25
    taking into account while working
        with improvisation, 134
    transitions between
        banners, 161–162
        fades, 161
        intercutting, 164–166
        narration, 162
        overdosing, 161

    overview, 159–161
    pre-laps, 163–164
    shot size, 162–163
Schmidt, Arthur, 3, 17, 69, 123
schneid, 32–33
science fiction
    compositing, 64–65
    computer-generated images, 64
    motion capture, 65–66
    overview, 61
    visual effects, 61–64
scores, 191
scrapping scenes, 25
screening
    dailies, 103, 104
    rough cuts, 168, 188–189
screenplay problems
    expository dialog, 145–146
    general discussion, 4
    montages, 143–145
    story problems, 145–146
    translation process, film as
        inherited traits, 140–143
        overview, 139
        Romeo and Juliet example,
            139–140
script supervisor, 98–99
script supervisor's notes, 99–100
scripts, 101–102 *See also* screenplay
    problems
ScriptSync, Avid editing system, 101
Searchers, The, 61
select rolls, 101, 103
select sequences, 103
selects, 102–103
sequences, 3
Serrurier, Iwan, 31–32
Serrurier, Mark, 33
Servant, The, 81
set up, in comedy, 68, 69, 70
setpiece, montage as, 145
7.1 surround sound, 66
Sharkey, Betsy, 72
Sherlock Holmes, 82–83
shock cuts, 49

shooting order, 96–98
shooting script, 100, 140
shot list, 106–108
shots
    achieving pace and rhythm
        through use of, 4
    length of, 113–114, 152–153
    pickups, 104–105
    rhythm, 158
    size of, and transitions, 162–163
    variety of in action adventure
        films, 72
"show don't tell" technique, 127–128
sight gags, 70–71
Silence of the Lambs, The, 83, 137
silent movies, 127–128
Silverado, 60
single roller mode, Avid editing
    system, 110
single stripe sprocketed sound film, 95
sit-coms, 67
slates, 98
Slide function, Final Cut Pro,
    110–111
Slip function, Final Cut Pro,
    110–111
slow motion, 75–77
Slumdog Millionaire, 58
Snapping option, Final Cut Pro,
    39–40
Social Network, The, 18
sound
    in action adventure films, 78
    audio tracks for documentaries, 85
    evolution of, 66
    film doctoring, 179–181
    pre-laps, 163–164
    quality of, and dialog substitution,
        132
    specialists, 190–193
    subjective influence of, 181
    in transitions, 162–163
    visual dominance, 12, 13
sound editors, 191–193
sound effects, 192–193

sound mix, in comedy, 71
Sound of Music, The, 25–27
soundtracks, 193, 193f
source music, 190–191
Source/Record toggle icon, Avid editing system, 103
special effects film, 162
Speed, 54–55, 153
splice-in edit, Avid editing system, 39
splices, 182, 183f
spotting sessions, 190–191
springboards, 94
Staenberg, Zach, 158
staggered clip method, for documentaries, 86, 86f
Stalker, 158–159
standard definition video, 30
Star Wars, 61, 137, 160
static master shots, 92
stealing shots, 22, 104–105, 143
Steenbeck flatbed editing machines, 33
stereophonic sound, 66
stock footage, 104–105
Stone, Oliver, 58
stop effect, 61–62
stories *See also* genre editing styles; rhythm; screenplay problems
  in documentaries, 87–89
  keeping in mind when organizing dailies, 97–98
  problems with in screenplay, 145–146
  reediting, 187–188
story order, 97–102
storyboard layouts, 100–101
Street of Crocodiles, 151–152
strength of weak ties, 174
student films, cliché in, 48
studio films, 140–141
stupidity, in comedy, 68
subclips, Final Cut Pro, 102–103
substandard coverage, 91–92
substitution, dialog, 132–133
subtext, 112, 122–128

success strategies
  overview, 1
  principles of medicine applied to film editing
    anatomy, 4–5
    bedside manner, 7
    cardiology, 4
    editor as doctor, 3
    film doctor metaphor, 2–3
    heredity, 4
    instruments, 6
    overview, 1, 2
    psychiatry, 5
    surgery, 5–6
Suicide Kings, 164
superfluous words, editing, 134
"surf the laughter" technique, 70
surgery, applied to film editing, 5–6
  See also lifts; trimming
surprise, versus suspense, 81
surround sound, 66, 193
surveys, audience, 189
suspense
  anticipation, 152–153
  and film time, 113–115
  films, 81–83
synchronizing
  dailies, 95–96
  dialog to picture, 132–133

T

tail slates, 98
Taken, 137, 145
takes
  circled, 98
  defined, 9–10
  multiple dialog, 128–129
Tarantino, Quentin, 113–115
Tarkovsky, Andrei, 158–159
technical necessity, and innovation, 47–48
Technicolor, 44
Techniscope, 41
technology
  and substandard coverage, 91

understanding of, 33
telecine, 95
television
  anamorphic process, 40–41
  exposition, 127
temp dub, 180–181, 190
temp music, 44–45, 151
temporality, in action adventure films, 73–74
Thank You for Smoking, 50–51
There's Something About Mary, 68
35 mm celluloid film *See* film
three strip imbibition process, 44
3D format, 66, 190
thrillers, 82–83
time, and rhythm, 158–159
timecodes, 87, 89, 111
timeline, Final Cut Pro, 39–40, 85
timing
  in comedy, 69
  editors as masters of, 154
  in thrillers and mysteries, 82
  in trimming process, 113
Totally Blonde, 53, 165
trailers, 161
Training Day, 134
transitions, scene-to-scene
  banners, 161–162
  fades, 161
  intercutting, 164–166
  narration, 162
  overdosing, 161
  overview, 159–161
  pre-laps, 163–164
  shot size, 162–163
translation process, film as
  inherited traits, 140–143
  overview, 139
  Romeo and Juliet example, 139–140
triage *See* film doctoring
Trim mode, Avid editing system, 110
trim tab, 32
trimming
  defined, 109

trimming (*Continued*)
  examples of in Tarantino films, 113–115
  fixing faulty lifts by, 117
  importance of, 112–113
  overview, 109
  practical considerations, 109–112
Trip to the Moon, A (*Le Voyage dans la Lune*), 63–64
Tucci, Jim, 34–35
Twain, Mark, 169
Twilight series, 81
two week trial periods, 177–178
2-shots, 94, 128
two-perf formats, 41
two-perf splices, 182–183
2001; A Space Odyssey, 64, 153
2010, 34–35

U
undercranked footage, 75–77
uninflected shots, 107
Up in the Air, 19, 159–160

V
vampires, 81
variety, in rhythm, 158
Variety magazine, 79, 147, 190, 194

video issues, film doctoring, 182–183
video tracks, for documentaries, 85–86
Video Transitions folder, Final Cut Pro, 160–161
videotape
  dupe detection, 154
  overlaps on, 125
Viewer, Final Cut Pro, 39
villains
  in action adventure films, 72
  in thrillers and mysteries, 82
VistaVision, 41
visual bridges, creating, 12–13
visual dominance, 12, 13
visual effects
  compositing, 64–65
  computer-generated images, 64
  development of, 61–64
  motion capture, 65–66
visual music, pace and rhythm as, 149–151
voiceovers, in documentaries, 84
volume, audio, 180, 181
von Stroheim, Erich, 180
Le Voyage dans la Lune (*A Trip to the Moon*), 63–64

W
Wall-E, 68
Wallerstein, Norman, 118
Walls, Tom, 52–53
weak ties, strength of, 174
wedges, 44
Westerns, 60–61
white gloves, 38
Wicker Man, The, 147
wide shots (WS)
  abbreviation for, 108
  and dialog substitution, 132–133
  general discussion, 92–93, 92f
  pace, 151
widescreen processes, 41
Wild Bunch, The, 75
wild sound, 192–193
Wilson, Larry, 62
Winters, Ralph, 172
wipes, 160
Wiseman, John, 187
workflow, filmmaking, 193–195
workprints, 95
World War II newsreels, 87
Wright, John, 54–55

Z
Zanuck, Darryl, 92–93